es of Easter Island (pictured on front jacket)

*about AD 1100 and for hundreds of years thereafter competing clans of Eas-
landers carved from volcanic rock magnificent statues of human heads on
s. These sculptures, or* moai *– about 900 in number – averaged 13 feet in
t and 14 tons in weight. To transport these monoliths from the island's sin-
uarry to ceremonial platforms along the coast, the people deployed tracking
ms made from tree trunks harvested from the lush forest. So extensive was the
e building and tracking system that by 1600 not a tree remained standing.
ecipitous decline in population ensued as the once flourishing civilization
nded into barbarism, civil war, cannibalism, and squalor. Easter Island,
gh its example of a civilization that, despite sophisticated art and technol-
depleted its resources and degraded its ecosystem so as to render its land virtu-
uninhabitable, is a warning to us all. We in Western civilization, too, have
tructed magnificent 'moai' emblematic of our own moribund way of life.*

CULTURE OF ECOLOGY:
RECONCILING ECONOMICS AND ENVIRON

ROBERT E. BABE

Culture of Ecology

Reconciling Economics and Environment

UNIVERSITY OF TORONTO PRESS
Toronto Buffalo London

Toronto Buffalo London
Printed in Canada

ISBN-13: 978-0-8020-3595-0
ISBN-10: 0-8020-3595-7

Printed on acid-free paper

Library and Archives Canada Cataloguing in Publication

Babe, Robert E., 1943–
Culture of ecology : reconciling economics and environment / Robert E. Babe.

Includes bibliographical references and index.
ISBN-13: 978-0-8020-3595-0
ISBN-10: 0-8020-3595-7

1. Ecology – Economic aspects. 2. Environmental economics. 3. Environmental degradation. I. Title.

HC79.E5B32 2006 333.7 C2005-905955-9

University of Toronto Press acknowledges the financial assistance to its publishing program of the Canada Council for the Arts and the Ontario Arts Council.

University of Toronto Press acknowledges the financial support for its publishing activities of the Government of Canada through the Book Publishing Industry Development Program (BPIDP).

In loving memory of
Edith Ruth Fenn
and for
David Andrew and Mary Noel Babe
and
Michael John and Daniel Stephen Babe

Lovely to see you again my friend
Walk along with me to the next bend.
–Justin Hayward

If I am not for myself, then who will be for me? And if I am only for myself, then what am I? And if not now, when?

– Rabbi Hillel, *Pirque Aboth*

Contents

Preface

Western culture since the Renaissance (and mainstream economic discourses in particular since Adam Smith) has misconceived humans' place in nature to such an extent that our activities are now destroying our life-support system. We need to radically reformulate our thinking and discussing, and a good place to start is our economics. Mainstream economics today, particularly the specialized school of thought known as *environmental economics*, is a harmful, destructive, anti-environmental discursive system that needs to be radically reformulated if we are to avoid the continued, accelerating deterioration of our life-support system. However, there are those with vested interests who profit in the short term from the propagation of standard economic doctrine despite the ruinous environmental consequences.

Chapter 1, 'Sustainable Development vs Sustainable Ecosystem,' documents the severity of environmental stresses within the context of 'sustainable development,' which too often is little more than a rhetorical ploy to justify continuous economic growth despite the ensuing environmental degradation.

Chapter 2, 'Economics and Ecology as Discourses,' discusses the evolution of the mainstream versions of these two disciplines, making special note of their intersections and interdependencies through time. The chapter also compares the main tenets and methodologies of today's predominant neoclassical economics with the ecosystem concept in ecology, arguing that the former is intrinsically anti-environmental and that to achieve a sustainable ecosystem, economics must be reformulated in accordance with principles of ecosystem interactions.

Chapter 3, 'Ancient Syntheses,' contends, contrary to Lynn White Jr and some other authorities, that Western culture generally and its economic discourses in particular were not in their origins fundamentally anti-environmental. Reviewing the economic writings of Aristotle and the ancient Jews, as well as certain medieval scholastics, the chapter establishes that these antiquarian authorities were actually profoundly pro-environment in their economic and other writings. The turn came, as argued in Chapter 4, 'Shattering the Synthesis: Hobbes, Smith, and Neoclassicism,' with the Renaissance, which for present purposes is typified by the writings of Thomas Hobbes and Adam Smith, whose major tenets are carried forth into today's mainstream, or neoclassical, economics.

Chapter 5, 'Environmental vs Ecological Economics,' reviews and critiques two present-day economic literatures dealing with environmental issues and policies. The first, *environmental economics*, is essentially mainstream neoclassical economics applied to environmental issues; the chapter argues that its conception of environmental issues and its proposed remedies, if pursued, will result in increased environmental degradation. The second, *ecological economics*, should be an important component of a culture of ecology.

Chapter 6, 'Information, Entropy, and Infinite Earth,' analyses and critiques the properties of 'information' as presented in the economics and other literatures in order to refute the mainstream doctrine of an infinite earth through applications of knowledge and technology. A brief concluding chapter closes the book.

As the term *culture of ecology* may make apparent, reformulating economics in order to make that discipline become more environmentally friendly is but a component of a much larger task entailing nothing less than an shift in our entire cultural paradigm. So much of our thinking and communicating – the pictures in our heads and our representation of these pictures in texts and conversations – is profoundly anti-environmental. We need, for example, to fundamentally reconsider our stance toward technology generally, and our culture's practice of defining 'progress' almost exclusively in terms of technological advancement. We need to reconsider also our stance toward life generally, and to non-human life in particular. We need to learn to critically appraise the content of our mass media – from movies and sound recordings to newspapers and video games – from the standpoint of ecosystem vitality, in the hope that these too will be reformulated in ways more consistent with a culture of ecology. And we need to repudiate the culture of armaments and of war in light of the interdependence of all life on our earthly home.

Acknowledgments

This book presents a comparison, and a critique, of economic and ecological discourses in the context of ecosystem vitality. It focuses mainly on present-day, dominant economic and ecological paradigms – namely, neoclassical economics and the ecosystem concept in ecology – but also pays attention to the evolution of mainstream economic and ecological discourses as well as to heterodoxies, particularly *ecological economics*. The major thrust of the book is that economics must not simply take into account environmental matters, as does the mainstream *environmental economics*, but, rather, it must actually become radically transformed so as to conform to principles of ecology.

This book was conceived as part of a larger work, which I refer to as 'Culture of Ecology,' by which I mean a culture thoroughly infused with principles of ecosystem interactions. Critiquing mainstream economics as a discourse is a starting point in the shift toward an ecologically sustainable culture; but it is just that, a starting point. There are many other aspects of our practices and discourses that warrant critical attention, and in the coming years I hope to look critically at some of these too: discourses on technology and technological practices; advertising and mass-media discourses; the formation and control of 'public opinion'; patent law and jurisprudence, particularly relating to DNA and the ideology of the gene; the culture of war and armaments. The list is almost endless, so anti-environmental is Western culture today. Yet I feel justified in using *Culture of Ecology* as the main title of the present manuscript, as it develops ecological principles and makes critical comparisons to one of the most significant anti-environmental discourses of our day.

Certainly public awareness and concern regarding the environment exist alongside accumulating evidence of escalating environmental deterioration. But individually and as a society we continue to maintain that no *fundamental* shift in our modes of valuation, organization, or activity is required. We tend to be lulled by rhetorical nostrums and placebos, such as 'sustainable development' that largely substitute for real action or real change.

This book was inspired, in part, by a 1996 conference in London, England, on cultural ecology, sponsored by the International Institute of Communications. Many thanks to Danielle Cliche, who organized the conference and edited my paper for inclusion in the Institute's volume, *Cultural Ecology: The Changing Dynamics of Communications* (1997). Even prior to that, however, Gary Hauch stimulated my interest in environmental matters, and in the problematic interplay of economics and ecology. *For the Common Good* by Herman Daly and John Cobb, likewise, was seminal in the preparation of this manuscript.

For the past fifteen years I have taught a course entitled 'Communication, Environment and Development.' To the students who have taken this evolving course at the universities of Ottawa, Windsor, and Western Ontario, thank you; you have contributed much to the clarity of my thought.

Leslie Shade and Edward Comor were graciously supportive in many ways. Angela Carter, Anne Dyer-Witheford, Gregory L. Walters, Jon van der Veen, Jim Winter, Stephen Kotowych, Warren J. Samuels, Daniel W. Bromley, and David Suzuki also commented on at least a portion of previous drafts. I benefited much, also, from reports of anonymous referees, and the present book is much the better as a result.

And, as always, heartfelt appreciation is extended to all my family for their love and support.

CULTURE OF ECOLOGY:
RECONCILING ECONOMICS AND ENVIRONMENT

1 Sustainable Development vs Sustainable Ecosystem

Infinite Earth, Infinite Wants, 'Sustainable Development'

Opening the 1947 Bretton Woods Conference, which set the world on a trajectory of globalization and 'free trade,'[1] the then U.S. secretary of the treasury Henry Morgenthau envisioned 'the creation of a dynamic world economy in which the peoples of every nation will be able to realize their potentialities in peace and enjoy the fruits of material progress on an earth infinitely blessed with natural riches.' Morgenthau called on all present to accept the 'elementary axiom ... that prosperity has no limits. It is not a substance to be diminished by division.'[2]

Morgenthau's declaration was followed up early in 1949 by President Harry Truman's inaugural address, which in turn 'inaugurated the "development age."'[3] Truman declared, 'We must embark on a bold new program for making the benefits of our scientific advances and industrial progress available for the improvement and growth of underdeveloped areas.' He continued,

> For the first time in history, humanity possesses the knowledge and skill to relieve the suffering of [impoverished] people. The United States is pre-eminent among nations in the development of industrial and scientific techniques. The material resources which we can afford to use for assistance of other peoples is limited. But our imponderable resources in technical knowledge are constantly growing and are inexhaustible ... Our main goal should be to help the free peoples of the world, through their own efforts, to produce more food, more clothing, more materials for housing, and more mechanical power to lighten their burdens ... Experience shows that our commerce with other countries expands as they progress industri-

> ally and economically ... Greater production is the key to prosperity and peace.[4]

In Truman's view, the application of technology and skill would transform an otherwise finite earth into an infinite resource that could be drawn upon indefinitely to meet humanity's material wants and needs. Even in the context of rapid population growth, Truman envisaged ever-increasing levels of material prosperity for industrialized and 'developing' countries alike.

In 1986 the General Assembly of the United Nations endorsed Truman's position by declaring development to be an inalienable human right.

In our day the application of science and technology continues to be regarded by many as the means of transforming the earth's crust into an unlimited resource,[5] although now the term 'sustainable development' is frequently invoked in mainstream government and business discourses to soften the proposal – an acknowledgment, at least, that economic growth to this point has proven problematic for the environment. 'Sustainable development,' however, is ambiguous, or polysemous – not quite one of 'the great empty vessels of contemporary political discourse,'[6] perhaps, but a 'motherhood' term nonetheless. As Carley and Christie write, 'There is still substantial disagreement on what [sustainable development] means and how to achieve it.'[7]

Broadly speaking, and at the risk of some oversimplification, there are two antithetical meanings or approaches to sustainable development. The first, the dominant, economically inspired meaning and approach, stems directly from the United Nations' World Commission on Environment and Development (Brundtland Commission), which, in its landmark report, *Our Common Future* (1987), defined 'sustainable development' as policies that 'meet the needs of the present without compromising the ability of future generations to meet their own needs.'[8] An essential component of Brundtland's program was its insistence that 'sustainable development' must entail 'a new era of economic growth'[9] – indeed, 'a five- to tenfold increase in world industrial output' over the next fifty years,[10] a target affirmed by the Secretary General of the Commission two years after publication of the report, who wrote that to achieve sustainability 'a fivefold to tenfold increase in economic activity would be required over the next 50 years.'[11] For the Brundtland Commission, moreover, this 'new growth' was to be based 'on policies that sustain and expand the environmental resource base.'[12] To be sure,

Brundtland did caution that 'Such growth has serious implications for the future of the world's ecosystems,'[13] one inference of which being that growth in the future must be planned more carefully than growth in the past.

Important though that qualification is, there is nonetheless a remarkable consistency, and continuity, of Morgenthau's vision of an infinite earth, Truman's call for 'development' through the application of science and technology and world trade, and Brundtland's call forty years later to expand the world's environmental resource base to achieve a five- to tenfold increase in world economic output over a fifty-year period.

Governments and corporations alike, by and large, accepted with open arms Brundtland's recommendation to sustain economic growth, and in publicity they have emphasized that they are indeed adherents to the program of sustainable development. In its report of 2001 on sustainable development, the Royal Dutch Shell Group, for example, exclaimed, 'We will grow the value of Shell by delivering robust profitability and leveraging our competitive edge. Our success will ensure highly competitive returns to shareholders and give us the financial flexibility to take advantage of new commercial opportunities. Profits are also a vital part of our ability to contribute to society and meet the economic, environmental and social requirements of sustainable development.'[14] In this document, focused on growth and profitability, Shell deployed the phrase 'sustainable development' fifty-five times.[15]

Likewise, in 2002 the International Association of Oil and Gas Producers published *Industry as a Partner for Sustainable Development,* in which the term 'sustainable development' appeared twenty-one times. According to the association,

> The world has moved on in the past decade and so have we. One of the drivers has been the demonstrable relationship between economic growth and greater social well-being and quality of life ... As public awareness grows, our business success is linked to performance in the areas of environmental protection and community affairs. Consequently, concerns in these areas, including assessments on potential social impacts of our activities, are factored into our decision-making processes ... We are companies and we are mandated to comply with the rule of law and regulations and to work in partnership with local authorities and communities to ensure sustainable benefit to all.[16]

In a similar vein, the World Bank's 1992 World Development Report,

Development and the Environment, attributed environmental deterioration mainly to poverty, not economic growth; hence its remedy for a deteriorating environment was not conservation but sustained economic growth – and growth not just in the poor South but in the rich North too. As summed up by former World Bank economist Herman Daly, albeit with irony, 'How else could the South grow if it could not export to Northern markets and receive foreign investments from the North? And how could the North provide foreign investment and larger markets for the South if it in turn did not grow?'[17]

Even a decade later, the World Bank was still championing continuous economic growth as the means to combat environmental degradation. In its 2003 World Deveopment Report, *Sustainable Development in a Dynamic World*, the bank declared that 'rising income can facilitate but not guarantee better environmental and social outcomes by permitting countries simply to "grow out of" pollution or civil conflict.'[18] It continued, 'Even the next 15 years (2003–2018) could bring a record period of economic growth in developing countries. Driven by growth in China and India, income in the low- and middle-income countries will almost double – accounting for more than a third of the 60 percent increase in world output. This period offers the opportunity to lay the foundation for inclusive growth – which will require confronting barriers to change.[19]

However, in its document, possibly for the first time, the bank did acknowledge disquiet on the part of many environmentalists regarding 'overconsumption.' But this concern was alluded to only briefly and in the context of the bank sceptically raising its own questions: 'But what kind of consumption qualifies as overconsumption,' it asked, and 'why is it harmful, and what should be done about it? ... On these questions, there is little clarity.'[20] The unwavering thrust, indeed, of the bank's report on 'sustainable development' was to endorse continual economic growth.

The Canadian government, too, in its 'sustainable development strategies' envisages continued economic growth, and while this is certainly not the only feature of its strategies, it is a major one. Note, for example, the consistency (albeit different emphases) regarding markets and growth in the following extracts from position papers from, respectively, Industry Canada and Environment Canada:

> Industry Canada's third Sustainable Development Strategy (SDS III), for 2003–06, has a vision of Canada as a leader in the development, commer-

> cialization and adoption of sustainable development tools, practices and technologies throughout the economy. This vision reflects the Department's mandate to help Canadians be more productive and competitive in the knowledge-based economy and thus improve their standard of living and quality of life. It also subscribes to the view that sustainable development, along with productivity, employment and income growth, is an integral part of growing a dynamic economy.[21]

> The updated Strategy [of Environment Canada] focuses on building a future shaped by a strong knowledge base that puts human and natural capital on an equal footing with economic capital, informs public debate and ensures integrated decision making. The Strategy calls upon the strategic use of market forces to ensure that good economic policy becomes good environmental and social policy. It emphasizes partnerships and governance models that enable horizontal decision making at the government, community and corporate levels. And, finally, the Strategy requires leadership by example in our departmental operations.[22]

In fact, by year's end 2004 so entrenched was the economic growth thrust of Canada's 'environment' strategy that the country's newly appointed minister of the environment, Stéphane Dion, was recommending to Cabinet colleagues that his department be renamed the Department of Sustainable Economy.[23]

In the dominant business and government perspective, then, 'sustainable development' is in large measure a code phrase for sustaining economic growth. This growth entails, in part, tapping new markets and new resource bases. It is, in large part, Morgenthau's doctrine of an infinitely expandable earth all over again.

The advisability and/or feasibility of expanding the resource base indefinitely is, of course, a major bone of contention between those that interpret sustainable development as privileging 'economic' ideas and goals, such as Royal Dutch Shell, Brundtland, the World Bank, and the government of Canada, and many ecologists and environmentalists. According to the environmental group Friends of the Earth, for instance, 'To achieve sustainability we ... need to reduce the total burden we place upon the environment to a sustainable level by cutting back on the amount of environmental resources, distribute access to those environmental resources fairly, and use them to increase quality of life.'[24] In 2003, Friends of the Earth responded directly to Royal Dutch Shell's publication on sustainable development with a document entitled 'Shell Record Profits at Expense of People, Planet.' There, Friends declared,

> Shell today boasted record profits for the first quarter of 2003, as well as the 'highest hydrocarbon production in recent history.' While Shell's directors and shareholders will be celebrating the figures, the profits may generate less enthusiasm among poor, vulnerable communities around the world whose health and local environment is suffering as a result of Shell's ageing and polluting refineries and depots. Shell's underlying profits in the first three months of the year almost doubled to a record 3.91 billion US dollars. Net income is up a massive 136% on the same period last year, to $5.3 billion. The news comes just one week after its Annual General Meeting was dominated by representatives from communities around the world who are suffering as a result of living next to the company's polluting refineries.'[25]

Friends of the Earth is certainly not alone among environmental advocates in maintaining that an ecologically sound economy can by no means tolerate indefinite economic growth. Lester R. Brown, president of the Earth Policy Institute, writes that 'an economy is sustainable only if it respects the principles of ecology.'[26] He adds, 'The larger the economy becomes relative to the ecosystem, and the more it presses against the earth's natural limits, the more destructive this incompatibility [between economy and ecosystem] will be.'[27] Brown provides no hint that human skills and technology can transform the earth's crust into an infinite resource.

Likewise, ecologist Robert Goodland cites evidence indicating that the economy, even at the time of the Brundtland Report, was too large vis-à-vis the ecosystem. He estimates that the human economy then used, directly or indirectly, 40 per cent of the net primary product of terrestrial photosynthesis (plant growth). Disregarding future desertification, urban sprawl, soil erosion, blacktopping of agricultural land, and pollution, this means that with only a single doubling in world population (in the absence of fundamentally altered consumption patterns – for example, a marked increase in vegetarianism – within just thirty-five years humans would be using 80 per cent of plant growth.[28]

Ecological economist Herman Daly has drawn perhaps the clearest distinction between the two views of sustainable development. Whereas business and corporate interests touting sustainable development equate 'development' with 'growth,' Daly insists that 'development' and 'growth' are by no means synonymous. For him, rather, 'development' means *qualitative* improvement, including, but not limited to, improvements in resource efficiency, whereas 'growth' means *quantitative* increase in resource use. For Daly, in fact, 'sustainable development' implies *no growth* 'beyond environmental carrying capacity.'[29] He adds, 'The whole idea of sustainable development is that the economic subsystem must not grow beyond the scale at which it can be permanently sustained or supported by the containing ecosystem.'[30] 'Development,' then, for Daly entails 'moral growth,' not quantitative increase; in his view, 'future progress simply must be made in terms of the things that really count rather than the things that are merely countable.'[31]

For Greenpeace, likewise, government and corporate rhetoric on 'sustainable development is, more often than not, merely a public relations scam: 'Governments pay lip service to environmental protection, while supporting economic growth – at least for the rich countries – above all else. The gap between rich and poor continues to increase in both developing and industrialised countries, and there are billions without access to the basics required to improve their lives. While people in industrialised countries buy more, and multinationals grow richer, natural environments – particularly those in developing nations – degrade rapidly.'[32] Interestingly, however, to more effectively prod governments and corporations into positive action on climate change, Greenpeace partnered with the World Business Council for Sustainable Development (WBCSD),[33] which describes itself as 'a coalition of 170 international companies united by a shared commitment to sustainable development via the three pillars of economic growth, ecological balance and social progress.'[34]

In any event, we see that 'sustainable development' carries different, often antithetical, meanings for those intent on sustaining economic growth as opposed to those who see a growing economy as a major threat to ecosystem vitality. The term 'sustainable development,' then, is emblematic of at best a precarious, if not indeed a false, synthesis in our day between ecology and economics, between environment and development.

Origins of 'Sustainable Development'

How and why did the rhetoric of 'sustainable development' arise and grow to such prominence over the last two decades? Certainly environmental discourses and the appreciation of pristine nature are of long standing and are readily detected even in writings from antiquity – in works by Lucretius, Aristotle, Theophrastus, and Virgil, for example. In the England of the 1800s, likewise, Romantic poets such as William Wordsworth and Percy Bysshe Shelley were paying homage to periwinkles and skylarks even as William Blake was denouncing the 'dark Satanic mills' of the Industrial Revolution; meanwhile, Gilbert White was making acute observations about the interdependence of all wildlife at Selborne. In the New World of the 1800s, too, the poetry of Walt Whitman and Ralph Waldo Emerson provided sublime accompaniment to the paeans to nature of Henry David Thoreau and George Parkins Marsh – counterpoints all to the then-dominant discourse of 'subduing, conquering, transforming, and controlling nature to man's purposes.'[35] In the early 1900s, U.S. president Theodore Roosevelt, by setting aside 150 million acres for national forest reserves and establishing five national parks and fifty-one refuges for wild birds, manifested the then-current progressive, conservationist outlook.[36] (On the other hand, it must be noted, the early twentieth-century American conservation movement was in large measure utilitarian, 'conservation' even being defined by the Chief Forester of the United States in 1905 as 'the development and use of the earth and all its resources for the enduring good of men';[37] as intellectual historian Donald Worster notes, one of the less laudable aspects of the conservation movement was a concerted effort to eradicate wolf, puma, and grizzly populations, and other 'noxious' wildlife.)[38] Given all this, both positive and negative, we must nonetheless agree with Neuzil and Kovarik when they note that an environmental awareness certainly existed long before 1962.[39]

Nonetheless, 1962 was a watershed year in terms of environmentalism. In the years leading up to 1962, notes former U.S. vice president Al Gore, '"environment" was not even an entry in the vocabulary of public policy.'[40] Exactly why environmental awareness and concern had dwindled to such an extent is subject to conjecture; perhaps two world wars, the Great Depression, the Cold War, and the economic boom of the 1950s, coupled with mass media's continual propagation of consumerism and lifestyles, induced people to focus on other, seemingly more pressing matters. Very likely the Darwinian revolution, positing an amoral nature 'red in tooth and claw,' had debased nature in the eyes of many to such an extent it was no longer to be admired, revered, or preserved.[41] Or perhaps, with Harry Truman, people actually believed that science and technology could transform the earth into an infinite repository of want-satisfying resources. Regardless of reasons Rachel Carson's *Silent Spring*, published in 1962, awakened the United States and much of the rest of the world to a renewed environmental awareness, thereby inaugurating the modern environmental movement. This was, according to Alex MacGillivray, 'the green manifesto that made ecology a household name'; it was 'by general consent, the first – and remains the only – manifesto on environmental issues.'[42] The story of Carson's book, and the tribulations of its author, are emblematic of certain themes in this present work.

Rachel Carson (1907–64) received bachelor's and master's degrees in zoology, the latter from Johns Hopkins University. For a time she taught university biology. In 1936 she became the first woman to take and pass the test for the U.S. civil service. Hired initially as a junior marine biologist with the U.S. Bureau of Fisheries, she rose through the ranks to become the chief editor of publications for the U.S. Fish and Wildlife Service. Evenings and weekends, though, she was an author – of three books, including the bestselling tome *The Sea Around Us.*[43] The remarkable success of that volume enabled her to forsake her civil-service post for full-time writing.

In her acknowledgments, Carson relates that she wrote *Silent Spring* in response to a letter from a friend, Olga Owens Huckins, which ascribed the deaths of birds in a sanctuary at Cape Cod to indiscriminant aerial spraying of the chemical, DDT. DDT had, in fact, concerned Carson as early as 1945 when she unsuccessfully proposed an article on the topic to *Reader's Digest.* Over the ensuing years she amassed a substantial dossier on the substance.

DDT (dichlorodiphenyltrichloroethane) was developed in 1939 and was widely used as a pesticide by the U.S. Army in the South Pacific during World War II to prevent typhus and malaria. So effective was the chemical in averting disease, its developer, Paul Muller, won the Nobel Prize in medicine and physiology in 1948. After World War II, on account of its low cost (22 cents per pound) and its seeming safety, this 'miracle compound' and related herbicides and pesticides were adapted widely for civilian use – particularly for agricultural applications. In the United States, DDT useage soared, peaking in 1959 at 35 million kg.[44] According to researchers at Case Western Reserve University, both governments and the chemical industry aggressively promoted its use. The U.S Public Health Department held demonstrations purporting to show DDT's safety and effectiveness.[45] Soon, public places and private backyards alike were routinely sprayed. The pesticide industry burgeoned – $200 million of pesticides were sold in 1958, the year Carson began her manuscript, and by 1962, the year of its publication, sales had soared to about $500 million.

In the first chapter of *Silent Spring*, entitled 'A Fable for Tomorrow,' Carson asked her readers to imagine 'a town in the heart of America where all life seems to live in harmony with its surroundings.' She painted images of white clouds, of bloom in the spring, of green fields in the summer, of a blaze of colour in the fall with foxes barking in the hills and deer silently crossing fields half hidden in the morning mists.[46] But then, she wrote, an evil spell settled on the community, a blight crept over the area, and everything began to change: domestic animals grew sick and expired; people grew ill; children were suddenly stricken and died in a few hours; the few birds that remained alive trembled violently and could not fly; apple trees came into bloom but there were no bees to pollinate them. 'In the gutters,' she continued, 'under the eaves and between the shingles of the roofs, a white granular powder still showed a few patches; some weeks before it had fallen like snow upon the roofs and lawns, the fields and streams.' Carson finished her fable by remarking, 'No witchcraft, no enemy action had silenced the rebirth of new life in this stricken world; the people had done it themselves.'[47]

Rachel Carson termed her story a fable. But it was not fiction. Like all fine myths, it generalized a multitude of actual occurrences: from Hinsdale, Illinois, to the Appalachian region of West Virginia, from the campus of Michigan State University to Whitefish Bay, Wisconsin, from Toledo, Ohio, to Syracuse, New York, birds *had* been silenced. 'Over increasingly large areas of the United States,' she summarized, 'spring now comes unheralded by the return of birds, and the early mornings are strangely silent where once they were filled with the beauty of bird song.'[48]

Rachel Carson described how DDT entered the trophic, or nutritional, structure, accumulated in the fatty tissue of animals, and rose up the food chain in ever-increasing concentrations (a process called *biomagnification*). She proposed that genetic damage, cancers, reproductive incapacities, and birth defects ensued. Carson claimed that although former scourges to human health – disease organisms such as smallpox, cholera, and plague – had been largely eradicated, the new hazards were ones that 'we ourselves have introduced,' namely, 'radiation in all its forms,' and the 'never-ending stream of chemicals,' of which pesticides like DDT are a part.[49] 'Their presence,' she declared, 'casts a shadow that is no less ominous because it is formless and obscure, no less frightening because it is simply impossible to predict the effects of lifetime exposure to chemical and physical agents that are not part of the biological experience of man.'[50]

The term 'ecology' does not appear often in Rachel Carson's book, although central ideas denoted by the word (the web of life, holistic analysis, interdependence, dynamic change, interacting populations, and so on) indeed permeate her thought. Her amplification of the term, however, is particularly compelling: 'There is also an ecology of the world within our bodies. In this unseen world *minute causes produce mighty effects*; ... a change at one point, in one molecule even, may reverberate throughout the entire system to initiate changes in seemingly unrelated organs and tissues.'[51] These remarks are poignant because, in the early spring of 1960, Carson was diagnosed with breast cancer. In April she underwent radical mastectomy, and continued to be treated through radiation until her death on 14 April 1964.

Portions of *Silent Spring* initially appeared in serial form in the *New Yorker*, and received immediate, serious attention: President John F. Kennedy ordered the Science Advisory Committee to study the effects of pesticides. The committee's report, issued in 1963, vindicated Carson, as it called for the eventual elimination of the use of persistent toxic pesticides and for greatly augmented federal research. In 1965 the President's Advisory Committee published *Restoring the Quality of Our Environment*, cataloguing pollution problems and their effects on human and environmental health. In 1969 the U.S. Congress passed the Environmental Policy Act, and in 1970 President Richard Nixon created the Environmental Protection Agency (EPA). In 1972–3, also, there was a flurry of activity: the use of DDT was banned in the United States, and many credit this action as being instrumental to the resurgence of such nearly extinct species as the peregrine falcon, the bald eagle, and the osprey. As well, the Endangered Species Act, the Clean Air Act, and the Clean Water Act were passed to establish regulatory safeguards and enable environmentalists to use the courts to protect wildlife, air, and water. But perhaps most significantly, Carson and her book implanted an awareness of certain environmental issues. Her book, certainly, was an instance in which a 'minute cause' produced a 'mighty effect.'

Prior to its publication in book form, however, *Silent Spring* provoked the chemical industry to rise up in arms. The Velsicol Chemical Corporation, for example, demanded that Carson's publisher, Houghton Mifflin, halt publication on account of purported inaccuracies and remarks disparaging two of the company's products. Carson's character was impugned through informal gossip. Her motives, competence, integrity, and sanity were all questioned. She was referred to derisively as 'a spinster,' 'a priestess of nature,' 'a fanatic,' and 'hysterical.' Upon publication, chemical giant Monsanto distributed a pamphlet to the various media parodying her book; entitled *The Desolate Year*, it described a world without chemical pesticides as being devastated by famine, disease, and insects. A major environmental public relations firm, whose clients included Monsanto, Dow Chemical, and the Agricultural Chemical Association, distributed damning reviews of the book to the press.[52] Meanwhile, chemical companies threatened to withdraw advertisements from publications carrying favourable reviews,[53] so great was the conflict in Carson's day between business and the environment, between economics and ecology.

While in some respects Carson won a great victory over powerful opposition, at another level she was far from victorious. Although use of DDT was banned in the United States, production for export continued apace. Moreover, as noted by Al Gore, the use of 'narrow spectrum' herbicides and pesticides, even more 'potent' (i.e., deadly) than DDT, escalated, and some tie this increase to alarming growth in the incidences of breast and testicular cancers. Even more basically, however, the thrust of Carson's book, which transcends the particular issues of DDT and other pesticides, has in practice been disregarded by large segments of the public, industry, and government.[54] Carson, most basically, disputed a main tenet of modern civilization, namely, 'that man ... [is] properly the center and the master of all things, and that scientific history [is] primarily the story of his domination.'[55] This orthodoxy, dating at least to the writings of Francis Bacon (1561–1626), if not indeed to Protagoras (c. 480–410 BC),[56] remains our culture's 'common sense, even though ecosystem tragedies should have made readily apparent to all the problematic nature of the doctrine. Carson, though, was explicit and insistent in denouncing this dominant world view. She concluded her book with these words: 'The "control of nature" is a phrase conceived in arrogance, born of the Neanderthal age of biology and philosophy, when it was supposed that nature exists for the convenience of man. The concepts and practices of applied entomology for the most part date from that Stone Age of science. It is our alarming misfortune that so primitive a science has armed itself with the most modern and terrible weapons, and that in turning them against the insects it has also turned them against the earth.'[57]

The contrast between the position of Rachel Carson and that of Harry Truman could hardly be more stark.

'Sustainable Development': Fragile, or False, Reconciliation?

In 1972 the United Nations held the first international conference on the environment (the Stockholm Conference), declaring: 'In our time, man's *capability* to transform his surroundings, if used wisely, can bring to all peoples the *benefits of development* and the opportunity to enhance the quality of life. Wrongly or heedlessly applied, the same power can do *incalculable harm* to human beings and *the human environment.* We see around us growing evidence of man-made harm in many regions of the earth.'[58] With this statement the UN proposed, in effect, a fundamental antithesis between environment and development, which is to say (at least with a narrow rendering of 'development') between ecosystem and economy, and by implication between ecology and economics. Although the term, 'sustainable development,' had yet to be invented, its basic thrust – meeting today's needs without sacrificing the capacity of future generations to meet theirs – was set forth, probably for the first time in an official policy document, as an approach to resolving both the world's economic woes and its burgeoning environmental crises. The UN Declaration continued, 'The natural resources of the earth, including the air, water, land, flora and fauna and especially representative samples of natural ecosystems, must be safeguarded *for the benefit of present and future generations* through careful planning or management, as appropriate.'[59]

A decade and a half later, with the report of the UN's World Commission on Environment and Development (Brundtland Commission), the proposal that economic growth and environmental health can be reconciled through careful planning and management was officially assigned the term 'sustainable development.' Remarking that 'many present development trends leave increasing numbers of people poor and vulnerable, while at the same time degrading the environment,'[60] the Brundtland Commission asked how 'development' could possibly serve the world in the next century, in which twice as many people would be relying on the same resource base. The issue, as the commission saw it, was to devise policies and revise activities that would bring about *development* that would be *sustainable* into the indefinite future for the entire planet.[61] As noted above, an essential aspect of its 'solution' was an expansion of the Earth's resource base to help bring about 'a new era of economic growth.'

Since 1987 the term 'sustainable development' has become a catchphrase of governments, transnational corporations, and some environmentalists. In 1994, for example, the Canadian Parliament established the National Round Table on the Environment and the Economy as 'an independent advisory body'[62] with a mandate 'to explain and promote sustainable development.'[63] Sustainable development, moreover, is an explicit goal of Canada's Environmental Assessment Act. As well, tabled in Canada's Parliament every three years are 'sustainable development strategies,' described as 'important tools that help guide departments and agencies within the Government of Canada in systematically integrating the principles of sustainable development into their policies, programs, legislation and operations.'[64]

Internationally, sustainable development is said to form a cornerstone of both public policy and corporate decision-making. In late August 2002, for example, the World Summit on Sustainable Development, held in Johannesburg, South Africa, assembled heads of state and leaders from government, industry, and civil society to reaffirm the commitment to sustainable development that had been made at the Earth Summit in Rio de Janeiro ten years earlier.[65] At the close of the conference, however – fifteen years after Brundtland's initial call for sustainable development and a decade subsequent to the Rio Conference – the UN issued a press release that began 'In the face of growing poverty and increasing environmental degradation, the World Summit has succeeded in generating a sense of urgency.'[66] It would seem from this statement, and more importantly from evidence cited immediately below regarding environmental deterioration, that attempts to safeguard the earth's ecosystems for future generations have met with at best limited success. It is suggested here, therefore, that the meanings businesses and governments assign sustainable development – predominantly that of expanding the earth's resource base to sustain economic growth – may well be a large part of the problem. Environmentalist Donella Meadows expresses the problem this way: 'A society that refuses to consider the idea that there are limits to growth is not going to bring forth a physical economy that fits within the constraints of the planet. A society that thinks there's an 'away' to throw things into is going to find itself choking on its own waste.'[67]

As a society and a culture, by and large, we continue to reject the idea that there are limits to growth. Corporate and governmental proposals for sustaining economic growth find ready support in the writings of many academics. Even Mark Sagoff, a philosopher of environmental ethics at the University of Maryland, declared baldly: 'It is simply wrong to believe that nature sets physical limits to economic growth – that is, to prosperity and the production and consumption of goods on which it is based.'[68] We will return on several occasions to Sagoff in the course of this book.

Likewise Julian Simon, until his death in 1998 a professor of business, also at the University of Maryland, insisted, 'The term "finite" is not only inappropriate but is downright misleading when applied to natural resources, from both the practical and philosophical points of view ... The more we use, the better off we become – and there's no practical limit to improving our lot forever.'[69] Sagoff and Simon, and others,[70] provide philosophical or theoretical support for the corporate/governmental program of sustaining economic growth indefinitely by insisting that the earth is infinite in its capacity to satisfy humans' material wants. They justify this claim essentially through a single line of argument, namely that resources, materials, the capacity of the planet to absorb wastes, are all a function of human knowledge and technology, which in principle can grow forever; furthermore, the price system effectively guides human innovation to counter scarcities.

We will have occasion in later chapters to critique this proposition, both in terms of the purported lack of constraint on human knowledge and technology, and the alleged efficacy of prices in guiding human endeavours in environmentally benign ways. For now, however, it suffices to turn to environmental indicators that fly in the face of the doctrine of an infinite earth, given centuries during which humans have applied knowledge and technology as guided by the price system.

Ecosystem Crises

Species Extinctions

At one time, at least in the context of the New World, the presumption that the earth is capable of sustaining economic growth indefinitely, although inaccurate, would at least have been understandable. When Europeans like Samuel de Champlain and John Cabot began exploring North America in the fifteenth century, cod were so plentiful at the Grand Banks off Newfoundland that they could be 'scooped out of the sea with buckets.'[71] Similarly, as late as 1854 a resident of New York State could write: 'There would be days and days when the air was alive with [passenger pigeons], hardly a break occurring in the flocks for half a day at a time; flocks stretched as far as a person could see, one tier above another.'[72] By the time of Morgenthau's speech in 1947, of course, the passenger pigeon – a bird that once numbered perhaps 5 billion – was extinct. The New World, evidently, was not large enough to sustain them! And today, as all Newfoundlanders know only too well, the codfishery is dead.

In fact, species extinctions have reached alarming proportions. According to the United Nations Environment Programme, 'global biodiversity is changing at an unprecedented rate, the most important drivers being land conversion, climate change, pollution, unsustainable harvesting of natural resources and the introduction of exotic species.'[73] Whereas the rate of extinctions during the past 600 million years averaged perhaps one species per year, present extinction rates, according to Oregon State University biologist Bruce Coblentz, are 'hundreds or even thousands of times higher.'[74] Estimates are that currently as many as five plant species become extinct every day; extinction rates of animal species are even higher. According to the World Conservation Union (IUCN):

- 15,589 animal or plant species are known to be threatened with extinction
- 1.9 million animal or plant species have been described out of an estimated 5–30 million species that exist
- One in every four mammals and one in every eight birds is facing a high risk of extinction in the near future
- One in three amphibians and almost half of all tortoises and freshwater turtles are threatened
- The total number of threatened animal species increased from 5,205 in 1996 to 7,266 in 2004[75]

The IUCN further estimates that by the mid-1990s, 12.5 per cent of vascular plants and 34 per cent of fish were threatened with extinction; of the 11,000 threatened species, 18 per cent were 'critically endangered.'[76]

From a biocentric viewpoint, loss of biodiversity is a tragedy of immense proportions. Even from an anthropocentric point of view it is hugely problematic. As ecologist David Suzuki has emphasized, 'Life itself has created the conditions hospitable to all creatures,' and species diversity enables life to continue and to diversify.[77] Environmental philosopher Mark Sagoff, however, citing biologist David Ehrenfeld, has dismissed the ecosystem importance of species extinctions with the following argument: 'There is no credible argument, moreover, that all or even most of the species we are concerned to protect are essential to the functioning of the ecological systems on which we depend. If whales went extinct, for example, the seas would not fill up with krill ... [Indeed] the species most likely to be endangered are those the biosphere is least likely to miss. "Many of these species were never common or ecologically influential; by no stretch of the imagination can we make them out to be vital cogs in the ecological machine.'"[78] Sagoff here presumes an ecosystem is like a machine, a dubious analogy addressed later on in this book. But even apart from that, he misses the main point. Granted, few species by themselves are vital for the effective functioning of the biosphere. When thousands of such species become extinct, however, biodiversity is reduced to such an extent that ecosystems become damaged irreparably.

Degradation of Arable Land

According to the United Nations Environment Programme, 23 per cent of all the earth's useable land (land excluding mountains and deserts) has been significantly degraded, the major causes being deforestation, overgrazing, agricultural mismanagement, urban growth, and industrialization.[79] About 2 billion hectares of soil (15 per cent of the earth's land – an area larger than the United States and Mexico combined) have been degraded through human activities. The UN Environment Programme notes that land is not only 'finite, fragile, and non-renewable,' but also that it 'aids in the preservation of terrestrial biodiversity, regulation of the hydrological cycle, carbon storage and recycling.'[80] The UN Environment Programme concludes that despite attempts to decrease soil erosion, 'there is no clear indication that the rate of land degradation has decreased.'[81]

Global Warming, Greenhouse Effect

According to the Intergovernmental Panel on Climate Change (IPCC), the 1990s was the warmest decade, and 1998 the warmest year, since measurements began in 1860. The IPCC calculates that average global surface temperature increases since 1900 of 0.3 to 0.6 degrees Celsius are attributable directly to human activities. These temperature increases have been accompanied by large decreases in snow cover and a rise in the sea level of ten to twenty centimetres.[82]

Temperature increases have been accompanied by significant increases in greenhouse gas emissions, particularly CO_2. Since 1750, atmospheric concentrations of carbon dioxide have risen by 31 per cent, and more than half of this increase has occurred within the last fifty years. Based on projected increases in CO_2 emissions, the IPCC anticipates that global average temperatures will rise by 1.4 to 5.8 degrees Celsius between 1990 and 2100. The average sea level is predicted to increase between 9 and 88 cm. Snow cover, sea ice, ice caps, and glaciers are expected to shrink. Moreover, 'even after greenhouse gas concentrations are stabilized, climate change will persist for many centuries, with surface temperature and sea level continuing to rise in response to past emissions.'[83] It is also anticipated that global warming will cause lengthened growing seasons in mid- to high-latitude regions, shifts in plant and animal ranges, and declines in animal and plant populations. Also endangered are glaciers, coral reefs, boreal and tropical forests, polar and alpine ecosystems, prairie wetlands, and remnant native grasslands. There is an increased risk of flooding for tens of millions of people due not only to rising sea levels, but also increased precipitation. Increases in the occurrence of droughts, floods, heat waves, avalanches, and windstorms are projected. Crop yields are expected to decline in most tropical and subtropical regions, and water is anticipated to become increasingly scarce in the subtropics.

Toxins in Air and Water

Unfortunately, there are no measures of the accumulation of toxins in the environment. Farmers worldwide, however, apply 2.5 million tons of pesticides, mainly synthetic chemicals, to crops annually. These pesticides 'are orders of magnitude more toxic than 50 years ago.'[84] According to the United Nations, contaminated water kills an estimated 2.2 million people a year and the effects of air pollution take 3 million lives annually around the world.[85] In Ontario, air pollution kills an estimated 1,900 people annually and costs the medical system about $1.1 billion annually.[86] Persistent organic pollutants (POPs) are long-lived toxins that collect and concentrate in the food chain. One of the major environmental achievements in the decade following the Rio Conference (1992) was the signing in Stockholm in May 2001 of the Convention on Persistent Organic Pollutants. The treaty bans production of ten POPs and specifies reduced emissions of two industrial by-products. The production of other POPs, such as polyvinyl chloride (PVC), however, continues apace. Nearly 25 million tons of PVC, associated with cancer, were produced in 1999. It is noted that every stage of the life cycle of PCV, from manufacture to disposal, creates 'dangerous chemicals, including some POPs.'[87]

Efforts have been made recently to measure the presence of chemical toxins in the human body. According to the U.S. Centers for Disease Control and Prevention, as published in its *Second National Report on Human Exposure to Environmental Chemicals* (January 2003),[88] pesticides were present in all the people tested. In releasing the report, experts speaking on behalf of the Department of Health and Human Services made the following points, among others:

- Overall, for specific chemicals, we have a mixed picture, some encouraging findings and some of concern. For lead, some encouraging data.
- Chlorpyrifos is an organophosphate pesticide that has been used heavily in the United States. Retail sales of chlorpyrifos for residential use were stopped in December 2001 ... Our data show that levels of chlorpyrifos in children are about twice as high as those in adults.
- The report presents serum levels of dioxins, furans and coplanar PCBs, polychlorinated biphenyls. In terms of their toxicity, furans and coplanar PCBs are dioxin-like compounds. All of these chemicals persist in the environment and in the human body for years. Most people who were tested for these compounds had levels of dioxins, furans and coplanar PCBS that were below the detection limits of our analytical method. These findings are encouraging and consistent with other data, indicating exposure to these chemicals has been declining in the past two decades.
- Phthalates are chemicals found in many consumer products including vinyl flooring adhesives, detergents, lubricants, food packaging, soap, shampoo, hairspray, nail polish, and all kinds of flexible or soft plastics. Animal testing has shown reproductive toxicity for some phthalates. The second report presents levels of seven separate metabolites or breakdown products of phthalates. One metabolite, monoethyl phthalate, tracks exposure to dimethyl phthalate, commonly used in personal care products such as soap, shampoo and cosmetics. The second report documents that levels of monoethyl phthalate were lower among children than among adolescents or adults. Another metabolite, mono 2 ethylhexel [ph] phthalate, tracks exposure to Dy 2 [ph] ethylhexel phthalate, which is commonly found in flexible or soft plastic products. Levels of mono 2 ethylhexel phthalate showed a different trend and were higher among children than among adolescents or adults. No generally recognized guidelines that indicate threshold values for adverse effects are yet available for levels of these phthalate metabolites.
- DDT was widely used in the United States until EPA banned its use in 1973. However, DDT is still being produced and used in limited quanti-

> ties in other countries. Both DDT and DDE – a major metabolite – persist in people and persist in the environment. The second report presents data showing serum levels of DDE that are three times higher in Mexican Americans than in either non-Hispanic whites or non-Hispanic blacks. Additionally, DDE levels were clearly measurable in people aged 12 to 19 years, even though people in this age group were born after DDT was banned in the United States. The national toxicology program has classified DDT as reasonably anticipated to be a human carcinogen. As yet, no generally recognized guidelines that indicate threshold values for other adverse effects are available. On the encouraging side, compared with levels found in several small studies of DDT exposure in selected groups in the United States before 1990, the DDT and DDE levels in the report are clearly lower.[89]

While the U.S. government agency reporting results found reasons both for encouragement and for concern, the activist organization Pesticide Action Network North America (PANNA) found little reason for optimism. It noted that the test results showed that

> All but five of the 23 pesticides and pesticide metabolites evaluated in this report were found in at least half of the study subjects. Among those tested for pesticide residues in both blood and urine, the average person had 13 pesticides in his or her body. Two chemicals found in nearly all the test subjects were TCP, a metabolite of the insecticide chlorpyrifos (found in 93% of those tested), and *p,p*-DDE, a breakdown product of DDT (found in 99% of those tested). Based on these data – which present results from testing for only a fraction of the pesticides that individuals are actually exposed to – it is clear that most people in the U.S. carry a significant body burden of pesticides and pesticide metabolites.[90]

Turning now to Canadian data, in December 2004 Pollution Watch (a joint undertaking of Environmental Defence and the Canadian Environmental Law Association) issued a report on trends in toxic emissions. Based on data released by Environment Canada, the study, *Shattering the Myth of Pollution Progress in Canada*, revealed the following:

- From 1995 to 2002 the amount of toxic pollutants reported released and transferred increased by 49%. Air releases increased by 21% and water releases increased by 137%.
- While air releases of chemicals designated as toxic under the *Canadian*

Environmental Protection Act (CEPA) and carcinogens have decreased (4% and 22% respectively), air releases of pollutants associated with reproductive and developmental harm have increased 10% from 1995 to 2002.

- Releasing chemicals into the air is still the main method of dealing with waste in Canada. In fact, of all chemicals generated at company sites, 71% ended up in the air in 2002, a total of 3,868,302,111 kilograms.
- In 2002, 7,007,091 kilograms of carcinogens were released into the air in Canada. About 176,030 kilograms were released into the water. [The four largest emitters of carcinogens into the air were: Vitafoam Products Canada Limited (Toronto facility), Inco Limited (Sudbury facility), Weyerhauser Canada Limited (Miramichi, New Brunswick), and Stelco Inc. (Hamilton).]
- In 2002, almost 1 billion kilograms of chemicals (968,107, 576 kilograms) known to cause reproductive and developmental harm were released into the air, the majority of this amount being carbon monoxide. A significant amount of the carbon monoxide is emitted into the environment is from cars and trucks – a source not tracked by NPRI. ... Once carbon monoxide was factored out, 14,386,091 kilograms of air releases known to cause reproductive or developmental harm remained. [In the list of the top 15 polluters, Shell Canada facilities appear three times, accounting for 1,564,007 of emissions, or 10.8 percent of the Canadian total].[91]

Ozone Depletion

Ozone in the earth's upper atmosphere shields organisms from the sun's ultraviolet rays, exposure to which is associated with skin cancer, cataracts, and immune-system problems. Significant decreases in the ozone layer covering over Antarctica were detected in the 1970s by a team of British scientists. Subsequently, an 'ozone hole' was also found over the Arctic. Depletion of stratospheric ozone has been attributed mainly to the release of CFCs (chlorofluorocarbons), but also to bromine compounds and nitrogen oxides. CFCs are used in refrigeration, air conditioning, aerosols, solvents, and some types of packaging; nitrogen oxides are a component of aircraft emissions and other combustion processes.[92]

Although world production of ozone-depleting chlorofluorocarbons fell by 87 per cent between 1988 and 1997,[93] current average ozone losses are 6 per cent in northern mid-latitudes, resulting in increases in ultraviolet radiation of 7 per cent.[94] According to the United Nations

Environment Programme, the thinning of the ozone layer not only threatens human health, but also affects flora and fauna and the planet's climate.[95]

Ironically, while ozone in the stratosphere shields organisms from harmful ultraviolet rays, ground-level ozone, created by the interaction of fuel emissions and sunlight, is a life-threatening pollutant. Yale University researchers, investigating air pollution and morbidity data for ninety-five large U.S. urban centres, attribute 3,767 premature deaths in the year 2000 to short-term exposures to ozone.[96] The authors add: 'This value is probably an underestimate of the total mortality burden from such an increase in ozone because it accounts for only the short term effects.'[97]

Population Growth

It took one hundred years for the world's population to double from 1.25 billion to 2.5 billion (between 1850 and 1950), but less than forty years for it to double again. By October 1999, it exceeded 6 billion. Some project that the world's population may stabilize at 8 to 14 billion over the present century.

It is thought that about 20 per cent of people now live in 'absolute poverty.' It is also estimated that each year half a million women die from complications of pregnancy and childbirth, that 4 million babies die annually in the developing world during their first week of life, and that diarrhoea kills about 2.2 million people each year, most of them children under five. It was a principal contention of the Brundtland Commission that population growth, environmental degradation, and poverty are inextricably linked.

Herman Daly and John Cobb have eerily depicted our present plight as 'living by an ideology of death': 'We human beings are being led to a dead end – all too literally. We are living by an ideology of death and accordingly we are destroying our own humanity and killing the planet.'[98] Unfortunately, their depiction is all too apt.

The antithesis of the 'ideology of death,' as developed partially in this book, is a culture of ecology.

Culture of Ecology

The disparate, indeed antithetical, interpretations of sustainable development noted previously point to the current bifurcation of economic and ecological thinking. Matters were not always thus, however, and the present book proposes (contrary to writers such as Lynn White Jr) that Western economic thought *in its foundations* (the Greek, Hebrew, and medieval writers) was actually profoundly environmentally sound. The book proposes further that the antithesis between 'environment' and 'development' arose only with the Enlightenment, and it investigates the writings of Thomas Hobbes and Adam Smith particularly to detect how this dichotomy arose.

At present, the antithesis between economics and ecology is even manifest in two dichotomous economic approaches to environmental matters. First, the dominant, orthodox approach, known as environmental economics, essentially applies mainstream economic principles and modes of analysis to environmental concerns; ecology becomes, in effect, a branch or an application of neoclassical economic theory. The main recommendation of environmental economists is to subject, so far as possible, human-environment interactions to market forces and price indicators. Sometimes these price indicators are to be 'adjusted' to reflect environmental impacts, but the belief persists among environmental economists that the system of relative prices, once adjusted, will be in principle sufficient to remedy, so far as is desirable (or 'efficient'), environmental degradations.[99] This approach, the present book argues, is quite problematic.

Second, the heterodox, marginalized approach, loosely known as ecological economics, places much less faith in the efficacy of the price system, and may even propose transforming economics itself in accordance with principles of ecology. Ecological economics, however, is very 'pluralistic.' According to Peter Söderbaum, who has written an overview of the field, 'The open-minded attitude [of the ecological economics movement] implies that even a neo-classical environmental economist can refer to her or himself as an ecological economist,'[100] a position validated by Richard Norgaard and other contributors to an anthology devoted to ecological economics.'[101] The scope of the term 'ecological economics' creates difficulties for summarizing or typifying the field. Nonetheless, chapter 5 attempts to do so, and elements drawn from ecological economics undoubtedly will constitute important components of a culture of ecology, defined as systems of symbolism, interpretation, and praxis largely conforming to ecological principles. The culture of ecology, then, encompasses economic as well as other discourses and practices, and implies that these all must become more harmonious with ecological principles.

Systems theorist Ludwig von Bertalanffy once remarked that the human being 'is a denizen of two worlds': a material world in which each person functions as 'a biological organism with the physical equipment, drives, instincts, and limitations of [the] species,' and a second, higher world wherein each one 'creates, uses, dominates, *and is dominated by* ... the universe (or universes) of symbols.'[102] The question, or problematic, for a culture of ecology generally, or for an ecological economics in particular, in the context of von Bertalanffy's insight, is this: Just how can the symbolic, communicatory, verbal, textual 'world' become more consistent with and supportive of the material, biotic 'world,' inextricably linked as they are?

One need not be a scientist (although scientific confirmations are important and abundant) to realize that our experience of external reality is not in accord with the 'dominant paradigm' (or system of meanings) instilled in us day by day and hour by hour by instruments of mass enculturation. It is within the common experience of most of us that the natural environment is deteriorating: Beaches are more often than not closed to swimming; air-quality advisories are continual and routine in the summer months; UV readings warn people to stay out of the sun; boil-water advisories make people apprehensive about the quality of even their municipal (chemically treated and filtered) drinking water; the asphalting of a favourite nature trail and the disappearance of a wetlands in the name of 'development' give people first-hand experience of disappearing ecosystems. In brief, we know experientially that the predominant discourses of business, governments, advertisers, economists, and most often journalists are inconsistent with ecosystem vitality. We do not live in an eco-culture.

These anti-environmental discourses, however, are largely the ones we live by. As Donella Meadows remarked, 'A paradigm is upheld by the constant repetition of ideas that fit within it.'[103] This book asks, in part, why do anti-ecological discourses generally, and neoclassical economics as a prime example in particular, persist in our era when our habitat is so obviously under siege?

As well as attempting to answer that question, the book proposes an alternative – a paradigm shift from the propositions and logics of mainstream (neoclassical) economics and its accompanying cultural supports (advertising, business news, government economic statements and strategies, etc.) to a culture of ecology, that is, a way of thinking and communicating, and ultimately of acting, that is more in tune with our habitat; this entails a shift, in turn, from 'sustainable development,' as the term is most commonly interpreted, to 'sustainable ecosystems.'

The culture of ecology is a vast topic for the simple reason that we are so far removed from ecologically sane thinking and acting. The present book, therefore, is but a beginning. It focuses on mainstream and heterodox economics. Although the discursive subject matter, namely economics, treated here is not the whole story, it is an important beginning, as the economy and the ecosystem are fundamentally in conflict.

Lessons from *Silent Spring*

Some aspects of our approach to current discourses and activities are already manifest in the story of Rachel Carson's book. I will close the chapter by reviewing these.

'Minute causes, mighty effects.' When Rachel Carson penned these words with reference to the human organism as an ecosystem, breast cancer was already ravaging her body. In her book, she also described what has come to be known as *biomagnification*: the manner whereby accumulations of toxic substances pass up the food chain in ever-increasing concentrations. That biological principle has few, if any, correlates in mainstream economic thinking, but it forms a cornerstone of the ecological mindset.

The dialectic of science and technology. Every innovation has both benefits and costs. Promoters tend to publicize the benefits but ignore or downplay the costs. Publicizing the latter, therefore, often falls to those who are quite diminutive compared with the powerful interests in society; this is especially the case if the costs are diffused widely but the initial benefits are concentrated and accrue to the innovator through patents and other monopoly rights. As a related point, once an innovation is in place, the public may grow accustomed to its services, and it may be difficult to wean them from it or to convince them of the harms, particularly if those harms are diffuse or abstract (for example, species extinctions and global warming). Carson's book demonstrates, however, that the general public *can* be made aware and become concerned, at which point public opinion becomes a powerful, corrective force.

The notion of discourse. Discourse is the communication of, or conversations within, a paradigm. Discourses are embedded with systems of assumptions, meanings, vocabularies, images, evidence, and criteria for evidence, propositions, beliefs, values, even heroes and mythic stories.

Rachel Carson told a mythic story – one, unfortunately, all too closely based on reality. The debates that take place within the context of a discourse tend to argue the fine points, not the fundamentals.

The notion of dominant and marginal (orthodox and heterodox) world views or discourses, and the rivalry between (among) them. Marshalling evidence is one way of supporting a discourse and undermining a rival one, but this is certainly not the only way. Mockery, satire, the courts, and publicity are others. One of the jobs of the public relations industry is to make or keep a discourse or way of thinking predominant, sometimes irrespective of its truth,[104] and to discredit or otherwise marginalize an oppositional paradigm or discourse, again irrespective of its validity or truth.

Anthropocentrism as an element of the dominant world view/discourse. Anthropocentrism is the position that humans are 'the measure of all things,'[105] a view quite antithetical to an ecological understanding whose major tenet is the mutual interdependence of all things.

The apparent antimony between economics and ecology, and between business and the environment. In view of their common prefix, *eco*, meaning household or habitation, the apparently antithetical relation between economies and ecology is highly ironic, as well as being of monumental importance. As we will see below, their antithetical relationship results, in part, from different time horizons, the former being very short term compared to the latter.

The notion of paradigms. Developed first by the historian of science Thomas Kuhn, paradigm theory holds that within cultures (including scientific cultures) there is a generally accepted way of viewing things which, when challenged by phenomena it cannot account for, is eventually overthrown and replaced. Nonetheless, those with a vested interest in the old paradigm will endeavour to retain it, modifying it if possible, to better fit the newer circumstances.

The political economy of knowledge and discourse. Some 'ways of seeing,' or paradigms, are profitable to those with wealth and power, and others much less so. Indeed, according to the eminent economic historian Harold Innis, change in the dominant paradigm ('monopoly of knowledge') can coincide with the replacement of one group of power holders by another. In any event, money is often – indeed, it is continuously

– spent to persuade people to think in ways advantageous to those dispensing the cash. Likewise, monetary and other pressures, especially in so-called democracies, inhibit thought and discussion inimical to vested interests (whereas in so-called totalitarian regimes threats are more often physical).[106]

The disjuncture between our knowledge/perception and the objects of our knowledge/perception. In semiotic terms, there is a dialectic of signifier and signified, or as journalist Walter Lippmann once expressed the same point, between the world outside and the pictures in our heads.[107] DDT was previously thought to be a miracle compound, even as it was imperceptibly poisoning unintended species, including humans.

The interaction between ways of thinking and ways of doing. Our thought systems guide our actions, and our actions have real-world consequences; these real-world consequences, in turn, impinge upon and modify our thoughts and perceptions. At one time DDT was thought of as a miracle compound, and hence was used indiscriminately in public and private spaces; when DDT was identified as a lethal chemical with unintended consequences, its use was banned.

The importance of rhetoric, or persuasion. It is not always the truth that wins, at least in the short run, and citizens should always be attuned to rhetorical ploys. Rachel Carson was herself skilled in rhetoric, as the title of her book and the parable she told well illustrate. One of the ploys of rhetoriticians, Walter Lippmann noted many years ago, is the use of 'binders,' by which he meant motherhood terms so broad as to be devoid of meaning; 'sustainable development' in our day is one such binder that this book hopes to expose as being virtually empty of environmental content.

2 Economics and Ecology as Discourses

Discourses

Economics and ecology are *discourses*, that is, verbal structures or literatures. Both bear some relation, albeit problematic, to the objects of their inquiry, respectively, economies and ecosystems. In making this point, we are opening up a huge area of speculation, namely, the relationship between the world out there and our verbal depictions and understandings of it. This is not an issue that can be pursued thoroughly here, but a few essential points can be made.

First, every discourse opens up some aspects of its subject matter while obscuring others. In the case of ecology, the arcadian, pastoral, or romantic view of nature, as espoused by figures such as the naturalists Gilbert White and Carolus Linnaeus (born Carl von Linné), for example, masked the extinctions, conflict, blood, and terror of the natural world. Likewise, the classic Darwin-Spencer model of 'survival of the fittest' obscures insights concerning interdependence among all organisms and the balance of nature. In a similar way, neoclassical economics, by emphasizing the purported beneficence of self-interest, obscures moral norms, communal values, empathy, and generosity. Moreover, by proposing harmony as the inevitable consequence of free markets and the dogged pursuit of self-interest, it veils opposition not only among individuals and among groups or classes of individuals, but even more importantly inconsistencies between the consumption/production practices of humanity and the vitality of the ecosystem.

Second, every discourse is an interacting assemblage of related 'texts.' Each discourse, moreover, comprises a verbal and visual framework that includes whole sets of ideas, words, concepts, images, models, theories, histories, and myths. As emphasized by literary critic Northrop Frye, as 'orders of words,' discourses – and by implication economics and ecology – have histories, internal consistencies, and internal dependencies. Both ecology and economics, in Frye's terms, are 'literatures,' and just as 'the new poem ... is born into an already existing order and is typical of the structure of poetry, which is ready to receive it,'[1] so too is the new scholarly journal article or book born into a world of discourse, and in a sense must 'fit' into that. This is not to say that discourses do not evolve, even perhaps to arrive at positions fundamentally antithetical to those from which they arose. Immediately below we touch on the evolution of mainstream economic and ecological thought, noting some marked twists and turns along the way.

Third, each discourse is a deep structure that patterns thoughts, beliefs, and practices. Discourses provide the general context within which phenomena, actions, objects, and people take on particular meaning or importance. According to Lisa Benton and John Short, 'society relies on [discourses] to make sense of the world [as these provide] a set of general beliefs about the nature of reality.'[2] In the case of ecology, as historian of ecological thought Donald Worster remarks, 'How the living world has been perceived through the aid of the science of ecology ... has had significant consequences for man's relation to the natural order.'[3] One's stance toward, and interactions with, nature will surely depend on whether one views it as a marvellous system of interacting components, say, or as inherently beset by violence, terror, and perpetual struggle.

It is equally true, however, that how the living world, including 'human nature,' has been depicted by economists has significantly affected humans' relations to the natural order. As Geoffrey Hodgson writes, 'Neo-classical economists have preached the doctrine that ... all people are motivated solely by self-interest and greed to millions of students around the world. Accordingly, generations of workers, business people, journalists and politicians have become disposed to belittle moral values and to favour policies based on such presumptions. By assuming the ubiquity of selfishness, such behaviour is legitimated, in turn encouraging more greed and adding to other forces of social, economic and environmental disintegration.'[4]

Analyses and comparisons of discourses, then, can aid our understanding of verbal, cognitive, symbolic, and belief factors which systemically induce activities that have deleterious effects on the environment. Analyses of discourses will shed light on implicit assumptions, preconceptions, values, ways of thinking, modes of analysis, even diction and figures of speech (or *tropes*), all of which make up the means whereby issues and events are presented, discussed, and interpreted, and from which actions ensue. A major goal of this book is to analyse various economic discourses, and to a lesser extent some ecological discourses, from the perspective of species interactions and ecosystem vitality.

Economics and ecology, both being discourses, certainly have important features in common. And over the last century or so, economics and ecology have in fact been intertwined in other interesting and important ways, as we shall see. However, economic and ecological discourses are not monolithic; in fact, there are several competing and often inconsistent economic as well as ecological discourses. That being said, the mainstream or predominant discourses of ecology and economics in our day differ significantly, even to the point that they can aptly be described as being largely antithetical to one another. It makes a huge difference to the future of humanity and the planet which of these discourses predominates.

One final, important point regarding the status of economics and ecology as discourses: the object of ecological discourse is, in the first instance, extrinsic to human thought and activity. True, human thought and activity affect ecosystems, often profoundly. But ecosystems existed long before humans came on the scene, and there will be ecosystem interactions long after humans depart. Such is obviously not true of human economies.

Definitions

Economics

'Economics' combines the Greek words *oikos* (meaning household or dwelling) and *nomos* (management, human law, or custom).[5] As used by Aristotle the term 'economics' meant 'home management' or 'rules of the household,' although that Greek sage also extended its meaning to encompass management of the polis, or city state: for Aristotle, the city, too, was 'home,' or at least a collection of homes, which he believed could be run on much the same principles as a single household. Aristotle's economics is treated in the next chapter.

Adam Smith, often identified as the founder of modern economic thought, described his discipline – he called it *political economy* – as the 'branch of the science' that helps government set conditions to stimulate economic growth.[6] His subject was *political* economy, because it was within the context of statecraft that he studied economic relations. Smith changed the focus of the discipline from that of Aristotle's (and, as we will see in the next chapter, from that of medieval theorists too) concern with issues of social justice (i.e., the distribution of wealth and income) to economic growth. Smith's *The Theory of Moral Sentiments* and *The Wealth of Nations* are compared in the context of ecosystem vitality in chapter 4.

For the modern era – from the rise of neoclassicism in about 1890 to the present – Lionel Robbins's definition is prototypical: economics, he declared, is 'the science which studies human behaviour as a relationship between ends and scarce means which have alternative uses.'[7] Robbins thereby opened the door for an 'imperial science' dealing not just with production, exchange, distribution, and consumption, but with all aspects of human behaviour. Most modern definitions of economics encompass the notion of allocating scarce resources among alternative or competing ends to help satisfy unlimited wants on the part of human actors. Neoclassicist Milton Friedman, more recently, defined the discipline as 'the science of how a particular society solves its economic problems,' such problems arising, according to Friedman, 'whenever scarce means are used to satisfy alternative ends.'[8] Only in Nirvana, Friedman continued, is scarcity not an issue.

The presumed pervasiveness and permanency of scarcity, upon which the 'science' of economics is based, it may be noted, is premised upon a particular, albeit controversial, view of human nature, namely, the proposition that humans inherently and inextricably possess unlimited wants. Unobtrusively embedded in definitions like Friedman's and Robbins's, then, are assumptions, beliefs, and modes of valuation that, as we will see, were never dreamed of except in the West after the onset of the Renaissance.

Also helpful is the definition provided by Alfred Marshall (1842–1924), who is regarded as a seminal figure in modern (neoclassical) economics. In his foundational text, *Principles of Economics* (1st ed. 1890), Marshall defined his discipline as 'a study of men as they live and move and think in the ordinary business of life.'[9] He added that economics 'concerns itself chiefly with those motives which affect, most powerfully and most steadily, man's conduct in the business part of his life.'[10] He acknowledged that humans can and do have motives other than pecuniary ones – personal affection, a conception of duty, and reverence for high ideals, for instance. 'But, for all that,' he continued, 'the steadiest motive to ordinary business work is the desire for the pay which is the material reward of work.' Loftier motives, principles, and ideals, for the purpose of economic analysis, he added, can safely be disregarded. In fact, he continued, 'It is this definite and exact money measurement of the steadiest motives in business life, which has enabled economics far to outrun every other branch of the study of man.'[11] Indeed, mainstream economics is, to a large extent, the study of money and prices.

Definitions are important for understanding neoclassical economics, and for contrasting economic orthodoxy with the ecosystem concept in ecology. Below I expand on neoclassicism's core assumptions, operating principles, and methodologies to draw out some implications for humans' interaction with other species and the natural order.

Ecology

Like 'economics,' the term 'ecology' derives from the Greek *oikos*, meaning 'habitation.' By its etymology, then, ecology is the study of the home or dwelling. The German zoologist Ernst Haeckel coined *oekologie* in 1866, and in 1873 its English translation first appeared in print. Prior to that time, what we now refer to as ecology was called the 'economy of nature.' For Haeckel, 'home' was all of nature. He insisted that economies (that is, human economic activities) are but a portion of, or are contained within, biotic systems. Indeed, he defined *oekologie* as 'the study of the economy, of the household, of animals with both the inorganic and organic environments.'[12] Today, a standard definition of ecology is 'the study of the interactions between living organisms and their environments.'[13] The related term 'ecosystem' denotes 'a unity of interacting organisms and environment.'[14] For ecologist Eugene Odum, the ecosystem constitutes the basic level of analysis for ecology.[15] Therefore, for Odum, ecology is the study of ecosystems.

Environmentalist David Suzuki has provided a more expansive and informative definition of ecology. For Suzuki, ecology is the study 'of the often invisible and mysterious web of relationships [or "pathways"] that connect living things to one another and to their surroundings.'[16] An ecological approach to understanding, he continues, sees the world as 'a set of relationships rather than separated objects.'[17] Suzuki proposes that three types of 'pathways' join each organism to the web of existence. First, there are energy pathways, all of which start with the sun. Upon contact with plant life, sunlight is transformed through photosynthesis into tiny stores of energy locked within the structure of plants, which, when eaten, enter new repositories within the bodily structures of animals. A similar process takes place when a plant-eater is consumed by a carnivore. These energy pathways, often termed the 'food chain,' are, according to Suzuki, 'meandering linear, one-way currents of sun-generated energy.'[18] The second type of pathway concerns the flow of matter. These pathways recirculate carbon, oxygen, nitrogen, phosphorous, and other life-sustaining substances.[19] The matter and energy pathways are, of course, interdependent, since it is energy that moves the matter. Indeed, at a certain level of understanding, matter and energy are but different states of the same substance, and physicists today therefore speak of 'matter-energy.' The third set of pathways, according to Suzuki, is communicatory. Through them flow the symbols associated with the forms or shapes or patterns that matter and energy assume.

Definitions such as the foregoing point to major differences in principles and approaches between the ecosystem concept in ecology and neoclassical economics. I investigate several of these differences below. For the moment, an interesting comment made by ecologist Eugene Odum may suffice: 'While energy can be thought of as the "currency" of ecology, energy and money [the latter being the currency of economics] are not the same because they flow in opposite directions.' Money flows in accordance with human production, through nodes of production from natural resources to finished products; energy, by contrast, flows in the opposite direction as it is transformed from high-grade (low-entropic) to low-grade (high-entropic) forms through production processes. Moreover, as Odum notes, 'money circulates while energy does not;'[20] consequently, money is unable to track the linear flow of high-grade light energy from the sun, which through a series of transformations is cast off through radiation as heat into the universe.

Evolution of Discourses

Economics

Economics, like other discourses, is not static. Moreover, at any given time there is an orthodox or mainstream version as well as heterodoxies or discourses of dissent. In addition, variations and controversies exist within both mainstream and heterodox schools, and lines of demarcation between or among schools of thought may therefore be blurred; indeed, over time, what was once an outsider position may become orthodoxy, especially if there is an accompanying shift in socio-economic power. This section looks briefly at the evolution of mainstream economics discourses. I will return to the evolution of economic thought and compare economic orthodoxies and heterodoxies throughout the book, and in chapter 5 I will contrast mainstream and heterodox economic discourses concerning the environment. For the present, however, I provide but a brief overview of the evolution of mainstream economic discourses.

Mainstream economics, as developed in Europe and introduced to North America over the last several centuries, may be said to have had three distinct stages, each based on a different theory of value. The *Physiocrats* – 'founders of economics as a science'[21] – held sway, particularly in France, in the last decades of an essentially agricultural, extractive economy (1756–76), a time when the landed aristocracy was still at the apex of the social-economic hierarchy. The Physiocrats affirmed the existing power structure by proffering a land theory of value; they maintained that all economic activity depends ultimately on agriculture and on resource extraction. Bountiful harvests, according to these theorists, give rise to surpluses that can be saved and reinvested, and that allow some workers to pursue non-farming activities, such as manufacturing. In contrast, all non-agricultural pursuits are 'sterile' as they yield no surplus.

With industrialism, however, the Physiocrats' influence waned. An economics endorsing rents to the landed aristocracy and belittling activities of the 'captains of industry' was not, after all, in tune with the changing economic climate. The major single *classical economics* text bolstering the claims of the emerging capitalist class was, of course, Adam Smith's *The Wealth of Nations*, first published in 1776. Smith's economic theory, like that of subsequent major classical political economists (Malthus, Ricardo, Bentham, Marx), was premised on a *labour theory of value.* At first this might seem paradoxical: a mainstream economics attributing all value to labour amid burgeoning capitalist power.[22] The paradox is partially resolved, however, once it is recalled that the classical economists defined *capital* as 'stored-up labour,' owned of course by 'capitalists.' Workers, in contrast, possess only 'labour power,' that is, their own capacity to do work, and to utilize that labour power they must generally attain access to the means of production (the 'stored-up' labour).

Marx went further, arguably sowing the seeds for the demise of classical economics. He claimed that if labour is the source of all value, then workers *should* receive that value. From the perspective of substantiating or 'justifying' existing power arrangements, then, classical economics was deficient, and in fact the eighteenth and nineteenth centuries were beset by strident demands to increase rights for the less privileged. The rather weak rejoinder on the part of conservative classical political economics to demands for political-economic reform and economic justice was that any movement toward equality in the distribution of wealth would merely serve to swell the ranks of the working class due to their innate propensity to procreate (Malthus's principle of population), driving wages back down to subsistence levels ('the iron law of wages'). The wealthier classes, by contrast, could reproduce profusely without unduly lowering average wealth and income due to their small numbers to begin with – a rather invidious argument and one ill-suited to placate revolutionaries and reformers of the day.

Neoclassical economics, by contrast, which replaced classical economics at the turn of the last century, makes no such invidious class distinctions, and indeed eschews class altogether in buttressing yet another theory of value. According to neoclassicism, the value of a commodity depends directly, not upon its land content, nor its labour content, but ultimately upon subjective considerations of 'utility.' True, 'land' and 'labour' are recognized as factors of production and hence enter the cost calculations, but it is fundamentally the aggregation of subjective preferences, ever shifting, that renders these factor inputs (and hence the products that embody them) 'valuable.' The neoclassical theory, therefore, *ostensibly absolves any individual or class from responsibility for bad outcomes*: if there is poverty or environmental degradation, it can be argued (and is), no individual or class is to blame, because ultimately the 'Market' expresses *every* individual's 'utility' (or rather, *marginal* utility). In fact, in the extreme, it could be (and often is) claimed that in principle nothing adverse can possibly happen since value is deemed to be synonymous with market valuations. (The present book critiques these contentions.) Further aspects demarcating classical and neoclassical economics will be addressed in subsequent chapters.

It may be noted briefly that since the 1960s some have claimed yet a fourth 'factor of production' to have become central, an implication being that we can perhaps anticipate yet another fundamental shift in mainstream economic theory. Fritz Machlup's 1962 book, *The Production and Distribution of Knowledge in the United States*, was seminal in conceiving information and/or knowledge production, processing, and distribution as important economic activities. Machlup calculated that nearly

29 per cent of U.S. output and 32 per cent of U.S. employment in 1958 were accounted for by 'knowledge industries' whose annual growth averaged between 8 and nearly 11 per cent. Machlup and Marc Porat, who extended Machlup's analyses, helped spawn a still-burgeoning literature on 'post-industrial society' or the 'information economy,' a topic treated in chapter 6.

Ecology

Ecological issues were discussed in antiquity by Aristotle and his pupil Theophrastus.[23] Although the *idea* of ecology dates back thousands of years, as a formal discipline it is little more than a century old. Even so, intellectual historian Donald Worster describes dramatic changes (or 'paradigm shifts') in ecology during that relatively brief time.

Worster suggests that ecology was inaugurated with the publication in 1789 of *The Natural History of Selborne* by the English pastor and naturalist Gilbert White (1720–93). The 'arcadian' perspective of that book, Worster claims, 'laid the foundations for the natural history essay in England and America.'[24] White's goal had been to describe how the wildlife in Selborne formed an interrelated system.[25] He saw divine planning everywhere, resulting in a harmony among the species. His was a holistic, organic view of nature, where individual organisms interact to form a *biotic community*.

A second pioneering figure was Carolus Linnaeus (1707–78). He too is sometimes credited with inaugurating ecology as a modern science,[26] due in part to his detailed classification of plant species into kingdom, phylum, class, order, family, genus, and species. But Linnaeus was more than a mere taxonomer. He also developed a philosophy of ecology, and his essay of 1749, 'Oeconomia Naturae' (The Economy of Nature), according to Worster, 'quickly became the single most important summary of an ecological point of view still in its infancy.'[27] Devoutly religious, Linnaeus nonetheless was also a product of the Enlightenment, and his ecological discourses reflect both a tension and a synthesis between these often disparate world views. On the one hand, Linnaeus 'saw a perfect hierarchy in the natural world'[28] and proposed that 'all things are made for the sake of man.'[29] On the other, he introduced the notion of the 'balance of nature' as a scientific theory.[30] Reminiscent of Newtonian physics, Linnaeus saw the biotic sphere as a grand machine, intricately composed of 'detachable, replaceable parts'[31] – a vision quite at odds with Gilbert White's organicism. Moreover, Linnaeus maintained that all species are linked through the great chain of being, and that the 'divine economy' assures abundance for all. Although acknowledging that in nature catastrophes occur and strife persists, Linnaeus also insisted that these are but details, and that at the level of the whole system there is harmony.[32] Linnaeus also proposed a cyclical pattern to all existence, whereby everything returns to its point of origin.

As the title 'Economy of Nature' suggests, even at this early stage in the development of ecological thought connections were being forged with classical political economy. For Linnaeus, the human economy was but an extension of ecological principles. Writing in 1746, he declared: 'Nature has arranged itself in such a way that each country produces something especially useful,' adding: 'The task of economics is to collect [plants] from other places and cultivate [at home] such things that don't want to grow [here] but can grow [here].'[33] Linnaeus hoped to transform Sweden into a self-sufficient state by applying principles derived from nature to politics and the economy. For example, he advocated naturalizing such unsuitable food crops as tea, rice, and olives to improve Sweden's economic self-sufficiency, a recommendation based upon his belief that every country is abundantly provided for by God and hence possesses sufficient resources for a 'multifunctional economy,'[34] and upon a utilitarian, mechanistic view of nature as destined to be 'managed' for the benefit of humans.

Linnaeus, then, saw himself not only as a biologist, but also as a political economist, and his writings were known to Adam Smith.[35] Indeed, there are close parallels between Smith's mechanistic view of the economy as coordinated harmoniously through the workings of the 'invisible hand' and Linnaeus's mechanistic view of nature whereby components interact harmoniously as a result of a divine plan. Moreover, Linnaeus maintained that the economy of nature was designed by Providence to maximize production and efficiency, just as Adam Smith saw increased production and efficiency as the goal for the human economy.

Even at ecology's beginnings, it may be noted, there was a rupture or fundamental dichotomy. On the one hand, White's metaphor for species interactions was that of an organism, and his interest was to depict how species interact to form an organic community that is greater than the sum of the parts. On the other hand, Linnaeus, although in accord with White regarding the overall divine harmony of the ecosphere, saw the interactions in mechanical terms, and the organic components as replaceable parts.

Romanticism in ecological thought is epitomized by the field ecologist and philosopher of nature Henry David Thoreau (1817–62).[36] Thoreau condemned the utilitarian spirit of his age, and with it the economists' insistence that humans, by nature, have infinite material wants. Like Gilbert White, he advocated a simple life and a close familiarity with nature. One of Thoreau's major contributions to ecological theory was the principle of ecological succession – the notion that through time ecosystems undergo change in their structure or composition. Even more significantly, however, Thoreau, like White and Linnaeus, helped inspire the ecosystem concept in ecology.

The science of ecology shifted ground abruptly with the Darwinian revolution. Charles Darwin (1809–82), a contemporary of Thoreau, deemed as no longer tenable the agency of a divine creator or mechanic, and proposed that competition in the struggle for existence was the first law of nature. With Darwin, moreover, connections between ecology and economics intensified. Darwin and Alfred Russel Wallace, co-originators of the doctrine of evolution through natural selection, each avowed indebtedness to Rev. Thomas Robert Malthus (1766–1834), a founding figure in classical political economy.[37] In 1798 Malthus published anonymously *An Essay on the Principle of Population as it Affects the Future Improvement of Society*, and thereafter economics was renowned as 'the dismal science.' For Malthus, in animal life there is an 'instinct' or propensity, uninterrupted by reason or concern for provisioning for offspring, that 'impels' species to increase and that unless 'checked' will outpace growth in the food supply. But 'checks,' according to Malthus, were in abundance: in the case of human beings, 'all unwholesome occupations, severe labour and exposure to the seasons, extreme poverty, bad nursing of children, great towns, excesses of all kinds, the whole train of common diseases and epidemics, wars, pestilence, plague, and famine.'[38]

Darwin read Malthus's *Essay* 'for amusement,' and was struck with an explanation for his surmised ascent of life forms. Malthus's *Principle of Population* was for Darwin a force in nature, lacking in the purpose or design of plant and animal breeders, but nonetheless 'selecting' organisms. Hence, Darwin wrote, the 'Struggle for Existence' is simply 'the doctrine of Malthus applied with manifest force to the whole animal and vegetable kingdoms.' 'For,' he continued, 'every organic being naturally increases at so high a rate, that if not destroyed, the earth would soon be covered by the progeny of a single pair ... Even slow-breeding man has doubled in twenty-five years, and at this rate, in a few thousand years, there would literally not be standing room for his progeny.'[39] Darwin's genius is all the more evident when it is recalled that the rules of heredity as developed by Gregor Mendel, and the concept of genetic mutation, were not known to him when he formulated his theory.

Despite manifest commonality between Malthus's principle of population and Darwin's theory of natural selection, Darwin departed significantly from Malthus. Malthus had been intent on defending the status quo, in nature and in society.[40] His population principle depicted nature as periodically restoring equilibrium or balance, the implication being that human 'interference' – for instance, by implementing social measures to alleviate human suffering – was vain and misguided; efforts to improve the lot of the poor would merely disrupt the natural cycles (the 'checks') put in place by a beneficent Providence. By contrast, Darwin's *principle of natural selection* (or 'survival of the fittest' as it came to be known) advanced the doctrine of sequential and cumulative change without limit and without a predetermined goal or destination. Whereas Malthus, moreover, viewed the struggle for existence as a regrettable, if not indeed tragic, existential condition, Darwin lauded the very same struggle because, he exclaimed, 'the most exalted object of which we are capable of conceiving, namely the production of higher animals, directly follows.' He added, 'There is grandeur in this view of life.'[41]

Darwin's makeover of ecology, stemming initially from classical political economy, had in turn a recursive impact on its progenitor, as manifested most emphatically in the Social Darwinism of Herbert Spencer (1820–1903) in England and William Graham Sumner (1840–1910) in the United States, and arguably in the free-market economics of our day. It was Spencer who coined the term 'survival of the fittest,' and he applied an evolutionary perspective analogous to natural selection in the biosphere to such otherwise seemingly disparate categories as ideas, institutions, societies, laws, customs, knowledge, artefacts, technology, and the economy. Likewise, Yale University political economist and sociologist William Graham Sumner was explicit with regard to the economic implications of Malthus's 'struggle for existence,' declaring: 'The law of survival of the fittest was not made by man,' and 'interfering with it [can only] produce the survival of the unfittest.'[42] Charles Dickens satirized classical political economists like Malthus and Sumner in such works as *A Christmas Carol.*

What has come to be known as the Darwinian view of ecology differed substantially,[43] of course, from that of Linnaeus and White. First, both Linnaeus and White proposed an essential harmony to biotic existence, whereas for Darwinists life was continuous struggle among antagonistic forces. Second, Linnaeus and White emphasized the cyclical nature of existence whereas Darwinists stressed linear, evolutionary change. Third, White's and Linnaeus's analyses were much more holistic than Darwin's, or at least the portion that had the biggest impact;[44] Darwin focused on the struggle for survival of individual organisms and species, and adaptation of species to changes in their environs, whereas Linnaeus and White emphasized interdependence among all species.

A third stage in the development of modern ecological thought began with the work of English botanist Alfred Tansley (1871–1955), who set forth the concept of the ecosystem in 1935.[45] Tansley defined the ecosystem as 'The whole system (in the sense of physics) including not only the organism-complex but also the whole complex of physical factors forming what we call the environment of the biome – the habitat factors in the widest sense.'[46]

Tansley's goal had been to create a mathematical science of energy flows. On the one hand his analysis was holistic as it took into account interactions among all organisms in an area; on the other hand, however, it was reductive, as his intention was to confine the subject matter of ecology to the working out of laws of physics and chemistry.[47] Eugene and Howard Odum were most responsible for expanding the circumference of Tansley's ecosystem concept into what it means for environmentalists today. Eugene Odum's *Fundamentals of Ecology* appeared in 1953 and went through several editions. Although he didn't eschew the mathematical and statistical approaches, Odum insisted, however, that a theory of the ecosystem must be holistic ('hological'), not just reductive ('merological'),[48] that it must treat systems as wholes as well as discuss the parts and endeavour to construct systems from them.[49] Odum viewed ecosystems as self-organizing entities, like organisms, and maintained that ecosystem vitality required mutualism and cooperation, not just predation and competition.[50] For him a basic principle of ecology was that over time organisms learn to cooperate to their mutual benefit. He proposed further that nature should be the guide for policies that would govern human behaviour, a project he termed 'human ecology.'[51]

Today, not all ecologists accept Odum's position, and some even deny the utility of the ecosystem concept[52] – an amazing position to assume given the virtually universal acceptance of hydrological and nutritional cycles and of plant-animal synergies. Equally amazing, however, is the fact that not all contemporary ecologists, perhaps only a minority, are environmentalists! A leading Swedish ecologist, Thomas Söderqvist, remarked that many ecologists today 'seem to do ecology for fun only, indifferent to practical problems, including the salvation of the nation.

They are mathematically and theoretically sophisticated, sitting indoors calculating on computers, rather than traveling out in the wilds. They are individualists, abhorring the idea of large-scale ecosystem projects.'[53]

Among environmentalists, however, including ecologists who count themselves as environmentalists, the ecosystem concept is fundamental. Henceforth, when I refer to the ecosystem concept as setting a pattern upon which human economic activity should be modelled, I will at least implicitly refer to the 'holistic ecosystem concept,' as formulated by the Odums and supported by environmentalists such as David Suzuki, Arne Naess, Aldo Leopold, Rachel Carson, Paul Ehrlich, E.O. Wilson, among others.[54] This concept is also consistent with general systems theory as developed by Ludwig von Bertalanffy, Norbert Wiener, Kenneth Boulding, and others. According to general systems theory, a 'system is made up of sets of components that work together for the overall objective of the whole'; the properties of a system are contingent not only upon the attributes of the components, but also upon the relationships among the components and among their attributes.[55]

The holistic ecosystem concept presumes that ecosystems constitute wholes that cannot be described adequately or completely by disaggregating them into their components, and that the components in interaction take on properties that could not have been foreseen from a knowledge of the parts alone. Further properties of the holistic ecosystem concept are detailed later in this chapter.

For at least part of its history, then, ecology, like its close cousin economics, has been inconsistent with sustaining viable ecosystems. The doctrine of survival of the fittest, for example, was often construed in a normative way as indicating that what endures 'deserves' to endure, and that 'might makes right,' seemingly justifying human despoliation of habitats and rendering extinct 'unfit' species. Darwin himself opined that humans should seek the extinction of the orang-utan on the grounds that they occupied similar niches.[56] The Darwinian model of ecology contributed to a vision of nature as hostile, malignant, and in need of being 'civilized' through the exercise of human power and control, a position not unrelated to massacres of indigenous peoples about the globe by those of European ancestry. The Darwinian model supported the notion that people 'in nature' are 'primitive' and inferior, and that to be detached from or 'above' nature is not only superior but is the only way of constructing a moral universe. Darwinism, furthermore, buttressed anthropocentrism by viewing humans in terms of a hierarchy of value.

Contemporary Economics and Ecology as Antithetical Discourses

At present, mainstream economics and the holistic ecosystem concept in ecology constitute fundamentally rival, even antithetical discourses or thought systems, even though their respective subjects – namely, the economy and environment/ecosystems – are inextricably linked.[57] The Brundtland Commission recognized this and stressed that environmental and economic problems must no longer 'be treated separately by fragmented institutions and policies.'[58] It also recognized, however, that institutions and policies will continue to be fragmented as long as economic and ecological discourses remain antithetical and inconsistent. According to the commission, 'Economics and ecology must be completely integrated.'

Without doubt, economics and ecology need to become more compatible, but how such compatibility is achieved is very much an issue. Today there exist two radically different approaches to forging such compatibility or integration. The first approach, which this book argues is quite problematic, is to extend the reach of mainstream (neoclassical) economics to encompass environmental concerns; this is the action plan of today's environmental economists, and it often finds favour with policy-makers. This approach essentially entails addressing environmental concerns and issues by means of mainstream economic theory, principles, assumptions, and modes of analysis; ecology becomes, in effect, a subdiscipline or application of neoclassical economics.

The second approach is to mould or transform economics by infusing it with holistic ecosystem principles and modes of understanding. Economics in this case would conform to the ecosystem concept. In past decades Kenneth Boulding and Nicolas Georgescu-Roegen made valiant efforts in this regard, and today that project is carried forward by a group of heterodox scholars known as ecological economists.

The present chapter identifies key, currently conflicting principles in economics and the holistic ecosystem concept. In subsequent chapters I investigate how and when these principles came into conflict, emphasizing also the harmony that existed in previous eras, as this may be helpful as we now endeavour to reintegrate or reconcile these two disparate world views or paradigms.

Major Traits of Neoclassical Economics Discourse

A major objective of this book is to establish that mainstream economics as a discursive system is, at its very core, anti-environmental. A listing and discussion of some of its anti-environmental traits follows, the implication being that neoclassical approaches to environmental problems should be studiously set aside and ignored.

ANTHROPOCENTRISM AND VALUE

Economics (like other of the social sciences) is an anthropocentric, or human-centred, discipline or world view. Economics is, and always has been, concerned with the human struggle to attain and allocate the material means of existence. That having been said, it is also true that today's neoclassical economics is far more anthropocentric than its precursors. The Physiocrats' land theory of value is an obvious case in point, and quite arguably much was lost when economists ceased attributing all value to nature. Likewise, however, the labour theory of value, while certainly anthropocentric and hence anti-environmental (nature not worked upon by humans by definition has no value), at least grounded value in something extrinsic to human whims and preferences.

ANTHROPOCENTRISM AND THE MEANING OF HOME

Since economics literally means 'home management,' an immediate question concerns the meaning for economists of 'home.' This frame of reference is key to understanding the divide between economics and ecology. Mainstream economists view the home as the sphere of human production, distribution, and consumption; they ignore ecosystem interactions except insofar as these provide immediate inputs (the 'primary sector') to processes of human production. Biotic activities beyond the sphere of human production are of little or no concern to neoclassical economists as these are outside the home. By contrast, for ecologist Ernst Haeckel, home was nature, and ecologists today understand that economies (that is, human economic activities) are an aspect of, and contained within, ecosystems.

HUMAN NATURE

The assumption that human beings possess infinite wants, a postulate of Thomas Hobbes (1588–1679), has characterized mainstream economics ever since the days of Adam Smith (1723–90). Indeed, individual maximizing behaviour is still emphatically encouraged by neoclassicism, due to the venerable presumption that such actions best contribute to the wealth of the nation. The assumption that humans are essentially unlimited appetitive machines, moreover, allows neoclassicists to focus on production instead of distribution (i.e., issues of equality/inequality): since wants are presumed never to be satiated, unconstrained accumulation is 'justified' and 'mere' distribution becomes at best a secondary concern. (See the discussion concerning Pareto optimality below.)

Here we come to a paradox in neoclassical thought. On the one hand, it presents itself as a doctrine of freedom[59] since the focus is on autonomous individuals wending their way through markets, selecting those goods and services that best serve their needs and wants, in contrast to systems in which the heavy hand of the state tells people what is good for them. On the other hand, neoclassicism sees itself as the 'physics' of the social sciences; given relative prices, people's 'decisions' are determined by their tastes and preferences – people are not psychologically 'free to choose.' Classical economist and utilitarian philosopher Jeremy Bentham (1748–1832) stated what has become the essential neoclassical position, and in stark terms: 'Nature has placed mankind under the governance of two sovereign masters, pain and pleasure. It is for them alone to point out what we might do, as well as to determine what we shall do. On the one hand the standard of right and wrong, on the other the chain of causes and effects are fastened to their throne.'[60]

The contention that humans inherently possess unlimited wants and that they cannot transcend the pleasure-pain principle would seem to be inconsistent with biospheric health on a finite planet. If the earth is finite in its capacity to supply resources and assimilate wastes, then the future of an infinitely grasping humankind is bleak indeed. As developed in the next chapter, however, this presumption concerning human nature is quite recent in the history of Western culture; it is, we could say, an invention of capitalism. Great thinkers of the past never dreamed of depicting human beings in this way. As proposed by political philosopher C.B. Macpherson, it makes great ecological sense to 'retrieve' antecedent conceptions of humans as, for example, developers of skills and exerters of talents, rather than infinite acquirers and consumers.[61]

MARGINAL ANALYSIS, MAXIMIZATION

Central to modern economic analysis is the principle of maximization, to be achieved by equating marginal (or incremental) costs and benefits. Indeed, this incremental principle is perhaps the single most important characteristic differentiating neoclassical economics from its classical precursor. Profits, for example, are maximized when the marginal, or incremental, cost of producing one more unit just approaches the revenues to be gleaned from the sale of that increment. Worker satisfaction, likewise, is said to be at a maximum when the 'disutility' (cost) in money terms of working one more hour just approaches (is just slightly less than) the incremental wage earned thereby. As long as the marginal benefit of producing more units or working extra time exceeds the incremental cost, the activity should (and, due to pecuniary incentives, will) be expanded; however, if the incremental cost exceeds the benefit, it should and will be cut back until cost savings fall just slightly below foregone revenue. For neoclassical economists, the maximization point is one of stability or equilibrium and the tendency for all economic actors is to move persistently toward that optimal point. (This economic notion of equilibrium, incidentally, recalls Linnaeus's notion of equilibrium in the biosphere.)

This incremental, or marginal, mode of analysis, however, is anti-environmental. Since it is the last dollar spent, the last item purchased, the last sale made, or the last hour worked that is of primary concern in this neoclassical economic model, little attention is paid to overall scale. Although the incremental approach may indeed inform individual consumers, firms, and workers regarding their optimal scale of activity, it is silent in terms of the optimal scale of the macro-economy. As Herman Daly and John Cobb attest, 'The market does not measure marginal costs and benefits of changes in scale, only marginal costs and benefits of exchanges and reallocations ... The notion of optimal scale is defined in terms other than efficiency, namely ecological sustainability. The market sees only efficiency – it has no organs for hearing, feeling, or smelling either justice or sustainability.'[62]

CONSUMER SOVEREIGNTY AND METHODOLOGICAL INDIVIDUALISM

Neoclassical theory applies the maximization principle to the decision-making processes of single consumers, producers, and workers – an approach sometimes referred to as 'methodological individualism,' the presumption being that the economy is additive. This basic tenet of modern economics dates back at least to the classical economics of Adam Smith, and the stance has permitted economists ever since to postulate that maximizing, egocentric individuals contribute, albeit non-deliberatively, to the benefit of the whole economy – to the 'wealth of nations.' While inequality and monopoly power make this proposition dubious even from a strictly economic point of view, in terms of the environment this axial principle of neoclassical economics can be lethal. A maximizing individual or firm (a Union Carbide at Bhopal, for example, or an Exxon at Prince William Sound, or even an urban resident spraying her lawn with pesticides) can cause substantial damage – not just in the present but also for future generations.

The neoclassical subfield of environmental economics is, in part, an attempt to maintain the ostensible autonomy of the economic actor (methodological individualism), albeit guided through prices that purportedly take into account environmental impacts. I argue below, however, that prices are insufficient guides to action as individuals are radically dependent upon each other and upon all other species for survival. The methodological individualism of neoclassical economics, including that of its offspring, environmental economics, flies in the face of this ecosystem reality.

Neoclassical economics' penchant for methodological individualism has pernicious environmental implications in another way too. As noted by Vatn and Bromley, 'Economists tend to overlook (or dismiss) the contextual [social] framing of individual preferences.'[63] In mainstream economics, individual preferences are simply presumed to be there, and are treated as 'sovereign' (the doctrine of *consumer sovereignty*). As Nobel laureates George Stigler and Gary Becker put it in the title of a journal article, 'De Gustibus Non Est Disputandum.'[64] Therefore the task of economic policy, according to neoclassicism, is to organize the economy in such a way that it will satisfy so far as possible these 'autonomous,' pre-existing, and not-to-be-disputed 'sovereign' tastes and preferences. However, as many social psychologists, anthropologists, and advertisers know, many tastes and preferences are learned; they are not genetically encoded. And they are learned, moreover, within a social context. In our day, that social context includes the mass media, which are largely devoted not simply to modifying existing tastes and preferences but to creating new ones. The media, in fact, are intent on reinforcing and promoting an ethic of accumulation and consumption. From an ecological perspective, therefore, mainstream economics misses the boat if and when it adheres to the maxim 'De Gustibus non est disputandum.' Should the momentary, and easily manipulated, subjective valuations of 'consumers,' for example, constitute the primary (sole?) basis upon which ultimate (i.e., irreversible) questions like species extinctions are decided? Strictly adhering to the neoclassical doctrine of consumer sovereignty would mean that such would be the case. An ecologically much saner approach would be to inquire into policies conducive to producing ecologically benign tastes and preferences.

But to question the sovereignty of tastes and preferences as they exist at any given moment is to undermine much of economic modelling as it currently exists. Once tastes and preferences are treated as contingent variables, nothing remains within the standard economics model to be maximized, and so the model itself becomes quite indeterminate! This makes the reluctance of mainstream economists to delve into this area quite understandable, if not laudable.

Finally, individual preference, the core 'justification' of price solutions, is based at least in part on knowledge. In terms of ecosystem interactions, however, human knowledge is overwhelmed by ignorance. E.O. Wilson has estimated that of all species extant on the earth, scientists have managed to name only perhaps 10 per cent. Simply identifying a species and naming it, of course, is but a first step toward learning about its interactions with other species. What we do not know, we cannot name, and what we cannot name we cannot value. According to Wilson's estimate, then, 90 per cent of species on the earth today are not and cannot be valued: they are, in fact, worthless according to our primary (pecuniary) mode of valuation, even though individually or in combination these species contribute to the fabric of biodiversity and thereby extend the capacity of the ecosystem to sustain human and other life. On this basis, we would expect economies emphasizing the price system as a medium of communication to experience alarming rates of species extinctions, and indeed estimates are that twenty thousand species worldwide disappear every year. Today we are making consumption and production decisions that carry irreversible consequences, but it is as if our ears were stopped and our eyes blindfolded as we exercise our 'consumer sovereignty.'

There are ways other than pecuniary or economic ones of valuing species. Environmental philosopher Mark Sagoff suggests that

> Species may be profoundly important for cultural and spiritual reasons ... Even those plants and animals that do not define places possess enormous intrinsic value and are worth preserving for their own sake. What gives these creatures value lies in their histories, wonderful in themselves, rather than in any use to which they can be put. The biologist E.O. Wilson elegantly takes up this theme: 'Every kind of organism has reached this point in time by threading one needle after another, throwing up brilliant artifices to survive and reproduce against nearly impossible odds.' Every plant or animal evokes not just sympathy but also reverence and wonder in those who know it.[65]

But even these thoughts are deficient from an environmentalist's perspective, as care and reverence for a species are evoked only 'in those who know it.' Sagoff's call to revere individual species must, therefore, be augmented by a reverence for the web of life itself.

EFFICIENCY

Every system of thought, I would suggest, privileges one or a few values or criteria above others. For Aristotle it was *eudaimonia* (happiness), while for the ancient Hebrews distributive justice was of great importance. For Adam Smith the transcendent goal was economic growth – to be achieved through increases in trade and in the division of labour. For modern neoclassicists the transcendent values, arguably, are consumer sovereignty and efficiency. We have touched on consumer sovereignty above; here I focus on efficiency, although as I will explain momentarily these two criteria in neoclassicism fold in upon one another.

In the neoclassical economics literature, there are several dimensions to the term 'efficiency':[66] *X-efficiency* is the effectiveness with which a given set of inputs are used to produce outputs, with no inquiry as to whether either the chosen inputs or outputs are appropriate. *Allocative efficiency*, by way of contrast, does enquire into the appropriateness of the selected inputs and outputs: Can the same output be produced more cheaply with a different array of inputs? Would a different mix of outputs have higher value? Finally, *Pareto Efficiency*, or *Pareto Optimality*, is defined as a situation in which no one can be made better off without at least one person becoming worse off. Pareto optimality, it is to be noted, has little or nothing to do with distributive justice, as even an economy in which a single person has all the wealth can satisfy the Pareto criterion of optimality.

A case can be made that 'efficiency' in the first two meanings of the term is pro-environmental. It is surely a good thing not to use more resources than needed to produce a given level of output. Problems arise with these notions of efficiency, however, once one asks which costs are included and how costs are calculated. In neoclassicism costs are determined by the prices times quantities of factor inputs. In other words, it is not the physical amount of resources that are to be minimized for efficiency, but the money value of these resources. The money system, in brief, is fully implicated in neoclassical definitions of efficiency.

Moreover, individual economic decision makers, intent on maximization, as intimated by Alfred Marshall, consider only costs to themselves. It is from this deficiency that the vast literature on 'externalities' arose.

Maximizing producers and consumers, neoclassicists acknowledge, can inadvertently impose costs on bystanders, and one way this can happen is through environmental degradation. As developed below, the approach most frequently recommended by environmental economists to rectify the externalities problem is to estimate the market value of these third-party costs, and either include them in prices or use taxes to constrain production and consumption. But the basis upon which modified prices are arrived at is generally the estimation of the value of these harms to consumers or other producers. In brief, the doctrines of consumer sovereignty and insatiable wants are fully implicated in economic definitions of efficiency and in neoclassical 'solutions' to environmental degradation.

THE NEOCLASSICAL TRIAD

In neoclassical economics, land, labour, and capital are set forth as the fundamental factors of production, and the entire edifice of microeconomic theory is premised on the validity of this taxonomy. In macroeconomics, too, the system of national accounts is based on these underlying productive factors. This classification (land-labour-capital) results in much different lines of analysis, however, than would more ecologically sensitive categorizations – matter-energy-information, for instance, a proposal set forth by Kenneth Boulding and addressed in chapters 5 and 6. As we saw from David Suzuki's definition of 'ecology,' matter-energy-communication corresponds more closely to the concerns and understanding of ecologists. Perhaps the greatest detriment to using land, labour, and capital as factors of production, however, is that these are defined in terms of markets: 'land' is the factor that receives 'rent'; 'labour' receives 'wages'; and 'capital' earns 'interest'; the summation of these rewards gives 'national income.' What is excluded from this taxonomy and mode of analysis, however, is not merely the human production that does not pass through markets (e.g., housework, underground economies), but 'nature's work' as in the propagation of organisms, and the recycling of basic materials.

PRICES AS INFORMATION

At the heart of neoclassical economics is the belief that prices are informational and that in principle they automatically guide economic actors into the most socially beneficial activities. Nobel laureate Friedrich von Hayek (1899–1992) is one who lauded the informational properties of the price system. The economic problem, Hayek maintained, is largely that of coordination, stemming from the fact that 'knowledge of the circumstances of which we must make use never exists in concentrated or integrated form, but solely as the dispersed bits of incomplete and frequently contradictory knowledge which all the separate individuals [in any economy] possess.'[67] How, he asked, can one use knowledge 'not given to anyone in its totality'?[68] His reply: market prices. Each price, Hayek proclaimed, is an 'index,' which is to say 'concentrated information,' reflecting the significance of any particular scarce resource relative to all others.[69] The index or price borne by each commodity, he added, permits autonomous economic agents to adjust their strategies 'without having to solve the whole puzzle [i.e., input-output matrix] *ab initio.*' For him, the main function of the price system is to serve as 'a mechanism for communicating information.'[70] As Hayek explained, 'In abbreviated form, by a kind of symbol, only the most essential information is passed on, and passed on only to those concerned ... The marvel is that in a case like that of a scarcity of one raw material, without an order being issued, without more than perhaps a handful of people knowing the cause, tens of thousands of people whose identity could not be ascertained by months of investigation, are made aware to use the material or its products more sparingly; *i.e.*, they move in the right direction.'[71]

The same theme, which can be found at least implicitly in virtually every microeconomics textbook, was taken up explicitly by Nobel laureate Kenneth Arrow. He, too, proposed that 'the competitive system can be viewed as an information and decision structure.' Buyers and sellers, he contended, with but limited knowledge save their own preferences and costs can make optimal decisions if and when confronted by 'correct' prices. Arrow continued, 'The prices are then, according to the pure theory, the only communication that needs to be made in addition to the information held initially by the agents. This makes the market system appear to be very efficient indeed; not only does it achieve as good an allocation as an omniscient planner could, but it clearly minimizes the amount of communication needed.'[72]

To be sure, Arrow is a much more critical neoclassicist than Hayek, and in publications like *The Limits of Organization*[73] he qualified the capacity of unadjusted market prices to allocate resources optimally. Nonetheless, he does adhere to the basic neoclassical premise: prices are conceptually sufficient to guide individual, maximizing economic agents into activities that are the most beneficial for the overall economy and society.

Given the foregoing, it becomes easy to understand why environmental economists spend so much time and effort theorizing about how best to implement price adjustments as a solution to environmental degradation. Generally, the neoclassical position today is that prices, perhaps after adjustments, are sufficient to inform and guide economic actors and policy makers in their decisions.

However, I will now argue that money and prices, whether adjusted or unadjusted, in and of themselves are 'biased' transmitters of information, and that this bias is profoundly anti-environmental. Some of the 'biases' include the principle of unconstrained, bidirectional substitutions, a shortened time horizon and present-mindedness, the notion of continuous exponential growth, the bias toward the exchange of private goods, and the doctrine of quid pro quo. These 'biases' of money and prices, treated briefly below, are endemic to neoclassical economics, which is, after all, the principal discourse 'justifying' money, markets, and prices.

Perfect Substitutes, Technological Change. Prices critically misrepresent ecological reality by suggesting that things are infinitely substitutable. The emphasis afforded substitutions by neoclassicists reflects, of course, the primary function of money to serve as a medium of exchange. Money makes possible the comparison of dissimilar things. Money is the common denominator for all commodities, and in theory it allows (in a famous example) guns to be converted into butter, and butter back into guns. Economists are forever depicting production possibilities frontiers (or 'product transformation curves,' like that between guns and butter [see Fig. 1]), as well as production functions (various combinations of land, labour, and capital to produce a given output) and 'consumer preferences' or 'utility functions'– all as systems of substitutions for which the 'optimum' trade-off is decided by the ratio of the prices of the items concerned.

Most economists, extrapolating the principle of infinite substitution from the symbolic world of price theory to the material world, argue that resources ('factors of production') are largely substitutable for one another, and that an effectively operating price system will raise the relative cost of scarce resources and thereby induce firms and consumers to shift into lower-cost substitutes. Should oil run out or become prohibitively expensive, there are other combustibles such as ethanol and hydrogen that can be used, as well as wind, water, nuclear, and direct solar power.[74] If cities become overcrowded, people can live and work in high-rise buildings or underground. Much of the faith of these theorists derives not only from their belief in the power of relative prices to direct the activities of economic agents, but also from their conviction that human knowledge is unbounded, making possible substitutions in the future that are unimaginable today. As a corollary, then, they propose that knowledge and technology can be applied indefinitely to increase the supply of land and other resources. Philosopher Mark Sagoff expresses this neoclassical economic view as follows: 'Reserves of resources "are actually functions of technology ... The more advanced the technology, the more reserves become known and recoverable." ... Although raw materials will always be necessary, knowledge has become the essential factor in the production of goods and services.'[75] Interestingly, Sagoff then remarks: 'If we assume, along with [Peter] Drucker and others, that resource scarcities do not exist or are easily averted, it is hard to see how economic theory, which after all concerns scarcity, provides the conceptual basis for valuing the environment. The reasons to preserve nature are ethical more often than they are economic.'[76]

Julian Simon is another proponent of the view that through technological change and an effectively functioning price system, resource scarcity becomes a non-issue, stating starkly: 'Natural resources are not finite':

> Heightened scarcity causes prices to rise. The higher prices present opportunity, and prompt inventors and entrepreneurs to search for solutions. Many fail in the search, at cost to themselves. But in a free society, solutions are eventually found. And in the long run the new developments leave us better off than if the problems had not arisen. That is, prices eventually become lower than before the increased scarcity occurred.
>
> It is all-important to recognize that discoveries of improved methods and of substitute products are not just luck. They happen in response to an increase in scarcity – a rise in cost.[77]

In *Scarcity and Growth: The Economics of Natural Resource Availability* neoclassicists Harold J. Barnett and Chandler Morse took this mode of thinking to the (ultimately absurd) extreme: Human knowledge, they proposed, has already transformed the earth's crust and broadened humanity's resource base to encompass 'such ubiquitous materials as sea water, clays, rocks, sands, and air.'[78] They continued, 'advances in fundamental science, in response to signals provided by the price system, make it possible to take advantage of the uniformity of energy-

Figure 1. Product Transformation Curve (adapted from Tibor Scitovsky, *Welfare and Competition*, 143)

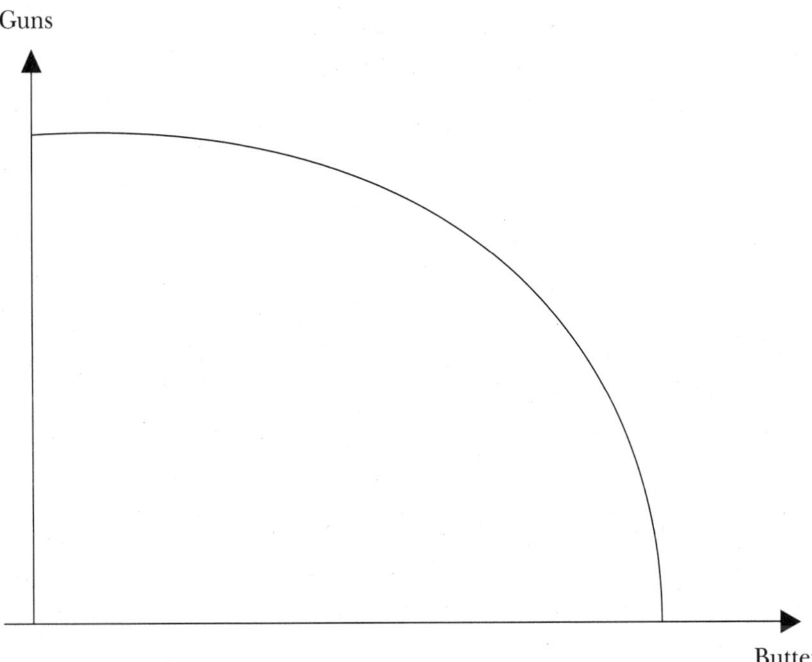

matter ... without preassignable limit, to escape the quantitative constraints imposed by the character of the earth's crust.'[79] Since for these authors the 'natural resource building blocks [are now] to a large extent atoms and molecules,'[80] conservationist practices and the naturalist ethic of a previous era are rendered, in their view, anachronous and perverse.[81] This is undoubtedly an extreme position among economists, but the tendency definitely exists to regard resources as eminently substitutable and human knowledge as potentially increasing forever. In chapters 5 and 6 I critique this neoclassical proposition, arguing that the presumption of infinite growth in knowledge is inconsistent with the law of entropy and seriously misconstrues information and knowledge.

For the present, however, it may be sufficient to note that the doctrine of infinite substitutability flies in the face of our environmental history to date, as reviewed in chapter 1, and is at odds with current ecological thinking. According to ecologists, there are limits, thresholds, and unique relationships, none of which the doctrine of infinite substitution can acknowledge. Nor does this neoclassical position account for the ecologists' principle of co-development or co-evolution; a shrinking biosphere, for example, will adversely affect the growth in human knowledge (more on this below).

Time. Money may be regarded as a medium of communication whose messages consist primarily of prices. Economic historian Harold Adams Innis maintained that all media of communication are 'biased' either toward time or toward space. Media that empower those who exercise control by calling upon time (in the sense of duration, continuity, history, culture, tradition), he termed 'time-binding' or 'time-biased.' Media that facilitate control over space (in the sense of empire or territory), he termed 'space-binding' or 'space-biased.'[82] Money in this sense is definitely biased toward space and away from time.

With regard to the past, it is axiomatic for the price system that 'bygones are forever bygones.'[83] The past is not a variable; it cannot be changed. Therefore, the past cannot affect the marginal conditions (that is, small or incremental changes) that, neoclassicists insist, are the bases upon which maximizing individuals make decisions. True, firms and individuals in the present can be encumbered with debts arising from past activities, even forcing some into bankruptcy, and in that sense the past lingers into the present. Likewise, others may have become rich, giving them a much larger array of options from which to choose. But these considerations are more a matter of wealth distribution (important though that is) than they are factors affecting the profitability or utility of choices in the present. A bankrupt company, for example, can be taken over by new owners/managers, be refinanced with the debt obligations altered if not wiped out altogether, and decisions then can be made in light of the present understanding of future flows of costs and revenues. Put briefly, it is difficult to summon up memories, loyalties, traditions, or a sense of belonging when one's mode of expression consists primarily of relative prices. Yet, as discussed below, from an ecological perspective, memories, loyalties, and feelings can be bonds of great importance.

It is not just the past that the price system neglects or obliterates; it also trivializes the future. Assuming a 10 per cent rate of interest (or discount rate), $1,000 payable 30 years from now would be worth only the equivalent of $57.32 today! (Stated alternatively, $57.32 invested for 30 years at 10 per cent compound interest would swell to $1,000.) A lower discount rate would raise the present value of the $1,000 somewhat, but even so note that the time period, considered in ecological terms, is extremely short – merely 30 years. The more remote the benefit (or the cost!), the more trivial it is to present-day economic actors making decisions on the basis of price information. A liability that the next generation weights at $1,000 is appraised by current reckoners at only $57.32.

Unfortunately, environmental trade-offs are mostly between consumption today (which receives a non-discounted value) against a sounder ecosystem in the future. More species extinctions, augmented global warming, increased ozone depletion, water and air pollution, and proliferation of radioactive wastes are examples of future consequences of present-day production/consumption activities – all of which monetary discounting trivializes.

Exponential Growth. Money is the lingua franca of contemporary society. It is simultaneously a language and medium of communication whose messages consist of relative prices. In this capacity, money induces expectations of limitless expansion, as opposed to satisfaction with current affairs or, more technically, a 'steady state.'[84] Through the 'magic of compound interest,' any principal, say $1,000, invested at a positive rate of interest, increases annually by ever-increasing amounts. After one year at a 10 per cent rate of return, a principal of $1,000 will grow by $100 to $1,100; after 2 years, it will amount to $1,210, an increase of $110 from the preceding year; after 3 years, the principal will be $1,331, an increase over the year of $121. After 30 years, the initial $1,000 will be worth $17,440, an increase of $1,586 from the preceding year. Given a 10 per cent rate of return, the principal doubles every 7 years; at a 5 per cent rate of return, it takes about 14 years for the principal to double; at 15 per cent, it takes only 5 years for money to double.

Since the Industrial Revolution, exponential growth has been realized in many sectors of the real economy. World coal extraction, for example, doubled on average every 27 years between 1800 and 1980, representing an average annual rate of growth of 2.6 per cent. Extraction of crude oil doubled on average every 9.8 years between 1880 and 1980, representing an average annual rate of growth of about 7.6 per cent. Between 1776 and 1976, the world's annual extraction/production of pig iron increased 1,556 fold, doubling every 18.9 years.[85] Accompanying, and partly inducing, these exponential increases in the extraction and use of resources were geometric (or exponential) increases in the human population. In

1776, when Adam Smith published *The Wealth of Nations*, the world's population stood at 790 million; by 1976 it was 4.24 billion (an average annual increase of 2.1 per cent); in 1999 it surged past 6 billion (an average annual growth rate between 1976 and 1999 of 2.7 per cent).

By living within the logic or mindset of money, by continually viewing the material world in money terms, one can easily construe (or, rather, misconstrue) the natural world whereby it seems to take on the infinite expansibility of the money system.[86] Or, equally as bad, one can lose sight altogether of the natural environment, so riveted is the mind on money.

Quid Pro Quo. Quid pro quo means an exchange of equivalences: 'What I give to you must be worth at least what you give to me.' A society functioning exclusively by quid pro quo will engage solely in commodity exchange/barter relations. Quid pro quo is, however, a perversion of biospheric reality. Arne Naess, founder of the deep ecology movement, described ecosystems as biospheric nets or fields of intrinsic relations.[87] An intrinsic relation for Naess is one so basic that, in its absence, the system's components are no longer the same things. Naess viewed organisms as 'knots' in these nets or fields.

The emphasis on quid pro quo implies also a linear understanding of relations – a series of production nodes from resources extraction, to various stages of manufacture, to distribution, and finally to purchase and consumption, each node being characterized by a commodity exchange. This logic of linearity supported by flows of money lies at the heart of neoclassical economists' faith that prices are/can be adequate guides to technological change and habitat preservation, and hence of environmental economists' recommendation that market prices be adjusted to induce or constrain as appropriate activities affecting ecological well-being. The presumption of linearity, however, is a major distortion of ecosystem reality. Previously we remarked that the ecological principle of biomagnification is quite incomprehensible from a neoclassicists' paradigm of commodity exchange. So too are emergent phenomena – properties of systems that are not predictable from knowledge of their components considered in isolation from one another. The existence of emergent properties implies, for example, that outcomes of large technological interventions may differ significantly from predictions based on extrapolations of consequences of small interventions. Ecologists likewise speak of thresholds or boundaries that, once transgressed, can cause an ecosystem to flip into an alternative state. For example, once the population of a species shrinks below its threshold (or 'minimum viable population') it will become extinct. Similarly, if an economy discharges effluent into an ecosystem beyond the ecosystem's absorption capacity, the ensuing build-up will affect the functioning of the ecosystem, possibly in unforeseen ways. More on these points below.

Quantification. As noted by Daly and Cobb, echoing Alfred Marshall, 'It is the commodity of money that makes possible the quantification of economics as an exact, deductive science.' However, they added immediately, 'features of this world that cannot be assigned a monetary price finally disappear from the present forms of economic science ... This means it abstracts from everything to which a monetary value cannot be assigned.'[88]

Above we noted that unnamed species 'disappear' from price system accounting. But, we can also ask, what are some of the other 'features of this world' that likewise disappear due to limitations in the messaging capacity of prices? There is a long list, but a good place to start is what Adam Smith, in *The Theory of Moral Sentiments*, termed 'sympathy' or empathy (see Chapter 4). We could speculate that in displacing sympathy (empathy) through a logic of quantification, present-mindedness, exponential growth, quid pro quo, infinite substitutability, individualism, and self-interest, money carries within itself the seeds of our, and hence its own, destruction. Justice, truth, beauty, health, friendship, peace, responsibility, taste, smell, touch, freedom, and dignity are but a few of the concepts that affect and are affected by everyday activities but that cannot be broken down into units and counted, and hence to which pricing is both inapplicable and nonsensical. All affect and are affected by, in one way or another, economic activity and technological innovation, and all relate to environmental well-being.

Private over Collective Goods. As John Kenneth Galbraith noted,[89] the bias in money-mediated societies is toward those goods and services that are consumed privately. In fact, the price system generates no information whatever regarding goods and services consumed or enjoyed collectively. Galbraith concluded that market-driven economies are consequently characterized by an undersupply of collective goods such as parks, education, and aesthetically pleasing architecture, for the simple reason that there is no market for them.

Ecosystems, of course, are rife with public goods, biodiversity being a perfect example, but one seldom mentioned in economic texts, which usually prefer to invoke as an example 'national defence.' But biodiversity fits the definition of a public good precisely: one person's or one species' benefit from biodiversity does not subtract from other people's or other species' benefit. This, however, means that there can be no market value (or exchange price) for biodiversity. Nor can there be ownership of it. Assuredly, an increase in the production of marketable commodities may cause a reduction in biodiversity through extinctions, and in that sense there is a 'substitution' or an 'exchange,' but no one owns the moribund species or is exclusively harmed by the ensuing ecosystem consequences and hence no one can insist on being compensated for the full amount of harms. Hence these 'costs' do not even enter market calculations. This despite the fact (or, rather, due to the fact) that all markets exist within, and are maintained by, the framework of biodiversity; it would actually be ridiculous even to attempt to set a 'shadow price' on biodiversity for that very reason, 'ecological economists' Robert Costanza and associates notwithstanding.[90]

Julian Simon, apostle of private exchanges as the preferred mode of economic governance, completely missed the boat when he remarked with satisfaction that over the course of human history the trend has been to make the earth 'ever more livable for human beings.'[91] He failed to mention that 'civilizing the wilderness' to make ourselves more 'at home' has resulted in massive extinctions of plant and animal species, making our planet thereby less habitable for humans.[92]

Clean air and water, good sanitation, an absence of undue UV or nuclear radiation, adequate rainfall, moderate climate, and so on, are all 'public goods' that the money system, premised on private exchanges, does not and cannot take into account. We would expect, therefore, societies driven by the logic of money to be instrumental in bringing about species extinctions, water, air, and soil contamination, detrimental climate and weather changes, and so on.

Main Principles of Ecology

A major objective of this book is to establish that mainstream economics as a discursive system is, at its very core, anti-environmental. Some of its fundamental anti-environmental traits have been identified above. It now remains in this chapter to identify some main ecological principles that contrast with the foregoing, and that a transformed economics needs to incorporate. Unless otherwise specified, ecology and ecological discourse henceforth denote the holistic ecosystem concept, as opposed to Linnaeusian, Darwinian, bioeconomic,[93] or other reductive ecological discourses.

The overriding implication of these two sections is that, contrary to the program of environmental economists, the reach of neoclassical economics should be sharply curtailed, certainly not extended to encompass environmental concerns. Stated more strongly, economics should be reformulated to conform to principles of ecology, some of which follow.

BIOCENTRISM

In contrast to the anthropocentrism of economics, ecology is *biocentric.* It regards human beings as but one of a multitude of species, co-evolving and interdependent, all of which seek the material means of existence and all of which depend for their well-being on interactions among the other species (*biocoenosis*) in their ecosystems.[94] The biocentrism of ecology is highlighted by such key notions as *ecosystem, biotic diversity* (biodiversity), *co-evolution, biomagnification, biotic community,* and *niche.* I now offer brief explanation of these terms in turn.

The *ecosystem,* according to Odum, is the basic unit of analysis in ecology.[95] The main function of the ecosystem concept in ecological thought, he continues, is to draw attention to 'obligatory relationships, interdependence, and causal relationships, that is, the coupling of components to form functional units.'[96] The founder of the ecosystem concept, A.G. Tansley, sought to model the new science after classical physics. All relations among organisms, he maintained, can be described in terms of material flows of energy and materials; as Worster summarizes, for Tansley 'these are the real bonds that hold the natural world together; they create a single unit [namely, the biosphere] made up of many smaller units – big and little ecosystems.'[97] According to systems theory, systems are more than just the sum of their parts or of the performances of the systems' elements.[98] As noted by Peter Sengbusch, professor of biology at the University of Bielefeld, Germany: 'Ecosystems with only a few system elements are extremely liable to break down ... They can only be kept in balance with the use of stabilizing, energy-consuming measures like the use of insecticides. They can, on the other hand, easily be rebuilt after complete destruction. Complex systems are very resilient, they have a large buffer capacity, but their destruction is an irreversible act. A destroyed tropical rain forest or a destroyed coral reef is lost forever.'[99]

Biodiversity, or the variety of life forms,[100] ecologists hold, contributes to the sustainability, balance, and equilibrium of each ecosystem. According to the United Nations Environment Programme, 'It is the combination of life forms and their interactions with each other and with the rest of the environment that has made Earth a uniquely habitable place for humans; biodiversity provides a large number of goods and services that sustain our lives.'[101] David Suzuki makes much the same point in declaring, 'Life itself has created the conditions hospitable to all creatures.'[102] He elaborates: 'Together, all species make up one immense web of interconnections that binds all beings to each other and to the physical components of the planet. The disappearance of a species tears the web a little, but that web is highly elastic. When one strand is rent the whole network changes configuration, but so long as there are many remaining strands to hold it together, it retains its integrity.'[103] There is growing concern today that the accelerating rate of species extinctions at some stage will cause irreparable harm to the web of life.

Co-evolution, according to Paul Ehrlich, occurs 'when two species are ecologically intimate, closely influencing each other's lives as do predators and prey or hosts and parasites.' In such cases, each species 'normally becomes a major source of selection operating on the other.'[104] Jane Jacobs, however, is much broader in her depiction of co-evolution, writing that: 'Development depends on co-developments.'[105] Discussed later in this book, co-evolution or co-development is a major argument opposing the doctrine of an infinite Earth. Growth in human knowledge and in applications of human knowledge (technologies) are constrained by co-evolutionary developments in ecosystems, and unless an accommodation is made to preserve species diversity, human knowledge and culture will ultimately decline.

Biomagnification refers to the manner whereby accumulations of toxic substances pass up the food chain in ever-increasing concentrations. Biomagnification is an example of an ecological principle completely bypassing economics' methodological individualism and its short time horizon.

Biotic community refers to the living organisms in a certain area. For some, such as ecologist John Phillips, the concept contains the notion not just of complex organization, but of a complex organism. He wrote: 'A biotic community in many respects behaves as a complex organism – in its origin, growth, development, common response, common reaction, and its reproduction ... The biotic community is something more than the mere sum of its parts; it possesses a special identity – it is indeed a mass-entity with a destiny peculiar to itself.'[106] Not all would agree, and Tansley evidently intended the ecosystem concept to substitute for, not extend, the notion of biotic communities as 'organic wholes.'[107]

Finally, *niche* in ecological thought, as developed by Charles Elton, denotes 'the status of an animal in its community ... its relations to food and enemies.' The term is used to indicate what an animal is doing, Elton explained, as opposed merely to describing its appearance. 'Animals have all manner of external factors acting upon them – chemical, physical and biotic – and the "niche" of an animal means its place in the biotic environment.'[108]

HOLISM

The holism of ecology, in contrast to the methodological individualism of neoclassical economics, is inherent in the notion of *ecosystem* – the idea that living beings interact with one another and with their abiotic environment. According to Eugene Odum, 'Since no organism can exist by itself or without an environment, our first principle [of ecology] may well deal with the "interrelation" and the principle of "wholeness."'[109] Another way of saying this is that ecology emphasizes relations among entities, whereas economics tends to focus on entities themselves, whether through the theory of the firm, the theory of production, or the theory of the consumer, and to presume that the whole is merely the aggregation of the parts. David Suzuki graphically drew out the distinction between holism and methodological individualism in writing that the basic elements – air, water, earth, and energy – mediate all life, as does life itself (biodiversity).[110] Suzuki believes that when the West forsook holism for a methodological individualism, there resulted dire environmental consequences. His hope is that by directing our attention to the fact that air, water, earth, energy, and biodiversity mediate all existence, we will be more careful about the effluvium we discharge, and we may also come to experience again our commonality with all other living beings.

HUMAN NATURE

Whereas economists propose an essentially static 'human nature' based on the principles of pleasure-pain (or on utility-disutility and the purported insatiability of individual wants), ecology points to an evolution in human nature as an adaptive strategy, and incorporates cultural evolution as part of this changing nature. According to Alfred Russel Wallace (1823–1913), an associate of Darwin and co-founder of the theory of natural selection, humans, unlike non-human species, can and do adapt to changing circumstances through technological, as opposed to genetic, changes.[111] Rather than growing warmer fur or a new covering of fat in order to adapt to the arrival of a new glacial age, for instance, humans devise 'warmer clothing' and build 'better houses,' leaving the 'natural body ... naked as before.'[112]

Paul Ehrlich, a contemporary ecologist, has extended Wallace's observations regarding the evolution of human artefacts as extensions of the human body, and applied them to human culture, which he defines as 'nongenetic (extragenetic) information embodied in stories, songs, tools, customs ... and so on.'[113] The body of extragenetic information, ecologists like Ehrlich maintain, contributes to, and alters, human nature. According to Ehrlich, 'human natures [sic] is the coevolution of genes and culture.'[114]

Part of the body of this 'extra-genetic information,' I argue here, is literature concerning what human nature is. This literature serves to modify human self-conception and activity. A culture of ecology requires a reformulation of the body of discourse concerning 'human nature' from that presented by neoclassical economists (and for that matter by behavioural psychologists, sociobiologists, and others); we need to 'retrieve,' as political philosopher C.B. Macpherson remarked, antiquarian conceptions of what it means to be human (more on this in the next chapter), and absorb indigenous people's conceptions of humans' place in nature.

Of course, obstacles abound to using extragenetic media to foster an environmentally sound human culture and human nature: political economists would point to issues of money, power, and control of media, and resistance by vested interests – no small matters to be sure. But the point remains that for ecologists it *is* possible to take hold of human nature as an adaptive strategy to ward off environmental collapse, whereas neoclassical economists, wedded to the belief that humans are inextricably selfish and infinite in their wants, per force place their chips on the doctrine of an infinitely expansible earth.

TIME

We noted previously that neoclassical economics, by placing great stock in money and prices, downplays both the past and the future. It is, according to eminent Canadian economic historian and communication scholar Harold Innis, a 'present-minded' mode of understanding.

Ecologist David Suzuki, however, insists that memory of and identification with one's ancestors and with the land is basic to ecologically sustainable land practices. Dune Lankard, head of the new Eyak Corporation of Alaska (the former Eyak Reservation), makes a similar point in remarking on changes in attitudes toward land once the system of prices and private property sets in:

> Incorporating the land and its people made us all shareholders of the land. You look out over the horizon and you see all this wonderful land that we have lived on and made our living on for thousands of generations. But when you become a shareholder, which means that you have ownership in the land, it changes your perspective on how you look at that land. Instead of seeing beautiful forests, you see acres of timber. Instead of seeing beautiful mountains, you see mines. You look at everything as a valuable resource rather than as a valuable way of life.[115]

Equally important, indigenous peoples historically have looked not just to the past, but also seven generations into the future in making decisions. Below we will note also how the concept of 'stewardship' permeated ancient Western and Hebrew thought. As well, there were proscriptions against usury in Greek, Hebrew, and medieval moral/legal codes; to completely ban interest payments is, in effect, to set a zero rate of interest, in which case there is no discounting of the future at all: present and future, in that circumstance, are valued equally – ecologically a condition far superior to our present mode of valuation. The tragedy of human history, from an ecological point of view, is that non-monetarized societies succumbed time and again to pecuniary cultures.

NATURAL SELECTION, SURVIVAL OF THE FITTEST, AND 'LIVE AND LET LIVE'

Seeds for the modern theory of 'natural selection,' we might say, were sown by Thomas Hobbes, who proposed that in 'a state of nature,' by which he meant humans lacking government but living in proximity to one another, life is a struggle of each one against all others. Classical political economist Thomas Robert Malthus took up Hobbes's notion of struggle for existence but argued that it pertained also to instances in which governments exist. Malthus is notable in the history of ecological thought, as discussed above, primarily because Charles Darwin invoked Malthus's population principle in formulating his own principle of natural selection. Darwin in turn recursively affected economics. Although today's neoclassical economists seldom employ the term 'natural selection' in their analyses, they do continuously invoke the concepts of market-based competition and the drive to efficiency; through competition the efficient are rewarded and the inefficient cease to exist.

However, placing survival of the fittest as a first principle of ecology, as Darwin did, arguably unduly emphasizes predator-prey relations and competition for resources, downplaying, for example, symbioses (such as plant-animal relations) and synergies arising from complexities. Even when attention *is* focused on predator-prey relations, 'Nature, red in tooth and claw'[116] can be an overstatement because, as noted by naturalist Guy Murchie, a predator that killed more than it needed would threaten its own food supply; such an activity would be suicidal.[117] Murchie continues:

> A herd of gazelles will graze peacefully within fifty feet of lions, because they instinctively know the lions are well fed and sleepy. But as soon as they sense a certain tension – perhaps just the twitch of a tail or a whiff of adrenalin imperceptible to man – they will be off for the horizon. This is perfectly natural, like breathing, to animals – something prey take for granted and practically never concern themselves about except at those relatively rare moments when action is vital.[118]

Arne Naess, founder of the deep ecology movement, interprets the struggle for life, not like Spencer, Darwin, Malthus, or Hobbes, as a struggle of each one against all others, but as an 'ability to coexist and cooperate in complex relationships.'[119] He continues, '"Live and let live" is a more powerful ecological principle than "either you or me" since the latter tends to reduce the multiplicity of kinds of forms of life, and to create destruction within the communities of the same species.'[120]

The ecological principle of 'struggle for existence,' therefore, is and has been subject to different, conflicting interpretations, and these are not without political, economic, cultural, environmental, and ideological import. The notion that higher life forms evolve through the struggle for existence resonates with neoclassical economics' contention that competition weeds out the inefficient and rewards the efficient with survival. On the other hand, there is precious little in mainstream economics that is analogous to Naess's position regarding 'live and let live,' and with the widely accepted ecological principle of 'intrinsic relations.' The intent here is not to romanticize nature, but simply to note that 'the struggle for survival' is more complex than the notion of 'survival of the fittest' allows.

THRESHOLDS, IMPERFECT SUBSTITUTES

Whereas neoclassical economic theory and the price system propose a world of substitutions, from an ecological point of view such is a grave oversimplification. There is, after all, no substitute for water or for oxygen to sustain life.

By unduly emphasizing substitutions, the price system and neoclassicism deflect attention away from limits and thresholds. A *threshold* denotes a point of no return, a place where bidirectional substitutions are no longer possible. Events have finality once a threshold is crossed. When the number of a species has been reduced to its threshold, or its habitat shrunk below a certain point, its extinction within nature is assured. In terms of *limits*, many ecologists insist, the *carrying capacity* of the earth has already been exceeded, meaning that there has already been a deterioration in water, air, and soil quality, explaining the pronounced decline in biodiversity that we documented earlier.

The logic of substitutions, furthermore, instils in people's minds the idea that 'every thing has its price,' a position fundamentally at odds with such vital concepts as uniqueness, sacredness, and intrinsic value. Sociologist Georg Simmel recognized that money turns human beings into strangers – into *res absolutae*, or mere objects;[121] hence, the commodification of life may well be fundamental to the equanimity with which middle-class people now confront poverty and homelessness in their cities. Uniqueness and sacredness, of course, imply an incapacity for, or inappropriateness of, substitutions, which is to say an absence or inappropriateness of price. But the absence of price, according to the logic of the market, means an absence of value. Economic and financial incentives always exert pressures to 'develop' land hitherto residing outside the bounds of commodity exchange, irrespective of the intrinsic value some may accord it.

ENTROPY

As noted previously, ecology concerns flows of matter, energy and information into, out of, and within ecosystems. *Energy* is the ability to do work, and is subject to the laws of thermodynamics, thermodynamics being the 'science of the conservation of the quantity and the change in quality of energy in a system.'[122] Two basic laws of thermodynamics were formulated in 1865 by Clausius.[123] The first, the law of conservation, maintains that matter-energy can be neither created nor destroyed, that in *isolated systems* (systems in which matter and energy can neither enter nor escape) the amount of matter-energy is constant.[124] The second, the law of entropy, states (according to one formulation) that a degradation of energy from a concentrated form to a dispersed form always accompanies an energy transformation.[125] In another formulation, the amount of free energy (energy capable of doing mechanical work) decreases continually in isolated systems. Free energy is lost, for example, when heat moves unidirectionally from warmer to colder bodies. Maximum entropy occurs when 'all energy is degraded to heat at a uniform temperature.'[126]

The laws of thermodynamics are accorded great importance in ecology. After all, life processes are to be understood as entailing energy transfers that produce growth, replication, and syntheses of complex relationships of matter, these energy transfers being, of course, subject to the laws of thermodynamics.

Entropy is not, however, a concept acknowledged by mainstream economics. One of the very few economists who actually tried to incorporate entropy in economic modelling, Nicholas Georgescu-Roegen, was considered a maverick, quite outside the pale of economic orthodoxy. I will review Georgescu-Roegen's contribution to today's ecological economics in chapter 5. According to ecological economist Herman Daly, the concept of entropy is sufficient to transform fundamentally the meaning of economic activity from that proffered by mainstream economists. Daly writes:

> The entropy law tells us that inevitably whatever resources we transform into something useful must disintegrate, decay, fall apart, or dissipate into something useless, returning in the form of waste to the sustaining system that generated the resource. The economy is thus an ordered system for transforming low-entropy raw materials and energy [such as fossil fuels] into high-entropy waste and unavailable energy, providing humans with a 'psychic flux' of satisfaction in the process.[127]

SCALE, GROWTH, CARRYING CAPACITY

Geophysicist M. King Hubbert once asked incisively, just how many doublings of population, resource extraction, and waste can the Earth support?[128] As a step to answering that question, ecologists have devised the concept of carrying capacity. In terms of human population, however, no definitive estimate of the earth's carrying capacity has been achieved. There are too many variables: per capita consumption and the nature of that consumption, income distribution, technological advance, estimates of the earth's resources and recycling capacity, and so on. Nonetheless, the concept of carrying capacity persists in the ecological literature, but it is virtually absent from mainstream economics. What *is* crystal clear is that civilizations in the past exceeded, for various reasons, the carrying capacity of their local environments – for example, those of the Tigris and Euphrates valleys, Easter Island, and the Mayan and Anasazi civilizations.[129] As Clive Ponting remarks, there are lessons to be learned from Easter Island: 'Like Easter Island the earth has only limited resources to support human society and all its demands. Like the islanders, the human population has no practical means of escape.'[130]

MORE THAN THE SUM OF THE PARTS

We saw previously that mainstream economics views the economy as being additive. For an economy consisting of two people according to the principle of Pareto optimality, for example, there is no significant difference if one person owns all the wealth or if the wealth is divided evenly between the two. It implies also that behaviour that maximizes the welfare of one individual necessarily contributes to the well-being of the economy or society. Finally, methodological individualism presumes that the characteristics of the whole economy can be understood adequately by investigating the properties of its components (the firm, the consumer, the worker).

Many ecologists – but not all[131] – by contrast, maintain that the whole is more than the sum of its parts, or at least that the parts in interaction produce properties that could not have been foreseen by studying the parts in isolation of one another. The terms 'synergies,' 'emergent properties,' and 'levels of analysis' all have applicability here. Eugene Odum, for example, remarks: 'Biologists discovered that each level had characteristics which knowledge of the next lower level explained only in part. In other words, not all attributes of a higher level are predictable if we know only the properties of the lower level. Just as the properties of water are not predictable if we know only the properties of hydrogen and oxygen, so the characteristics of ecosystems cannot be predicted from knowledge of isolated populations; one must study the forest (i.e., the whole) as well as the trees (i.e., the parts).'[132] Similarly, Frank Golley summarizes that 'ecosystems are wholes, in the definitional sense proposed by philosophers,' adding, 'The ecosystem [concept], for some at least, has provided a basis for moving beyond strictly scientific questions to deeper questions of how humans should live with each other and the environment.'[133]

Recapitulation

Enough has been said to demonstrate profound incompatibilities between mainstream economic and holistic ecosystem discourses. It is also clearly evident that these competing, conflicting discourses must somehow be reconciled, because economies and ecosystems are inextricably linked. We have mentioned two current, antithetical plans of action for such reconciliation: neoclassical economics to subsume ecology, and holistic ecology to transform economics. Jane Jacobs is instructive as to which is the wiser course to pursue: 'Natural processes aren't founded on human behavior ... Instead, nature affords foundations for human life and sets its possibilities and limits.'[134]

3 Ancient Syntheses

As I have argued in chapter 2, mainstream or neoclassical economics and many of our economic practices are incompatible with biospheric vitality. Neoclassical economics and the ecosystem concept in ecology today are also largely antithetical. This chapter and the next look at the roots of this problem. Acquaintance with this discursive history may prove valuable in forging a new synthesis between economics and environmentalism.

Some have argued, however, that a synthesis never existed. They blame the current spate of environmental crises on the foundational texts of Western culture. Historian Lynn White Jr, for example, in an oft-reprinted article that first appeared in *Science* in 1967,[1] blamed present-day anti-environmental practices on the lingering influence of Judaism and Christianity. Likewise, Eugene Hargrove pointed an accusing finger at Greek philosophy.[2] In this chapter I inspect these claims closely, and I conclude that those ancient texts were actually profoundly pro-environmental, that their economics was quite consistent with environmental vitality, but that through time meanings of key concepts narrowed (or 'mutated') and counterbalances atrophied, eventually resulting in the contemporary anti-environmentalism of mainstream economic discourses. The implication is that for biospheric health, counterbalances as in a previous era must be restored.

Aristotle

Ancient Greek philosophy has been criticized for purportedly lacking environmental sensitivity, thereby setting the West on a trajectory of environmental ruin. John Passmore, for example, claims that the Greek influence on Christianity was responsible for introducing an ethic of domination to Western thought.[3] Likewise, Eugene Hargrove states baldly, 'Greek philosophy is the primary source of the philosophical perspectives that have historically inhibited the development of appropriate environmental and preservationist attitudes';[4] for him, the Greek position that the world is essentially rational in its make-up induced the view that only objects of reason are worth enquiring into, inhibiting in the West an interest in ecology and the natural environment.[5] David Suzuki elaborates: 'Many thinkers trace the origins of our particular and violent fall from grace, our exile from the garden, back to Plato and Aristotle, who began a powerful process of separating the world-as-abstract-principle from world-as-experience – dividing mind, that is, from body, and human beings from the world they inhabit.'[6]

There is among the ancient Greek philosophers, of course, a wide range of positions. It would appear that Democritus, for example, although rejected for centuries on account of being dismissed by both Plato and Aristotle, exerted a strong influence on Thomas Hobbes regarding the presumed mechanical nature of reality flowing from the motion of particles. Likewise, anthropocentrism was anticipated by Protagoras, to whom is ascribed the statement 'Man is the measure of all things.'[7]

To canvass the whole of ancient Greek philosophy is well beyond the scope of this book. Among Greek philosophers, however, none has had greater influence on Western thought and culture than Aristotle. He was 'the greatest collector and systematizer of knowledge whom the ancient world produced,'[8] and his legacy affected profoundly the course of Western thought and civilization. Thomas Aquinas (1225–74), foremost among medieval writers, is said to have lived his mature years in the 'confluence and reconciliation of Aristotelian learning and Christian teaching.'[9] Medieval thought, in brief, is based primarily on the Bible and Aristotle.

Aristotle has been called 'the father of animal ecology.' As summarized by Gerhard Wiegleb of Brandenburg Technical University Cottbus, Aristotle 'studied behavior and habitat of birds, seasonal influence on reproduction, animal geography, hibernation and migration, colour change, feeding habits, and symbiosis.' Like Linnaeus, however, Aristotle also 'favored the idea of prestabilized harmony.'[10] Aristotle's student Theophrastus transcribed and extended Aristotle's work, and so it is often difficult to know exactly what were their respective contributions. Wiegleb notes that Theophrastus is often thought of as 'the father of botany,' and he considers Theophrastus also to be 'the founder of ecology.'[11]

Defending Aristotle, as I do here, from the perspective of environmental vitality is challenging on account of a key passage that critics quote repeatedly to 'prove' his anthropocentrism and hence anti-environmentalism: 'Plants exist for [the] sake [of animals] and ... the other animals exist for the sake of man, tame ones for the use he can make of them as well as for the food they provide ... If then nature makes nothing without some end in view, nothing to no purpose, it must be that nature has made all of them for the sake of man.'[12] If the foregoing fully represented Aristotle's thinking, environmental critics of Greek philosophy would certainly have a strong case. With Aristotle, however, things are much more complicated. In addition to proposing a hierarchy of living beings, with a certain class of humans at the apex and all other living beings subservient, he also recognized a continuity between the rest of nature and humanity. Humans share with plants and other animals a 'vegetative' aspect, by which he meant the automatic processes of our physical bodies – growth, circulation of nutrients and fluids, and so forth. Humans also share with other animals an 'appetitive aspect,' that is, instinctual desires and responses. And in *De Anima* (*On the Soul*) Aristotle maintained further that all objects possessing powers of movement and sensation have souls.[13] Where humans do differ from other beings, Aristotle wrote, is in their capacity to reason.

Aristotle maintained that due to rationality there can be a unique conflict besetting humans – between one's 'appetitive' or instinctual desires and what reason tells us is 'good.' Excellence in a human life consists, in part, in making appetitive desires obey reason; this, for Aristotle, *is* moral virtue. Humans, then, are 'rational animals'; although humans possess animal or appetitive desires and needs, human rationality can and should rule these appetites, the morally excellent person being one who seeks a balance between excess and deficiency. On the other hand, he declared, the 'bad and unnatural condition of a permanently or temporarily depraved person will often give the impression that his body is ruling over his soul.'[14] Note the contrast here with today's neoclassical economics, which maintains that human intelligence, far from restraining acquisitive inclinations, is to be applied in service of accumulating goods and satisfying an unlimited array of wants.

Moreover, Aristotle proposed that since humans possess language, they are unique in being able to understand and perceive good and evil, and hence in being able to distinguish justice from injustice. Based on this awareness, and being capable of rational thought, humans also possess the capacity to choose – to act according to principles, for example, and not merely in response to impulse or appetite.[15] To give in to appetite, even if one uses rational faculties to pursue appetitive ends, Aristotle believed, was to be less than fully human. Again, we find here a sharp contrast with classical and neoclassical economics, which, to recall, maintain that human behaviour is quite predictable; in the words of Bentham, 'Nature has placed mankind under the governance of two sovereign masters, pain and pleasure.'[16]

Although credited with but a minor tract devoted to economics,[17] Aristotle broached the subject in other works, particularly Book I of *The Politics* and Book V of *The Nicomachean Ethics.* In the latter tome Aristotle took up the question of *justice,* which he defined in terms both of *personal character* and *social justice.* For Aristotle, a prime indicator of injustice in a person's character is that he is 'grasping' ('The unjust man is grasping').[18] To be grasping, Aristotle maintained, is to be focused unduly on making money: 'All other unjust acts are ascribed invariably to some particular kind of wickedness, e.g. adultery to self-indulgence, the desertion of a comrade in battle to cowardice, physical violence to anger; but if a man makes a gain, his action is ascribed to no form of wickedness but injustice.'[19] Regarding social justice, Aristotle wrote: 'We call those acts just that tend to produce and preserve happiness and its components for the political society.'[20]

Aristotle further distinguished among three types of social justice: *Distributive justice* requires that wealth, including honours, be distributed equally among those of equal merit, while those of greater merit should receive greater wealth.[21] *Rectificatory justice* is a product of litigation; it restores wealth to those afflicted by past injustices.[22] Finally, *reciprocal justice* entails fairness in exchange. In this latter regard Aristotle advanced rudiments both of a *labour theory of value*[23] and of the *just price,* defined as a midpoint between the lowest price a seller would accept and the highest amount a buyer would pay. For Aristotle, justice and goodness always involved finding a *virtuous mean* between unjust extremes.[24]

In *The Politics* Aristotle took pains to distinguish between *oeconomica* and *chrematistike,* the former referring to the entire field of household (and community) management, the latter to the mere acquisition of goods and wealth.[25] To be sure, Aristotle maintained that *chrematistike* (or chrematistics) is a part of household management since, after all, households must acquire the necessities they do not produce. Nonetheless, for good household (and community) management, he believed, acquisition must remain only a part of household activity and should never become an end in itself.

Stated differently, acquiring goods for Aristotle should always be subject to limitations. Otherwise, acquisition descends into mere money making. He was opposed to mere accumulation for several reasons. First, he noted, accumulation is in principle without limit, whereas in nature there are always limits. For Aristotle (as for Plato, Xenophon, and other of the Socratic philosophers), to live a good life, wants must be limited. Once a person has wealth sufficient to allow participation in the life of the polis, there should be no further accumulation. Indeed, high levels of consumption or concentrating efforts on accumulation detract from one's capacity to participate in the democratic life of the community. Second, he insisted, the incentive for unlimited acquisition arises 'from men's gaining from each other,'[26] an inherently undesirable if not entirely unavoidable state of affairs. Finally, he wrote, when people turn their attention toward accumulating, they lose sight of the greater good, which is happiness.

It was on account of the tendency of money to foster the accumulation of wealth through its capacity to serve as a medium of exchange that aroused Aristotle's scepticism regarding its ultimate net benefit. Anticipating Adam Smith and Karl Marx, he distinguished between *value-in-use* and *value-in-exchange*, and proposed that when money came into being, 'what started as a necessary exchange became trade,'[27] that is, exchange for the base motive of accumulation. For the same reasons Aristotle opposed interest ('usury'). 'The gain [from interest],' he wrote, 'arises out of currency itself, not as a product of that for which currency was provided.' He continued, 'currency was intended to be a means of exchange, whereas interest represents an increase in the currency itself ... And of all types of business, this is the most contrary to nature.'[28]

Aristotle displayed an understanding of what we might call the 'semiotics of money': money is a 'sign' that attains its meaning by convention; it represents demand or wealth, but is itself devoid of intrinsic value. Money, therefore (as argued in the previous chapter), is of the order of language: 'Money has become by convention a sort of representative of demand; and this is why it has the name "money" (*nomisma*) – because it exists not by nature but by law (*nomos*) and it is in our power to change it and make it useless.'[29] Aristotle also recognized the possibility of a severe disjuncture between signifier and signified, that is, between the physical presence of the sign (money) and what it purports to represent (wealth): 'And it will often happen that a man with wealth in the form of coined money will not have enough to eat; and what a ridiculous kind of wealth is that which even in abundance will not save you from dying with hunger! It is like the story of Midas: because of the inordinate greed of his prayer everything that was set before him was turned to gold.'[30]

According to Aristotle, human beings are not only rational animals; they are also political animals.[31] It is natural for humans to be dependent upon, and to live in community with, other human beings. He wrote that a village is an association of households, and the state (polis) an association of villages; these larger units form 'naturally' as a result of people attempting to satisfy wants over and beyond daily needs. Once the city state has been formed, he maintained, 'self-sufficiency has been reached ... [and] for all practical purposes the process is now complete.'[32]

In Aristotle's view, the village and the city state could form only because households were already in existence, yet he insisted that the larger unit took priority over the smaller: 'the whole must be prior to [or more important than] the part.'[33] In this regard Aristotle displayed what we would today regard as a keen ecological understanding. He knew that individual units become transformed and take on new characteristics through association with other units, and that systems therefore have properties different than the parts studied alone. 'Separate hand or foot from the whole body,' Aristotle declared, 'and they will no longer be hand or foot except in name, as one might speak of a "hand" or "foot" sculptured in stone; that will be the condition of the spoilt hand, which no longer has the capacity and the function to define it.'[34] Aristotle, therefore, eschewed the rugged individualism championed by modern economics: 'The final good [i.e., happiness] is thought to be self-sufficient. Now by self-sufficient we do not mean that which is sufficient for a man by himself, for one who lives a solitary life, but also for parents, children, wife, and in general for his friends and fellow citizens, since man is born for citizenship.'[35]

It is important to note that Aristotle was not a 'determinist' in the modern sense of the term. Certainly, he looked for causes: to understand something, he declared in *The Physics*, one must know its cause. However, causation in Aristotle's thought is not confined to antecedents that necessarily foreordain outcomes. Rather, he proposed that purpose, too, is a 'cause.' He wrote: 'The end of something is what that thing is for.' For example, 'the end of taking a constitutional is to be healthy.'[36] By invoking purpose as a 'cause,' Aristotle insisted that we are not prisoners of our past, and that people can change trajectories by imagining alternative futures.

Modern environmental critics of Aristotle charge that he, and other Greek philosophers, descacralized nature. The ancient philosophers insisted, after all, that the natural world is understandable through human reason, whereas the mythic polytheism characterizing the writings of Homer, for example, served to protect nature from wilful degradation.[37] The Greek philosophers, at least according to some modern environmentalist critics, substituted 'impersonal forces ... codified only as scientific generalities' in place of the spirits,[38] making (it is alleged) nature bereft of intrinsic value and of a moral dimension. This fateful disjuncture between knowledge and value, between science and art, purportedly characterizing ancient Greek philosophy certainly characterizes thought systems in our day, and hence we arrive at another reason for the suggestion that the Greek philosophers set the West on a trajectory of environmental destruction.

However, here again there is more that needs to be said. In fact, Aristotle advocated no disjuncture between knowing and value. To the contrary, he proposed that all living beings have value insofar as they all serve a purpose or function. True, the most important function was to serve human purposes, raising once again the question of anthropocentrism and an incipient utilitarianism. But value for Aristotle was not limited to this: rather, all entities possess an intrinsic value as they fulfil or act out their inherent purpose or design. Moreover, he insisted that all things should be valued for their beauty as well as be studied to attain understanding.[39]

In fact, Aristotle was very much a cosmologist. He maintained that a continually acting cause ('the Unmoved Mover') is required to keep bodies, including the celestial spheres, in motion. For him, there is a final cause for everything that nature does. For Aristotle, therefore, human activities, including economic activities, take place within a grander context of natural law.

Viewed from the perspective of modern economics, Aristotle seems at best to be rather quaint, fussing over such metaphysical questions as 'just price,' distinguishing between value-in-use and value-in-exchange, condemning money making and mere acquisition, insisting that in the cosmos there is a natural order into which each part is fitted for a purpose, proposing that society is more than the sum of its parts, and that humans are naturally political (i.e., communal) animals. From the perspective of modern ecology, however, Aristotle displays much wisdom. He insisted on limitations, on balance, and on integral relations of parts to wholes. He was opposed to mere money making, for at least two reasons: money is inadequate as a measure (or sign) of value, and money encourages accumulation without limit. He was outraged at individualism in the sense of hedonistic self-seeking, and proposed an intrinsic value to everything in existence. These are fundamentally ecological positions.

The Bible

As noted above, historian Lynn White Jr[40] contends that Western civilization is inherently anti-environmental on account of its Judaeo-Christian roots. Others, such as Clive Ponting,[41] William Leiss,[42] and Donald Worster,[43] seem by and large to have accepted White's claim. White writes: 'Christianity is the most anthropocentric religion the world has seen.'[44] He backs this assertion up in several ways. For one thing, he remarks, according to biblical accounts, all non-human life was created solely for the benefit of humans. In Genesis 1:28, God instructed Adam to 'fill the earth and subdue it; and have dominion over the fish of the sea and over the birds of the air and over every living thing that moves upon the earth.' For another, White attests, Judaism and Christianity descacralized nature: whereas pagan religions maintained that gods are everywhere – in trees, hills, streams, plants and animals – in Judaism and Christianity God transcends nature, and since humans, according to the Bible, are created 'in God's image,' they participate in this transcendence. Whereas pagans sought to placate the spirits before cutting a tree, slaughtering an animal, or damming a brook, Jews and Christians, according to White, were satisfied that they could exploit natural objects with equanimity. Indeed, they believed it was God's will that they do this.[45] Finally, according to White, Judaism and Christianity introduced to Western thought and action 'an implicit faith in perpetual progress.'[46]

The idea or belief in perpetual progress, he continued, arose from the linear, non-repetitive conception of time proffered in the Bible, which is to be contrasted with the cyclical conception of time characterizing other belief systems. According to Old Testament stories, time had a beginning when God created in sequence light and darkness, the stars and planets, the earth and life on earth, and (finally) the first human beings. Moreover, the Old and New Testaments unfold a narrative of human existence: from an idyllic beginning, to the Fall of humankind, to the long and arduous quest to be reunited with God, and finally to the prospect of reunification upon the creation of a New Jerusalem at the end of time. There is, then, in the Bible (as White noted) the prospect of a final outcome or goal, and movement toward that outcome can indeed be regarded as 'progress' – a 'Pilgrim's Progress.' The Western idea of, or faith in, progress, however, White insisted, is 'indefensible apart from Judaeo-Christian teleology.' Pagan religions, according to White, are/were non-teleological (i.e., having no final goal or set outcome); rather, they are/were cyclical, proposing eternal recurrences, and hence are/were non-progressive.[47] Belief in progress, White concluded, meant that Western people set about 'improving' their material conditions, and indeed nature itself, thereby embarking on a trajectory of severe environmental degradation.

Let us take at closer look at these pronouncements. The argument developed here is that although the seeds of modern-day economics' anti-environmentalism can perhaps be found in the Bible's linear conception of time and in its anthropocentrism, there are other, countervailing factors at work too. We consider first White's position concerning biblical anthropocentrism.

Anthropocentrism

Jeremy Cohen, after exhaustively tracking down interpretations and uses made of Genesis 1:28 in ancient and medieval texts (including sermons, law, theology, mysticism, and popular poetry), concluded: 'The ecologically oriented thesis of Lynn White and others can now be laid to rest; rarely, if ever, did premodern Jews and Christians construe this verse as a license for the selfish exploitation of the environment.'[48]

There are reasons for Cohen's findings. In the first chapter of Genesis the claim is made that God laboured five days over the rest of Creation and 'saw that it was good.' Then, having created humans on the sixth day, 'God saw everything he had made, and behold, it was very good.' The 'goodness' of Creation at least implicitly constrains humankind's moral authority to wantonly exploit and degrade nature.

The second chapter of Genesis offers a different Creation story. There, the first man is said to have been made from the dust of the ground. After creating Adam, God planted a garden in Eden 'and out of the ground the Lord God made to grow every tree that is pleasant to the sight and good for food.' We are told that God intended the man to till the soil and maintain the Garden, that is, to be a steward or caretaker of the Garden. Later in Genesis, humans-as-stewards of creation is emphasized again with the story of Noah and the Flood; following God's command, Noah built an ark and assembled all species two by two to preserve them from the devastation. The concept of stewardship implies that property rights are never absolute; God retains sovereignty over creation. Although property is to be enjoyed, in the context of stewardship, it is to be used for benign purposes, not selfish ones, and with an eye toward the future and not just the present.[49]

As if anticipating the split between economics and environment, the second Creation story also states, however, that after Adam and Eve ate of the forbidden fruit, God cast them from the Garden, declaring: 'Cursed is the ground because of you; in toil you shall eat of it all the days of your life; thorns and thistles it shall bring forth to you ... In the sweat of your face you shall eat bread till you return to the ground, for out of it you were taken; you are dust, and to dust you shall return.' On the one hand, the notion that people now must scratch out a living from the land adds to the concept of nature being 'wild' and needful of being tamed or subdued. On the other, although the ideal harmony said to exist before the Fall is broken, humanity's identity with and dependence upon the earth is again affirmed: humans are born of the earth, shall return to the earth, and depend during their lifetimes on the fruits of the earth.

Even more basic, however, is the reason for the Fall in the first place: the serpent's temptation was that by eating the fruit, the eyes of the first humans 'will be opened, and you will be like God, knowing good and evil.' According to the story, the first humans chose power (to become 'like God') over the harmony and simplicity of the Garden. In fact, the Bible rather consistently condemns an ethic of power or domination (the story of the Tower of Babel, for instance), and advances instead what Herman Daly and John Cobb Jr have termed the 'principle of subsidiarity,' that is, the notion that those with wealth or power are supposed to serve those without. This theme occurs time and again in stories of the Old Testament, the Commandments ('Love your neighbour as yourself'), in the teachings of the Hebrew prophets, and in the sayings of Jesus: 'Every one who exalts himself will be humbled, but he who humbles himself will be exalted' (Lk 18:14).

It is true that the Old Testament depicts humans as being created 'in God's image,' and in the New Testament Saint Paul refers to people as being 'a little lower than the angels.' White therefore is correct in concluding that the biblical writers propose that humans 'transcend' the rest of creation. But the Bible is also replete with accounts of a close synchronization between the moral condition of humans and the state of the land: accordingly, if the ancient Hebrews acted in accordance with

God's will, they would attain a land 'of milk and honey,' but when people defied God, they were beset with poisoned water, locusts, flies, and plagues. In Deuteronomy 15, for example, the promise is made that the Lord will bless the land if the needs of the poor are cared for – a doctrine tying ecology directly to social justice. As Philippe Crabbé notes, 'Land is central to the spirituality of Israel'[50] – a condition remarkably similar in some respects to pagan animism.

Nature in the Bible belongs to God, and humans are to hold nature in stewardship and do God's will. And what is 'God's will'? There are many formulations, but a number of them have a direct bearing on the environment. In Leviticus 25:3–4, the Hebrews are told: 'Six years you shall sow your field, and six years you shall prune your vineyard, and gather its fruits; but in the seventh year there shall be a Sabbath of solemn rest for the land.' Likewise, every fiftieth year the land is to rest. Moreover, trees are not to be harvested for their produce until they have matured (Lv 25:11–12). As noted by Crabbé, one of the laws of warfare (Dt 20:19–20) forbade the destruction of trees while laying siege to a town.

J. Philip Wogaman claims that the notion of stewardship is a 'point of entry' today for those with religious inclinations to assess economic and environmental policy. He writes: 'Property is to be enjoyed; but understood as stewardship, it is to be used for loving purposes, not selfishness, and with an eye toward the future and not only the present ... Stewardship recognizes the linkages of all generations through the common source of all being, and it accepts responsibility to the ultimate design of things and not only to oneself and a narrow frame of loyalties.'[51] This is all, of course, a much different view than that forwarded by White.

To conclude, the Jewish law was a moral or divine code that governed, among other things, economic affairs and which had far-reaching ecological implications.[52] For the Jews and early Christians, economics was bound up with a larger system of morality, some of the elements of which have been discussed above.

Progress and Time

Consider next White's position concerning linear time and the accompanying notion of progress. In actual fact, the Jews invented neither one. Robert Nisbet observes that the first recorded statement of the idea of progress in the West is by Xenophanes in the sixth century BC, who declared: 'The gods did not reveal to men all things from the beginning, but men through their own search find in the course of time that which is better.'[53] Nisbet demonstrates that the idea of progress is evident also in Homer, Hesiod, Protagoras, Aeschylus, Sophocles, Plato, Aristotle, Epicurus, Zeno, Lucretius, and Seneca.[54] For all these ancient Greek and Roman writers, it was the accumulation of knowledge and successive technological developments that enabled perpetual material progress.

The notion of progress maintained by the writers of the Old and New Testaments is, in fact, in stark contrast to that implied by White. For the Hebrews and early Christians, progress was not material but spiritual. A continuing theme of the Old Testament is that sojourners on earth improve their spiritual health by obeying God, and in so doing their material needs are then met. This is a basic meaning of the story of the manna in the desert, provided as nourishment to the Jews; as the manna lasted only a day, it could not be accumulated, making the Jews utterly dependent on God's provision. In the Old Testament, there is a clear distinction between pursuing wealth, an activity that is condemned, and enjoying the wealth that ensues from following God's commands. The same theme is continued in the New Testament.[55]

Indeed, there is much in both Testaments warning people *not* to devote themselves to accumulating material wealth ('progress' in White's sense of the term). On the seventh day of the week, for example, the Jews were to rest and refrain from work. They were also to celebrate numerous feasts, and bring the first fruits of the land as a sacrifice to God. A proud, acquisitive spirit was deemed sinful; rather, the Jews were to 'Do justice ... love kindness, and ... walk humbly with your God' (Mi 6:8). They were not to 'covet [their] neighbour's house ... or anything that is [their] neighbour's' (Ex 20:17); and they were admonished not to charge interest on loans to the poor (Ex 23:21–5). Every fifty years, those indentured (i.e., those who had sold themselves into slavery to pay debts) were to be set free and all losses from economic dealings were to be restored; this Law of Jubilee is presented in Leviticus 25:10 and elsewhere.

The Jewish moral law governing economic affairs emphasized empathy and kindness in business dealings, and maintained that those with wealth had responsibility for caring for those without – an ethic, that is, of social justice: 'And if your brother [neighbour] becomes poor, and cannot maintain himself with you, you shall maintain him; as a stranger and sojourner he shall live with you. Take no interest from him or increase, but fear your God; that your brother may live beside you. You shall not lend him your money at interest, nor give him your food for profit' (Lv 25:35–7). Likewise, in the New Testament, it is emphasized repeatedly that the accumulation of wealth and failure to share one's riches with the poor jeopardizes salvation.[56] To care for, rather than exploit, those weaker and poorer than oneself is indicative of a caring posture toward nature as well.

There are numerous passages in both Testaments regarding trade and the commodification of life: The love of money is the 'root of all evil' (1 Tm 6:10); 'You cannot serve both God and mammon (Mt 6:24);[57] Jesus 'upset the tables of the money-changers' (Mt 21:12); and so on. Undoubtedly, the most bitterly ironic statement in the Bible, however, is from Jeremiah, as cited by Matthew: 'And they took the thirty pieces of silver, the price of him on whom a price had been set by some of the sons of Israel, and they gave them for the potter's field' (Mt 27:9–10); this can be viewed as the definitive biblical position on the inadequacy of money, of prices, and of markets to represent value.

Even into the fifth century AD, Saint Augustine, whose *City of God* is credited with being the first work to devise epochs or stages of human history, based his schemata on the spiritual development of humankind, not on material, technological, or organizational factors.[58] For Augustine, human attention was to be focused on the divine kingdom. Indeed, according to historian Paul Johnson, 'Augustine saw the human race as helpless children ... Humanity was utterly dependent on God. The race was prostrate, and there was no possibility that it might raise itself by its own merits. That was the sin of pride – Satan's sin.'[59] In brief, there was no materialist progress principle here.

To summarize, White is correct in noting the presence of both a linear conception of time and a progress principle in the Judaeo-Christian foundations of Western culture, and these may be regarded as seeds that, undergoing 'mutation,' contributed to the anti-environmentalism of modern economics. Over the centuries, the meaning of 'progress' changed, coming to be defined more in material than in spiritual terms. Indeed, the history of the Church itself illustrates the interplay and tension between these at times conflicting notions of progress. Likewise, linear time is presented in the Bible as existing or unfolding within the context of eternity or unchanging time; however, with secularization, rather than events being understood as being contained within an eternal order of goodness, time became merely history,[60] that is, the sequential unfolding of secular events.[61]

From the standpoint of ecological principles, Aristotle and the biblical writers have much in common. Both speak of human action within the context of a transcendent 'goodness,' implying that economic conduct takes place only within a moral framework. Both denigrate money making, accumulation, and charging interest. Both eschew an egoistic, individualist frame of mind, and recommend altruism, a sense of community, the common good, and responsibility for the plight of others. Both indicate that human welfare is not bound up with commodities and deny that value is co-extensive with prices. Nature, of course, represents non-commodified relations, and both Aristotle and the biblical writers emphasize that human well-being depends upon values that cannot and should not be commodified.[62]

In the writings of Aristotle and in the Bible, moreover, we see the same tensions or dialectic at play: human dominance vs the intrinsic goodness of nature; anthropocentrism vs the continuity or similarity of humans and the rest of nature; linear time in the context of eternal time and natural (or divine) law. Eco-critics of the Bible and of Aristotle have chosen to emphasize but one side of these polarities, rather than the tension between the two. Perhaps this is due to the fact that modern thought systems, such as economics, have lost sight of the constraining side, emphasizing anthropocentrism and the uniqueness (superiority) of humans, and hence use/exchange value rather than intrinsic value.

A major turning point in Western thought occurred, therefore, when value came to be deemed coextensive with commodities and prices; in no way were either the Bible or the Greeks responsible for this conception of value. A further turning point took place when communities and societies were no longer deemed to be organic, but merely collections of individuals. We saw indicators of this principle in Aristotle and Democritus, but also noted that for Aristotle the community transcended the individual.

Middle Ages

The Middle Ages span the thousand years between the end of the ancient world with the fall of Rome (476 AD) and the onset of the modern period in the middle of the fifteenth century. The period is characterized by the church as a dominant institution.

In its history the church made many and continuous compromises with mammon, pursuing with great interest and energy its own material well-being. In this regard, two events stand out as emblematic. First was the Edict of Milan, resulting from the conversion to Christianity of

Emperor Constantine in 313, ending the official hostility of the Roman Empire toward Christianity and setting up the marriage of church and state. One of Constantine's first acts was to privilege the clergy, exempting them from taxes and compulsory public office, helping thereby to support the emergence of a 'separate and exclusive clerical class.'[63] With time the State took on the role of enforcer of Christian orthodoxy, and Christianity became the state religion. The church changed a great deal as a result, adapting to worldly ways and accepting a range of secular responsibilities in exchange for state protection.[64]

A second noteworthy date was Christmas Day 800, marking the coronation of Charlemagne. At Saint Peter's Basilica in Rome, the pope celebrated mass, placed a crown on Charlemagne's head, and immediately 'prostrated himself in an act of emperor-worship.'[65] Thus was born the Holy Roman Empire, and for centuries the church was beset by inner conflict between the lure of wealth and privilege and the principle of subsidiarity.

Yet none of this is to suggest that the intellectual, philosophical, or moral foundations of Judaism and Christianity justified or advocated unlimited acquisition and consumption, or defined progress in the narrow sense of improved material well-being. The greatest of medieval writers was Saint Thomas Aquinas (1225–74).[66] For Schoolmen like Aquinas, all activity should be consistent with a moral framework in order to sustain well-being, including by implication ecological well-being. According to Aquinas, 'the maker and manager of the whole universe wills what he sees to be good for the whole of that community.'[67] Prominent in medieval thought, therefore was the notion that the cosmos is an inherently moral order ensuring the common good.

However, according to Aquinas, mere mortals are often unable to see the big, indeed cosmic, picture, and hence interpret goodness on a much smaller, even local scale. 'So it can happen,' he continued, 'that a good will can want something, for a particular reason, that God does not want on universal grounds, and vice versa.' People therefore have a duty to 'conform' their willing to 'the common good,' namely, 'the general good that is God's.'[68] Aquinas added that this conforming might not be as difficult as it sounds since 'even the parts of a natural whole instinctively desire the common good of their whole.'[69]

A key characteristic of Aquinas's thought, and of medieval thought generally, then, is its holism. All activities were thought to be enclosed within a grander end, sometimes termed the 'common good,' from which they derived their significance.[70] The economy and economic thinking, therefore, were always related to, and understood as existing within, this larger context. Although medieval thought emphasized contrasts and antitheses (as between the common good and lesser goods, between good and evil, between the body and the spirit), these oppositions, too, were comprehended as existing only within a larger synthesis or unity.[71]

Furthermore, medieval thinkers maintained an organismic view of society, and indeed of all creation. Like the human body, society was conceived as comprising different parts, each working for the benefit of the whole. ('In civic relationships, all men who belong to the same community are regarded as one body, and the whole community as one man').[72] Some members were to be devoted to prayer, others to defence, others to trade, and others still to agriculture. Because society needed them all, Aquinas maintained, people should be content with the class or occupation into which they were born. But, equally, all were entitled to receive enough to sustain their lives in that station.

Mere money making in medieval thought was regarded with great suspicion. Aquinas maintained that engaging in trade signified one's fall from grace. However, he continued, since trade is necessary, it would be tolerated as long as the seller charged only the 'just price.'[73] Although the conception of the just price changed somewhat during the course of the Middle Ages, its essence remained fairly constant:[74] it was the price that allowed each person to 'have the necessities of life suitable for his station.'[75] The church fathers agreed that justice was violated whenever monopolists charged prices in accordance with their advantage. The concern was that trade, in the absence of moral control over prices, could deprive some of the means of living even while raising others beyond their natural station within the social hierarchy.

Likewise, a person was not permitted to charge interest for loans (usury). As described by Herbert Heaton, the sentiment was that since a lender parts temporarily with money for which she has no immediate need, she should allow the borrower, the one in need, to use the money freely.[76] Greed and the accumulation of wealth, in other words, were denigrated during the Middle Ages, in both selling and lending.

In formulating and enforcing these proscriptions, R.H. Tawney notes, the church was hardly a disinterested party. Indeed, precisely the opposite: 'Practically,' he writes, 'the Church was an immense vested interest, implicated to the hilt in the economic fabric, especially on the side of agriculture and land tenure, itself [being] the greatest of landowners.'[77] Regarding the sale of indulgences by the Roman Catholic Church,

Lewis Mumford remarked that the practice 'announced more brazenly than by words that henceforth there was nothing on Earth or in Heaven that could not be bought for money.'[78]

That being said, the point remains that during the Middle Ages the economy (and all else) was theorized and discussed as being contained within a moral framework that was to govern the activities of all participants. Regarding economic activity, that moral framework was opposed to undue trading and to excessive accumulation. There was no notion of humans as unlimited appetitive machines. Nor was there disharmony between economic understanding and what we today conceive to be ecological understanding. Precisely the opposite. Everyone and everything were seen to serve a purpose within the overall design of creation. Each person, plant, and animal was part of an intricate web of creation, and each part was to function not according to its own interests alone, but to the benefit of the whole, that is, the common good. This evidence contradicts completely White's contention that Christianity was inherently anti-environmental from the outset.

The Protestant Ethic

At this point mention must be made of Max Weber's famous thesis that the Protestant Reformation was closely aligned with the emergence of capitalism.[79] Weber maintained, on the one hand, that Catholicism was inimical to capitalism, due in part to its idealization of otherworldliness and the monastic life.[80] On the other hand, he proclaimed that Protestantism, and in particular Calvinism, by maintaining that success in one's 'calling' in this world is a 'sign' of salvation in the next, encouraged hard work, frugality, and the accumulation of wealth. Thereby Calvinism, Weber opined, gave rise to a new 'spirit' – the 'spirit of capitalism.' Weber quoted sayings by Benjamin Franklin, such as the following, to indicate the content of this new 'spirit':

> Remember that time is money. He that can earn ten shillings a day by his labour, and ... sits idle, one half of that day ... has really spent, or rather thrown away, five shillings.
>
> Remember, that credit is money. If a man lets his money lie in my hands after it is due, he gives me the interest.
>
> Remember, that money is of the prolific, generating nature. Money can

beget money, and its offspring can beget more, and so on. Five shillings turned is six, turned again it is seven and three pence, and so on, till it becomes a hundred pounds.

Remember this saying, The paymaster is lord of another man's purse. He that is known to pay punctually and exactly to the time he promises, may at any time, and on any occasion, raise all the money his friends can spare.[81]

Franklin's maxims, Weber noted, constitute a 'philosophy of avarice,' since accumulation 'is assumed as an end in itself.'[82] According to Weber, Franklin issued not merely advice on how to make one's way in the world, but he also set forth an 'ethos,' 'a peculiar ethic,' a 'duty,'[83] indeed a system of morality based on expediency: 'Honesty is useful,' Weber summarized, 'because it assures credit; so are punctuality, industry, frugality, and that is the reason they are virtues.'[84] Weber then continued: 'A logical deduction from this would be that where, for instance, the *appearance* of honesty serves the same purpose, that would suffice.'[85] Nearly a century later, Jane Jacobs essentially expanded upon Weber's analysis of Calvinistic business 'morality.'[86]

It is interesting to note that no less an authority than John Wesley (1703–91), founder of Methodism, essentially agreed with Weber's depiction of Protestantism. Wesley pointed to a gaping contradiction between the ethic of Protestantism and its religious base, which, unless and until rectified by a spirit of benevolence, would doom Christianity:

But how astonishing a thing is this! How can we understand it? Does it not seem (and yet this cannot be) that Christianity, true scriptural Christianity, has a tendency, in process of time, to undermine and destroy itself? For wherever true Christianity spreads, it must cause diligence and frugality, which, in the natural course of things, must beget riches! And riches naturally beget pride, love of the world, and every temper that is destructive of Christianity. Now, if there be no way to prevent this, Christianity is inconsistent with itself, and, of consequence, cannot stand, cannot continue long among any people; since, wherever it generally prevails, it saps its own foundation.

But is there no way to prevent this? – to continue Christianity among a people? Allowing that diligence and frugality must produce riches, is there no means to hinder riches from destroying the religion of those that possess them? I can see only one possible way; find out another who can. Do you gain all you can, and save all you can? Then you must, in the nature of

> things, grow rich. Then if you have any desire to escape the damnation of hell, *give* all you can; otherwise I can have no more hope of your salvation, than of that of Judas Iscariot.[87]

The Protestant ethic, then, for Wesley, consisted in gaining all one can and saving all one can – certainly a far cry from Aristotle, the Jewish writers of the Testaments, and the medieval scholastics – but, he insisted, these traits were to be modified by benevolence. Soon, however, the acquisition and diligence aspects of the Protestant ethic, as formulated by Calvin, permeated secular thought and practice unmodified by a 'an ethic of benevolence.' This constituted the 'Spirit of Capitalism' in the raw. Exemplars in formulating this new world view or discourse were Thomas Hobbes and Adam Smith.

4 Shattering the Synthesis: Hobbes, Smith, and Neoclassicism

To locate the origins of modern economics' anti-environmentalism we need look no further than the writings of two exemplars of the Enlightenment: Thomas Hobbes and Adam Smith. These acclaimed authorities helped inaugurate an economics discourse in tune with 'the spirit of capitalism,' as described by Weber, but bereft of the mitigating ethos of benevolence that, according to Wesley, is so essential. This chapter reviews anti-environmental elements in the writings of these two authors and connects them to today's neoclassical economics. As Peter Dickens remarks, to this day 'the Enlightenment is casting a shadow.'[1]

Thomas Hobbes's *Leviathan*

Thomas Hobbes (1588–1679) was the son of a 'low-grade,'[2] alcoholic clergyman. His father abandoned the family when Thomas was a child, and the largely literary education of this brilliant student was attained only through the beneficence of an uncle. Well versed in the classics, Hobbes's first book, published in 1629, was a translation of Thucydides, while his last, written when he was in his eighties, was a complete translation of Homer. Many of his ideas on the individual and society were set out in *Elements of Law, Natural and Politic*, written in 1640 and circulated widely in manuscript form, but unpublished until 1650. His most famous tome, said to be 'one of the most influential books on political theory in the English language,'[3] was *Leviathan*, published in 1651. Hobbes wrote it in Paris during a decade of self-imposed exile from England – this because *Elements of Law*, circulating at the start of the English Civil War, supported the King, not Parliament, and Hobbes feared for his life and freedom.[4] When he finally returned to England, Hobbes was more circumspect about what he published: *Behemoth*, for example, his political history of the period of the Long Parliament (1640–60), although written in 1668, was published only after his death.

Hobbes lived during a time of unprecedented change in cosmology. Copernicus (1473–1543) had previously undermined the geocentric understanding of the universe, ushering in the scientific revolution. According to this new world view, the motion of bodies on earth and in the heavens can be understood through mechanical laws. As historian of economic thought Roger Backhouse remarks, with the scientific revolution there arose 'a coherent and complete alternative to medieval cosmology.'[5]

Hobbes also lived in a time of 'extraordinary [political] instability and savagery.'[6] By 1500 much of the old feudal nobility in England had been killed off in the Wars of the Roses, enabling the first Tudor monarch, Henry VII (1485–1509), to centralize government.[7] Hobbes's period of exile in France was also a time of violence as the English Civil War (1642–51) raged between forces supporting Charles I and Parliament.

Hobbes's work also appeared during a time of unprecedented economic transition and dislocation. For one thing, England was in the midst of a centuries-long enclosure movement. Prior to the enclosures, as noted by Karl Polyani, land was bound up with 'kinship, neighborhood, craft, and creed – with tribe and temple, village, gild, and church'[8] – in brief, with the whole of human life. Although officially entitled to the Crown, nobility, or church, much of the land in practice was held through custom by peasants who made periodic payments to the landlord for its use.[9] When the enclosures were imposed, however, customary rights were routinely abrogated. Peasants were denied access to the commons, which was bundled up into blocks for sale in the emerging real-estate market. Cottagers without legal proof of ownership were dispossessed without compensation, while those with documented claims retained only a small parcel insufficient for subsistence.'[10] It was, E.P. Thompson writes, 'class robbery, played according to fair rules of property and law laid down by a parliament of property-owners and lawyers.'[11] Many of the dispossessed fled to the cities in quest of employment in the new, centralized sites of production (factories) and emerged as a class of often unemployed industrial labourers (proletariat), who were forced by necessity to work (when they could find jobs) for mere subsistence wages.

This period was marked as well by the onset of new technologies (circa 1540–1640). The textiles, mining, and metal industries, among others, grew rapidly, as power shifted from the ownership of land to the control of capital.[12] One of the landmark inventions was the printing press (mid-fifteenth century), which was instrumental in spreading the ideas of religious dissidents such as Luther and Calvin. The Protestant Reformation (beginning in 1517) may in turn have played an important part in industrial development;[13] although Calvin was certainly more attuned to the temper of the emerging economic order than Luther.[14]

In addition to experiencing scientific, agricultural, and technological revolutions, England was also in the midst of a commercial revolution: a merchant class was born, which organized domestic and foreign trade ('mercantilism,' or merchant capitalism). Leading economic thinkers of the day – Thomas Mun (1571–1641), Charles Davenant (1656–1714), and others – advocated a centralized power in the state, which should concentrate on achieving a favourable balance of trade in order to accumulate gold and silver; specie, it was felt, represented real wealth for a nation, and the more of it a country had relative to its rivals, the greater its security. Mercantilist thinking was manifested particularly in the quest by the great powers (England, France, Spain) for colonies. Mercantilists believed the world's total wealth was fixed (a doctrine of a finite earth!), and that what one nation achieved was inevitably at the expense of others. They also concluded that colonies provided a superb way of increasing national wealth. Colonies made available vast reserves of minerals and other raw materials outside the reach of foreign governments, and constituted markets secured from foreign competition for the export of manufactured goods.[15]

Instrumental to all of the foregoing disruptions and changes in the social structure and mode of production was the rise to predominance of money as a medium of communication. According to historian of economic thought Wesley Mitchell, it was the proliferation in the use of money that 'broke down the old medieval scheme of organization.'[16] To be sure, Mitchell points out, money had circulated long before the dawn of the commercial and industrial ages. Indeed, it had been in use before the Norman Conquest.[17] But the commodification (monetarization) of daily life had proceeded slowly until the reign of Elizabeth (1558–1603), and thereafter accelerated, becoming a major factor in the disintegration of the medieval orders of society – to such an extent that there was a flaying about for new principles of organization.

As concomitant to these events and transformations, then, there was also, necessarily, a discursive revolution. Hobbes helped pioneer this revolution, lending philosophical support to mercantilism and anticipating capitalism, and he did this in at least two closely related ways.

One was his methodological individualism and rejection of the hitherto prevailing organic conception of society (except as manifested in *Leviathan,* or the totalitarian state). The other was his thoroughgoing materialism, which he applied to social and political affairs. Each of these related positions has had dire environmental implications, and so we now look at them in turn.

Methodological Individualism

We noted previously that methodological individualism ('atomism') was present in certain strains of Greek thought, but that this understanding was dismissed by Aristotle, and hence did not form a main current in the ancient and medieval discourses. Hobbes in a sense resuscitated Democritus, as both philosophers sought to explain complex phenomena by mechanistic interactions among basic parts. Hobbes proposed conceptions of both the individual and society at odds with Aristotle, and in the process helped launch the West on a trajectory of environmental degradation.

Hobbes learned his basic methodology, termed the 'resolutive-compositive method' (in the social sphere, it is more commonly known today as 'methodological individualism'), from the astronomer Galileo. It entails 'resolving' complex phenomena (for Galileo, the solar system; for Hobbes, both society and the individual human being) into components, and then recomposing these elements through logic based on assumptions to re-form a whole.[18] The recomposition that is achieved, however, depends fundamentally on the presumed properties of the individual components; that is to say, the whole takes its characteristics from the parts, rather than being understood to have emergent properties that derive from interactions among the parts. Here I will consider, in turn, Hobbes's analysis of society and the individual.

To break society down into its individual members, Hobbes imagined a primeval 'state of nature' where no authority existed to enforce laws or contracts. This condition, he proposed, would be a *bellum omnium contra omnes* – a war of each against all others.[19] In the absence of a supreme authority to keep the peace, he maintained, each person would be in a constant state of conflict with everyone else on account of jealousy, fear, and the desire for material gain, personal reputation, or glory.[20] For Hobbes, then, humans were not at all the naturally social, communitarian, political beings they were for Aristotle. According to Hobbes, it is human nature 'to love ... Dominion over others.'[21]

Therefore, in Hobbes's view, collectivities of humans did not constitute a community as they did for Aristotle, or a people, as they did for the Old Testament writers. Rather, society was composed essentially of autonomous, selfish individuals, each a proprietor of his or her own capacities (skills, labour power),[22] and each possessing unlimited appetites or wants. In these circumstances, without an overseeing authority to keep the peace and resolve disputes, Hobbes surmised, people would possess only such limited security as their strength and cunning could provide, and in the circumstances, he proposed, 'the life of man [is] solitary, poore, nasty, brutish, and short.'[23]

In this 'state of nature,' moreover, Hobbes deduced that there could be no conception of justice or injustice.[24] For him, natural law in a state of nature meant simply that 'each man [may] ... use his own power, as he will himselfe, for the preservation of ... his own Life.'[25] Hobbes added as corollary to this *jus naturale* the principle that 'in such a condition, every man has a Right to every thing; even to one another's body.'[26]

As antithesis, and antidote, to the insecurity of the 'state of nature,' Hobbes proposed the 'COMMON-WEALTH,' which he defined as a society governed by a despotic ruler mandated to keep the peace. He argued that individuals, recognizing the radical insecurity of their existence in the 'state of nature,' once afforded the opportunity, would eagerly forfeit their freedom in exchange for security of person and possessions. Hobbes termed also a 'law of nature,' the principle that 'a man be willing, when others are too ... to lay down this right to all things; and be contented with so much liberty against other men, as he would allow other men against himselfe.'[27] When a 'multitude' of like-minded individuals had thus surrendered their freedom to a person or an assembly of persons, Hobbes declared, power would reside in the hands of 'a COMMON-WEALTH, in latine CIVITAS,' which incorporates [i.e., embodies], and represents, all the people.'[28] In return for securing the safety of its subjects, this 'LEVIATHAN' was to command and receive total obedience. It is from this 'social contract' (or what Hobbes termed 'Covenant') that all notions of injustice and justice for him arose: 'For where no Covenant hath preceded, there hath no Right been transferred, and every man has right to every thing; and consequently, no action can be Unjust. But when a Covenant is made, then to break it, it is Unjust: And the definition of injustice, is no other than the not Performance of Covenant.'[29]

In his thought concerning human nature, the war of one against all others, and the emergence of the Leviathan, Hobbes was, at the very least, in tune with, if not indeed a progenitor of, mercantilist thought and policy.[30] Mercantilists believed that in international affairs, it was each nation against all others, that nations had an insatiable appetite for acquisition, and that in international affairs 'might makes right.' He also foreshadowed the principle of population as set out by the Malthus, and Darwin's principle of natural selection

Hobbes's Materialism

According to intellectual historian Jacob Bronowski, Hobbes's major contribution to Western thought was the application of the materialist conception of the universe, as formulated by Galileo and others, to social affairs.[31] All that mattered, Hobbes maintained, were phenomena that could be observed and forces that could be measured;[32] there was little difference, for example, between animate and inanimate objects: 'For seeing life is [nothing] but a motion of Limbs, the beginning whereof is in some principall part within; why may we not say, that all *Automata* (Engines that move themselves by springs and wheels as doth a watch) have an artificial life? For what is the *Heart*, but a *Spring*, and the *Nerves*, but so many *Strings*, and the *Joynts*, but so many *Wheels*, giving motion to the whole Body.'[33] Hobbes wished to apply the 'laws of motion,' which pertain to inanimate objects, to animate creatures, including human beings, declaring: 'When a thing lies still, unlesse somewhat els stirre it, it will lye still for ever ... When a thing is in motion, it will eternally be in motion, unless somewhat els stay it.'[34]

Hobbes identified two broad categories of forces (or 'Motions') that stir and stay animate beings generally, and humans in particular. One he called 'Appetite, or Desire'; this Motion, he explained, operates when the tendency is *toward* something (food, drink, etc.). The other he called 'Aversion,' and it is present when the tendency is to move away from something.[35] Things for which people have neither desire nor aversion he labelled 'Contemne,' or contempt, this 'being *nothing else but* an immobility, or contumacy of the Heart, in resisting the action of certain things.'[36] Humans are born with some appetites and aversions (appetites for food and for excretion, for example), but many others are learned. One of the principal desires or appetites of people, Hobbes proposed, is for security. We have aversions, moreover, not only for things we know will hurt us, but also for things we are uncertain about.

Hobbes applied also his materialist methodology to *value*. 'The *Value* or Worth of a man,' he proclaimed, anticipating modern economics, 'is as of all other things, his Price; that is to say, so much as would be given him for the use of his Power.'[37] Hobbes defined 'Power' as the capacity 'to obtain some future apparent Good.'[38] And 'Good,' for Hobbes, meant anything toward which someone has an appetite or desire. For him, therefore, there is no intrinsic or 'absolute' value to a person, or to anything else for that matter.[39] Hobbes also premised his theory of good and evil on a mechanical conception of human nature, again departing markedly from Aristotle, to say nothing of the Hebrew prophets. Hobbes equated goodness with desire, and evil with antipathy.[40]

Like Aristotle, Hobbes elaborated on the likenesses and differences between humans and other animals. By his account, humans are unique in possessing the capacity to detect causal sequences.[41] Moreover, humans alone, according to Hobbes, are capable of speech. Hence, only humans are able to make contracts ('Covenants') [42] to obtain their security by voluntarily surrendering their liberties.[43]

To summarize, although Hobbes listed a number of axioms that he termed 'natural laws,' these are mostly contingent upon the prior creation of an 'artificial person,'[44] known as Leviathan, which makes the laws; thus, these are really 'positive laws.' The main exception to the foregoing – the 'real' natural law in Hobbes's work – is the doctrine that in a state of nature, one may do anything, which when you think about it is not a 'law' at all since it proscribes nothing.

Hobbes also minimized the medieval notion of the 'common good.' Whereas bees and ants live sociably one with another, he asserted, that is because their common good is virtually indistinguishable from the good of each individual member. As far as people are concerned, however, one person's gain is another's loss – the sole but monumentally important exception to that principle being, he contended, the common interest of everyone in peace and security. Thus, the totalitarian state and its policies are deemed by him to be the embodiment and manifestation of the 'common good.'

Hobbes also proposed a new view of human nature. For him, as documented thoroughly by C.B. Macpherson, humans are appetitive machines, mechanically driven by wants and aversions. No hint here, as in Aristotle, that the perfection of human nature entails applying intelligence to curb instincts and appetites so that one can participate more fully in the life of the polis. However, Hobbes did credit humans with enough intelligence to constrain in the short term their appetites for acquisition by submitting to the laws of the despot; note, however, that this submission was deemed a means of furthering acquisitions over the longer term – a far cry from Aristotle indeed.

Hobbes was certainly a forerunner of modern economic thought: methodological individualism, materialism, utilitarianism,[45] and the priority accorded economic growth over distribution or social justice are all features characterizing Hobbes's work that resonate with modern neoclassicism. He also anticipated behavioural psychology (pleasure-pain, reward-punishment, conditioning) and, of course, the Darwin-Spencer principle of 'survival of the fittest.' We can see from all this just how current in the first decade of the twenty-first century are the thoughts of Thomas Hobbes.

Adam Smith

Adam Smith (1723–90), the father of economic liberalism, extended some tenets of Hobbes and reversed others, but in the end he, too, contributed mightily to the anti-environmental thrust of neoclassical economic discourses. Before delving into these matters, however, it is worth recalling the interesting and controversial relation between two of Smith's major works: *The Theory of Moral Sentiments* (*TMS*), a treatise on moral philosophy that went through six editions between 1759 and 1790; and the much larger and, in our day, more influential *The Wealth of Nations (WN)*, characterized by Max Lerner as 'undoubtedly the foundation-work of modern economic thought,'[46] of which there were five editions between 1776 and 1789, the year before Smith's death. *Moral Sentiments*, the smaller work, 'contains' the larger one in at least the chronological sense: *TMS* was Smith's first book and he revised it after *WN*'s final (in Smith's lifetime) edition.

Moral Sentiments has been said also to 'contain' *The Wealth of Nations* in yet another, more profound, way. Following the precedent established at Glasgow University by his predecessor and mentor, Francis Hutcheson, Smith taught political economy (the subject matter of *WN*) as but one component of moral philosophy, the others being natural theology, ethics (the subject matter of *TMS*), and jurisprudence.[47] Thus, according to historians of economic thought Roger Backhouse, Warren Samuels, and others, *Moral Sentiments* sets out the ethical framework that is required for a market economy, while *Wealth of Nations* describes the operations of such an economy.[48] But none of this is clear from reading Smith, who seldom cross-references the two books, although he does remark that both volumes were intended to be part of 'tripartite system of social science covering the domains of moral rules, government and law, and market.'[49]

In the context of the present discussion, these two books epitomize the split in the West between economics and environmental concerns. First, I will argue, *The Theory of Moral Sentiments* sets forth an environmentally sound world view, whereas *The Wealth of Nations* is profoundly anti-environmental. Second, whereas *Moral Sentiments* 'ought' to contain *Wealth of Nations,* just as ecology 'ought ' to contain economics, the conversation between the two books is virtually non-existent, and *WN* has far surpassed the smaller tome in influence so as to render the latter but a curio among specialists. The position taken here on the relation between the two books is not without controversy. Smith's modern editors, Raphael and Macfie, for instance, endeavour to minimize the contradictions by claiming that the two works are 'complementary.'[50]

Over the centuries, however, the contradictions between the books have been subject to much speculation and comment. *TMS,* after all, lauds 'sympathy,' defined by Smith broadly as 'our fellow-feeling with any passion whatever,'[51] and more properly as 'our fellow-feeling with sufferings, not that with the enjoyments, of others';[52] *WN,* in contrast, points to 'self-love' as the main force driving human activity and praises it as the engine of economic prosperity. Smith himself, in a passage referencing Hobbes, denied that sympathy can in any way be considered the same as self-interest or self-love: 'Sympathy, however, cannot, in any sense, be regarded as a selfish principle. When I sympathize with your sorrow ... I consider what I should suffer if I was really you. ... My grief therefore, is entirely upon your account, and not in the least upon my own. It is not, therefore, in the least selfish.'[53]

Raphael and Macfie, editors of *TMS,* miss the point when they argue that of course the books have different emphases because *WN* 'concentrates on self-interest,' dealing as it does primarily with economic activity, whereas sympathy in *TMS* is a criterion for moral judgment.[54] For as we have seen, Aristotle and other ancients addressed 'economic activity,' too, but they did so without focusing on self-interest; their centre of attention, rather, was the common good, a position much more closely aligned with Smith's *TMS.* In other words, had Smith chosen to follow antiquarian precedents in his political economy, 'sympathy' would have been afforded a central position.

There is yet another major reason for deeming *WN,* in veering from the positions articulated in *TMS,* as being anti-environmental. In *WN* Smith defined political economy as an investigation into which government policies can best increase material well-being – what he called 'the wealth of nations.' (His answer, laissez-faire, was a complete reversal from Hobbes: in place of Hobbes's despot, Smith proposed 'governance' by the price system and the market).[55] In formulating this definition, however, and this is the central point, Smith refocused the subject matter of political economy from the antiquarian topic of distributive justice (the just price, the law of jubilee, laws proscribing usury, the just wage, charity and benevolence, proscriptions against accumulation of wealth and so on – all matters that relate closely to 'sympathy' as defined in *TMS*) to that of economic growth. Smith therefore contributed mightily not only the currently exaggerated belief in the efficacy of self-interest and markets to promote individual and collective well-being, but also to common acceptance of the notion that well-being is dependent primarily upon the material wealth of individuals and on the continual growth of that wealth. Both these changes are environmentally problematic in the extreme.

Perhaps most significantly, by writing these books as *separate* works, with negligible cross-referencing between them, even while in effect arguing that from a moral standpoint the engine of economic prosperity ('self-love') is deficient, Smith figured powerfully in separating political economy from moral philosophy. Since the separation of political economy from moral philosophy and the redefinition of political economy as the study of wealth creation rather than distribution or economic justice are key in the shift in economics from being environmentally benign to becoming anti-environmental, we shall now take a closer look at these two works of Adam Smith.[56]

Theory of Moral Sentiments

Smith's *Moral Sentiments* proposes that 'sympathy' (in modern terms, 'empathy') for one's fellow human beings is the highest of human virtues:

> And hence it is, that to feel much for others and little for ourselves, that to restrain our selfish, and to indulge our benevolent affections, constitutes the perfection of human nature ... As to love our neighbour as we love ourselves is the great law of Christianity, so it is the great precept of nature to love ourselves only as we love our neighbour, or what comes to the same thing, as our neighbour is capable of loving us.[57]

Here, in *Moral Sentiments*, is an utter repudiation of Hobbesian 'morality,'[58] of Hobbes's claim that selfish individualism is unalterably at the heart of human nature, of Hobbes's denial of community, and of his denunciation of organic collectivity except in the person of a despot. Smith says, rather, echoing Aristotle, that a person does not become fully human ('perfection of human nature') until he or she comes into relationship with another or others, and 'relationship' for Smith is not mere reciprocity (or, worse, utilitarian expediency), but rather 'sympathy,' a capacity of putting oneself in the place of another or others. Although proposing that selfishness *is* inherent to the make-up of human beings, Smith in *TMS* insists that there also resides within the heart of each person 'some principles ... which interest him in the fortune of others, and render their happiness necessary for him, though he derives nothing from it except the pleasure of seeing it.'[59] Whereas for Hobbes the predominant natural law was the right of each of us to preserve and improve our existence in any manner that seems expedient, even though this may harm others, for the Adam Smith of *Moral Sentiments* it is our capacity and need to empathize with others that is a 'precept of nature.'

Moral Sentiments, then, very much helped reinvigorate antiquarian ethics and morality from the trashing they had received from Hobbes. Compared to *Leviathan,* hence, there is an ecological soundness to *Moral Sentiments.* Conceiving that people are bound together in networks of interrelationships through sympathy is an 'ecological perspective' insofar as a basic principle of ecology is mutual interdependence and normally an absence of the will to dominate.[60] An environmental implication of Smith's *Moral Sentiments* is that one should never pursue material welfare without regard for the effects of this activity on others; rather, the 'perfection of human nature' requires each person to prioritize the welfare of others, including (we may say) their environmental welfare.

The Wealth of Nations

In *The Wealth of Nations,* however, Smith emphasized self-love or self-interest; indeed, the words 'sympathy,' 'compassion,' and 'pity' do not even appear in the index of Cannan's authoritative edition. Note, for example, how starkly the following famous passage from *The Wealth of Nations* contrasts with the words quoted above from *Moral Sentiments,* particularly in terms of how Smith conceives human nature and the principles whereby humans should, and do, relate one to another:

> In almost every other race of animals each individual, when it is grown up to maturity, is entirely independent, and in its natural state has occasion for

> the assistance of no other living creature. But man has almost constant occasion for the help of his brethren, and it is in vain for him to expect it from their benevolence only. He will be more likely to prevail if he can interest their self-love in his favour, and shew them that it is for their own advantage to do for him what he requires of them. Whoever offers to another a bargain of any kind, proposes to do this. Give me that which I want, and you shall have this which you want, is the meaning of every such offer ... It is not from the benevolence of the butcher, the brewer, or the baker, that we expect our dinner, but from their regard to their own interest. We address ourselves, not to their humanity but to their self-love, and never talk to them of our own necessities but of their advantages. Nobody but a beggar chuses to depend upon the benevolence of his fellow-citizens.[61]

Not only did Smith, in this passage, neglect sympathy, benevolence, or the common good as means of organizing society, he in fact celebrated the opposite. Indeed, later on he proclaimed that if empathy or goodwill should in fact encroach upon narrowly conceived calculations of self-interest, this could be harmful. Why? Because, he asserted, each individual knows better than anyone else what he or she needs; even more importantly, by pursuing only one's own gain a person is 'led by an invisible hand to promote an end [namely, wealth for the nation] which is no part of his intention.' He continued: 'By pursuing his own interest he frequently promotes that of the society more effectually than when he really intends to promote it. I have never known much good done by those who affected to trade for the public good. It is an affectation, indeed, not very common among merchants, and very few words need be employed in dissuading them from it.'[62]

Smith anticipated neoclassical economics not only in his celebration of self-interest and his thoroughgoing materialism, but also in his characterization of markets and prices as modes or media of communication. He did this, for instance, by comparing humans to puppies and other animals, writing: 'A puppy fawns upon its dam, and a spaniel endeavours by a thousand attractions to engage the attention of its master who is at dinner, when it wants to be fed by him.'[63] Humans likewise, he continued, on occasion may use 'treaty,' especially when they have nothing to offer. But, he advised, it is impossible for most people to attain all or even most of their wants this way; there simply are not enough opportunities or time. Rather, he proposed, people use one or other of two remaining strategies, namely, barter and purchase. (He neglected to mention theft, threat, and force.) In both these instances, he explained, the stratagem is to show another or others that one possesses something that the other wants, and to offer to exchange that for what the self wants. With barter, the exchange is of one article or commodity for another; with purchase, the exchange is money for a commodity.

Not only are markets a medium of communication for Smith since traders come together, let their desires be known, negotiate, reach agreement, exchange possessions, and then go their separate ways; according to him they also reconcile individual greed with the common good: one can best increase one's private wealth by offering goods and services that others want.

Smith recognized, however, that markets are not neutral. They do not merely transmit information concerning pre-existing wants and preferences and signal availability of items. Rather, they affect profoundly the availability of items. In other words, markets are biased transmitters of information since they affect the condition of those things concerning which they transmit information. (In this, it may be noted, Smith anticipated Harold Innis's media thesis, alluded to earlier.)

In particular, Smith drew attention to the propensity of markets to stimulate the production of items intended not for home consumption but for trade, and thereby to intensify specialization, or what he termed 'the division of labour.' Specialization, he declared, increases markedly the output of each worker, and he illustrated that claim through his famous example of pin making:[64] by dividing and combining operations in the manufacture of pins, output increased by an order of perhaps 4,800 to 1 compared to what individual workers each doing the complete operation could produce.[65] Specialization, Smith insisted, is *the* major source of increases in the wealth of nations, and it was his view that through trade based on the division of labour, economic growth is, in principle, without limit.

Smith also remarked, however, that the division of labour is essentially dehumanizing. He proposed that job specialization renders the worker 'altogether incapable of judging ... the great and extensive interests of his country,' that it 'corrupts the courage of [a worker's] mind, ... [and] corrupts the activity of his body.' He concluded, 'In every *improved and civilized society* [*sic*] this is the state into which the labouring poor, *that is, the great body of the people* [*sic*], must necessarily fall, unless government takes some pains to prevent it.'[66]

To his credit, Smith's remarks on the debilitating consequences of the division of labour are contained within his extended chapter titled 'The Education of Youth.' There he recommended that the state teach the young children of the 'common people,' before they enter the labour force (which in Smith's time was at a very young age), how to 'read, write and account,' staving off perhaps the full dehumanizing consequences of the division of labour.[67] Nonetheless, it was also Smith's position that

> The understandings of the greater part of men are necessarily formed by their ordinary employments. The man whose whole life is spent in performing a few simple operations of which the effects too are, perhaps, always the same, or very nearly the same, has no occasion to exert his understanding, or to exercise his invention in finding out expedients for removing difficulties which never occur. He naturally loses, therefore, the habit of such exertion, and generally becomes as stupid and ignorant as it is possible for a human creature to become. The torpor of his mind renders him, not only incapable of relishing or bearing a part in any rational conversation, but of conceiving any generous, noble, or tender sentiment, and consequently of forming any just judgment concerning many even of the ordinary duties of private life. Of the great and extensive interests of his country he is altogether incapable of judging.[68]

It is doubtful, then, that even Smith believed that a little reading, writing, and arithmetic at an early age could stave off these dire consequences of the division of labour.

For Smith, however – and this is the essential point – dehumanization through the division of labour was a necessary, albeit regrettable, price to pay for steadily increasing material abundance. For him, well-being depends much more on per capita income and consumption than on job satisfaction, a sense of wholeness, or even a capacity to participate in democratic society. Note the total reversal from Aristotle here – and from his own position regarding 'the perfection of human nature' as articulated in *TMS*. Smith's view regarding the greediness of human nature and the willingness of people to sacrifice things of great importance in order to secure material abundance recalls Hobbes, of course, and the sacrifice of liberty in the name of security, and likewise is a harbinger of principles defining modern economic analyses and public policy. In Smith we find, then, support for yet another deleterious axiom of the economics of our day, namely, that economic growth (today often termed 'sustainable development') is to override other important considerations.

If markets encourage specialization, Smith insisted, the converse is also true: specialization is limited 'by the extent of the market.'[69] Smith explained: 'When the market is very small, no person can have any encouragement to dedicate himself entirely to one employment, for want of the power to exchange all that surplus part of the produce of his own labour.'[70] Anything that hinders market expansion, therefore, Smith surmised, inhibits growth in a nation's wealth.

Note also, very significantly, that Smith, anticipating the doctrine of Pareto optimality, considered a nation's wealth to be simply the aggregate of the wealth of its individual members; he did not, in other words, consider (as he well might have, given his position in *Moral Sentiments*), that each person's well-being may depend fundamentally on the well-being of others, an implication being that a nation beset with ghettos, homelessness, poverty, and other social ills is less 'wealthy' than a more egalitarian society, even if the per capita or 'average' wealth and income of the two are identical. This, then, is an example of Smith's methodological individualism, which is quite consonant with Hobbes's 'resolutive-compositive' method, but which is a far cry from Aristotle, the Hebrew prophets, the medieval writers, and indeed Smith's *Moral Sentiments.* Smith's assumption that the wealth of a country is merely the sum of the wealth of its inhabitants is, in fact, a cornerstone of his economic analysis, as it is of neoclassical economics today. That assumption allowed Smith to propose that whatever effectively promotes the wealth of individuals also contributes most to the growth of a nation's wealth[71] – an extremely anti-environmental position to adopt.

Smith discussed several factors that he believed help to increase the extent of markets, and thereby the division of labour, and hence the wealth of a nation. Three of these are improved transportation infrastructure to facilitate the movement of goods and bring buyers and sellers into proximity;[72] heightened self-interest (as opposed to 'sympathy') as this increases the circumference of market forces;[73] and money.[74] For Smith, money complicates the exchange process compared to barter. He distinguished different kinds of prices, as well as various kinds of value. He proposed first an 'ordinary' or 'natural' price of commodities, which he defined as the price just sufficient to cover the costs of production.[75] Costs of production, he maintained, consist of wages to workers, rent to landowners, and profit to investors, and these too have 'natural rates ... [depending on] the time and place.'[76] Moreover, the natural price is 'the central price, to which the prices of all commodities are continually gravitating.'[77] The 'market price,' on the other hand, may be subject to continuous fluctuation according to market conditions, but Smith believed it tends to gravitate toward the natural price. And here we see, in its infancy, the modern economic theory of pure competition, and the notion of the competitive market as an automatic, non-deliberative, and effective allocator of resources. We also see the incipient collapse of value into market price. Moreover, Smith delineated the triad – land-labour-capital – as the factors of production, a schemata still widely used, even in the system of national accounts. I will suggest in the next chapter that this schemata, too, is anti-environmental.

A final point concerns the power dimension, or instrumentalism, evident in *Wealth of Nations* compared to *Moral Sentiments.* For Smith, labour was not only the main source of value, it was itself also a commodity. Reminiscent of Hobbes, Smith wrote: 'It is in this manner that the demand for men, like that for any other commodity, necessarily regulates the production of men.'[78] As remarked by Jacob Bronowski, coupling a labour theory of wealth with the view that labour is itself a commodity, implies a 'very inhuman kind of civilization.' And, Bronowski continued, 'the implication became reality in the years after Smith's death.'[79]

Others continued on the path set by Smith: Malthus, Bentham, Ricardo, James Mill – in many ways even Marx. But, by the early twentieth century, for reasons we could speculate on,[80] classical economics gave way to a new, or neoclassical, economics, to which I now turn.

Neoclassical Economics

As noted above, Adam Smith described his discipline – political economy – as the 'branch of the science' that helps government set conditions to stimulate economic growth.[81] His subject was *political* economy because it was within the context of statecraft that he studied economic relations. Smith was ever cognizant of actual laws and policies, institutional arrangements and business practices; he addressed concrete issues in the context of real-world power plays.

By the early 1900s, however, mainstream economists had narrowed their analyses;[82] they began addressing exchange relations virtually in 'total abstraction' from the social and political setting.[83] Stanley Jevons (1835–82), one of the principal architects of neoclassical economics, remarked, 'My theory is purely mathematical in character ... The theory consists of applying the differential calculus to the familiar notions of wealth, utility, value, demand, supply, capital, interest, labour.'[84]

Today's neoclassical economics continues in the vein of Jevons and other founders (Leon Walras, Vilfredo Pareto, Francis Edgeworth, Alfred Marshall), and is quite distinguishable from classical economics. First, as just noted, it abstracts from the social, political, and institutional setting, whereas the classical economists were fully engaged with the political economy. Economics became largely a 'logical mathematical' science, meaning that 'truth' is defined primarily according to the soundness of the logical deductions from a given set of axioms.[85]

Second, whereas classical economists like Adam Smith attempted to anchor value in the concrete (i.e. in terms either of the labour or, in the case of the Physiocrats, in the land content of commodities), neoclassical economists ascribe value to the interaction of supply and demand, where demand is attributed to the often fleeting tastes and preferences of consumers.[86] Another way of saying this is that the classical economists distinguished between value and price, maintaining that the former is based on the labour or land content of a commodity and that price fluctuates around value according to market conditions, whereas neoclassicists make no such distinction: value is price, and price is value.

Third, whereas classical economists like Smith looked at the *average* labour (or land) content of commodities to explain value (an exception being David Ricardo's theory of 'rent'), neoclassicists employ the method of *marginal* analysis, maintaining that key determinants of prices are the cost of producing an additional unit, and the additional or incremental satisfaction to be derived from acquiring one more unit.

These differences are certainly important. However, neoclassical economics and classical economics also bear at least four important traits in common. Both presume insatiability to human wants; both believe in the efficacy of Smith's 'invisible hand'; both are anthropocentric; and both are methodologically individualist – assumptions and positions all serving to make neoclassical economics, in its very fundamentals, an immensely anti-environmental discourse. Consider each of these traits in turn.

First, the assumption that humans by nature have limitless appetites for acquisition is obviously inconsistent with a finite world beset by declining biodiversity. As proposed by C.B. Macpherson, it makes great ecological sense to 'retrieve' the ancient conception of humans as developers of skills and exerters of talents; or, in Aristotelian terms, to regard as the perfection of human nature the use of intelligence to moderate appetitive desires; or, in Judaeo-Christian terms, to seek first spiritual growth in the confidence that material needs will be met – and to organize society accordingly. As shown by Macpherson, the view of human nature as infinite appetitive machine arose only with Hobbes and other early English political economists (Locke, Smith); no one had ever conceived human nature in this way before. What this new conception did, however, was to provide an essential 'moral' justification for the emerging system of private property (the enclosure movement) and unconstrained capital accumulation.

Second, like classical economics, neoclassicism proposes an inherent efficacy to market activity, or what Smith termed 'the invisible hand.' Unlike Smith, however, neoclassicists explain this efficacy through a marginal mode of analysis that is, arguably, even more anti-environmental than Smith's. For neoclassicists it is the last dollar spent, the last item purchased, and the last sale made that are of primary concern; there is little attention afforded to the whole. But ecosystem health is largely contingent on interacting populations of both organic species and human artefacts; it is not the additional automobile that produces the noteworthy environmental impact, but the total field of automobiles in interaction with all other species.

Third, modern economics is anthropocentric, with no countervailing principles, such as existed in Greek and Judaeo-Christian discourses. Anthropocentrism means it looks at economic activity solely from the viewpoint of human wants, not from the standpoint of empathy (in Smith's terms, 'sympathy') for other creatures. The radical anthropocentrism of neoclassical economics is exemplified by its insistence that there is no intrinsic value, only relative value, and that market price, based in part on market demand, is an adequate indicator of value.

Finally, neoclassicism, like the political economy of Adam Smith, is methodologically individualist, since the analysis proceeds by hypothesizing a single consumer and aggregating to the whole population, and a single firm and again aggregating. The method of aggregation, however, denies that wholes have properties different from the sum of their parts; it denies, for instance, that people in relation with one another differ from isolated individuals. People, however, when considering themselves as part of a group, may feel a certain responsibility for the welfare of the group, over and beyond their individualist maximizing tendencies; they might even voluntarily curb excesses in consumption and pollution for the betterment of the whole. In *The Wealth of Nations* Smith explicitly denigrated all such socially conscientious activity on the grounds it interfered with the benign operations if the 'invisible hand.' Likewise in the modern era, neoclassicist Milton Friedman has berated business leaders who voluntarily cut back on pollution and who in the process lessen profits for the corporation.[87]

The real danger of economic models is not that they may describe reality inaccurately (Friedman agreed that they do);[88] rather, it is that they 'justify,' and hence may induce, socially and environmentally deleterious behaviour. Economic models are templates to which real life may, over time, conform.

5 Environmental vs Ecological Economics

From its beginning at the turn of the twentieth century, neoclassicism has grown into a mighty force, challenged only at the fringes by such heterodoxies as institutional and evolutionary economics, marxian economics, and ecological economics.

To be sure, over the century 'fissures' in the mainstream doctrine became evident, but these invariably spawned new subdisciplines to address the problems within the bounds of the neoclassical paradigm.[1] For example, the basic neoclassical model presumes 'perfect competition,' whereas the real economy is characterized in certain sectors by monopoly and oligopoly; *public utility economics*, however, proposes that even in the face of monopoly, competitive results can be simulated through 'marginal cost pricing' as enforced by a regulator; the problem of monopoly is reduced to a question of appropriate pricing. Again, once it was acknowledged that the real world is beset by uncertainty, *information economics* arose to proffer as a 'solution' the commodification of information, so that it too would be produced and sold in markets in optimal amounts;[2] although a vast literature on the topic exists, nowhere have economists conceptualized information in a way that lends rigour to this proposal. Yet a third fracture, the one addressed in this book, has concerned 'externalities,' and again there arose a new subfield – *environmental economics* – which, like the aforementioned, endeavours to salvage neoclassicism through policies that induce 'correct' prices.[3]

In this chapter, I carry neoclassicism's story forward into the present as it concerns this last-mentioned problem – 'externalities' – which I then compare to an emerging but still heterodox discourse, ecological economics. These are, we will see, disparate discourses concerning economy-ecosystem interactions. The former focuses on prices and market exchanges, and sees in these both the source of and solution to environmental problems. The latter views environmental issues as being too complex to warrant merely price adjustments, and hence recommends a panoply of non-market, non-price-based policies – including a phasing back of market activity.

The present chapter assesses these two discourses in the context of ecological principles, that is, from the standpoint of a culture of ecology. It bears emphasizing, however, that neoclassical approaches remain the orthodoxy; as John Foster bluntly puts it, 'The mainstream neoclassical version [being] the only version of green economics with a respectable pedigree in terms of "economic science," has commanded the field.'[4]

Environmental Economics

A core assumption of neoclassical economics is that humanity consists of rational, utility-maximizing individuals with given tastes and preferences. 'Rational' in this context means that people know what they want and are able to act in ways that best satisfy their wants, given such constraints as the size of their income. This presupposition, dating back to the utilitarianism of Jeremy Bentham and others, engenders policy approaches hinging on the presumption that tastes and preferences are sacrosanct ('De Gustibus non est disputandum').[5] In terms of the environment, neoclassicists treat such fundamentals as air and water quality as 'preferred goods and services.' Anything that reduces the availability of these environmental amenities is an 'externality,' the avoidance of which is likewise treated as a 'preference.' In elaborating this approach, there are essentially two traditions, the first inaugurated by A.C. Pigou, and the second, decades later, by Ronald Coase.

Forerunners

A.C. PIGOU

Retrospectively, A.C. Pigou's landmark tome, *The Economics of Welfare* (1920), marked the birth of environmental economics. Pigou had been inspired by his mentor, Alfred Marshall, who in *Principles of Economics* (first edition, 1890) opened the door for economists to consider economy-ecosystem interactions. There, Marshall introduced the concept of *external economies,* which he defined as cost savings per unit of production accruing to a firm as a result of increases in industry-wide production.[6] Marshall conjectured that a more highly skilled labour force, higher health standards, and improved infrastructure might accompany industry-wide growth, and that the ensuing cost savings would redound to individual firms. It needs to be noted, however, that from an ecosystem perspective, Marshall's conception of external economies, seminal though it was, is quite deficient insofar as he posited only third-party savings or benefits, omitting entirely consideration of third-party costs or harms. For that reason Marshall cannot be credited with inaugurating environmental economics.

Subsequent to Marshall, the notion of external economies (and hence, of course, diseconomies) remained largely dormant within the mainstream literature until Pigou reintroduced them in 1920 through the term 'externalities.' Pigou focused on discrepancies between individual economic interests and those of the community, explaining that even in purely competitive economies, private and social interests can diverge. He defined an externality as a cost or benefit that is not considered by the person taking the action. For instance, Pigou elucidated that smoke from a factory imposes costs on third parties in terms of 'injury to buildings and vegetables, expenses for washing clothes and cleaning rooms, expenses for the provision of extra artificial light, and in many other ways,'[7] but, he noted further, the egoistic, maximizing producer will be undeterred by such occurrences. In all such instances, Pigou proposed, collective well-being can be increased if governments intervene by implementing a system of taxes and subsidies – taxes in cases of negative or harmful externalities, subsidies in instances of beneficial ones – to narrow the gap between 'marginal social net product' and 'marginal private net product.' Running through Pigou's analysis, then, is an appeal for an activist government; Pigou simply did not believe that market forces automatically generated optimal prices.[8]

As well, however, his analysis supported the contention that, in principle, corrected prices are sufficient to resolve issues posed by externalities. It is this presumption that qualifies Pigou as a neoclassicist, and the founder of environmental economics.

RONALD COASE

Nobel laureate Ronald Coase's classic piece, 'The Problem of Social Cost,' published in 1960, may be regarded as a libertarian economist's rejoinder to Pigou. Coase's preference was very much for unadulterated market prices; he had an obvious antipathy to taxes and subsidies. Coase prepared the ground for a long line of environmental economists by delineating the extension of private property rights as a means of addressing environmental issues.

According to Coase, a polluter cannot inflict damage unless people are present to suffer injury, which is to say, in his view, that polluter and victim are *reciprocally responsible* for environmental harms, the former for producing noxious emissions, the latter by virtue of mere propinquity. Therefore, Coase concluded, justice does not require that parties *emitting* pollution should bear legal liability; victims are also to blame.

Coase turned next to the criterion of economic efficiency, contrasting two situations. The first was characterized by 'perfectly functioning markets' (i.e., pure competition, perfect knowledge, zero transactions costs), for which, Coase opined, all possibility of externalities, by definition, is precluded. He 'proved' his contention with a simple numerical example of cattle destroying neighbouring crops. If legal liability for damages resides with the polluter (here, the cattle rancher), free contracting would enable the polluter to bribe those harmed into agreeing to the harm, and the polluter will have incentive to proffer a bribe of such magnitude that the marginal benefit of being able to continue the noxious activity at any given level (i.e., number of cows) just compensates for the added costs experienced on account of having to pay additional money in a bribe. Likewise, those harmed by pollution will find it advantageous to accept a bribe of such magnitude that the last dollar received just slightly more than compensates for damages wrought by the incremental pollution. Conversely, if the legal system does not impose on the polluter liability for damages, free contracting, Coase averred, will nonetheless permit those being damaged to bribe the polluter into cutting back production (i.e., decrease the number of cows); and, moreover, aggrieved parties will find it beneficial to offer bribes of such magnitude that the marginal benefit they attain from a small decrease in pollution just exceeds the cost of bribing the polluter into cutting back the activity (here, the herd by one more cow). After comparing the two situations– the first with liability residing with the polluter, the second envisaging no such liability – an obviously satisfied Coase exclaimed: 'The ultimate result (which maximizes the value of production) is independent of the legal position if the pricing system is assumed to work without cost.'[9] For 'perfectly competitive' markets, Coase (and other neoclassicists) concluded, it does not matter whether or not the law ascribes liability for pollution, since markets will commodify pollution, ensuring thereby that only 'optimal' amounts of pollution are produced.

Coase next addressed imperfectly competitive markets, and in particular ones beset by transactions costs (the costs of concluding an agreement between polluter and victims). In such circumstances, he conceded, private bargaining will not automatically bring about 'optimal' results. Nonetheless, he cautioned, it could still be better for governments *not* to act than to impose liability on the polluter, as recommended by Pigou. The imposition of such liability, Coase remonstrated, would affect third parties (employees, suppliers, and customers) as 'externalities.'[10] Better, perhaps, that those experiencing the consequences of pollution bear the full cost.

Coase of course can be critiqued on several grounds. Objections can be raised, for instance, to his rather infantile conception of justice (blame the victim), and to the blind eye he casts, perhaps unwittingly, on the prospect of extortion ('Bribe me or I'll pollute').

In any event, those suffering ill effects from pollution are not necessarily just those living near the site of production – a circumstance Coase presumed and upon which he based his doctrine of co-responsibility. In the case of Chernobyl, for example, nuclear fallout extended far beyond the USSR to the Netherlands, Belgium, Great Britain, the Balkans, Austria, eastern and southern Switzerland, parts of southern Germany, and Scandinavia.[11] More generally, as Rachel Carson has informed us, contaminants spread globally through the food chain as well as through wind and water currents. The polar ice caps, likewise, are melting due in part to automobile emissions from Southern California. The Earth is effectively a single, integrated ecosystem; thus the victims include all of humanity, both present and future generations.

Second, even assuming that purely competitive conditions exist, the Coasean system of bribery can *increase* pollution levels. As noted by Fisher and Peterson, 'under plausible assumptions, though the bribe does indeed reduce emissions *per* firm, it will tend to *increase* them at the industry level.' New firms will find it profitable to enter an industry now enriched by bribes.[12]

Third, the Coasean examples were all typically trivial. In addition to cattle trampling a neighbour's crops, Coase explored, for instance, a case where damages were inflicted 'by a person keeping an unusual and excessive collection of manure in which flies bred and which infested a neighbour's house,' for which Coase pronounced that the economic problem centred on 'ownership of the flies.'[13] In the Coasean world, in other words, there are no Three Mile Islands, no Love Canals, no Persian Gulf Wars, no Chernobyls, no Exxon Valdezes, no Bhopals. Coase's marginalist techniques confined him to weighing the merits of one less cow versus one more cow; a slightly smaller or a slightly larger pile of manure. As well, there are no thresholds or limits in Coase's schemata. One can always reverse the consequences of pollution, he implied, by simply reducing the size of, for example, a herd of cows or a pile of manure.

Fourth, Coase did not incorporate in his analysis considerations of ecological balance. Indeed, his illustrative benefit/cost example presumed perfect knowledge of outcomes flowing from alternative courses of action, a most inappropriate assumption for ecosystem relations that, by their very nature, are complex, evolve, and are in many respects unpredictable. He was concerned, rather, only with felt irritants on the part of human agents from whom assent had not been attained. As a related point, he presumed that all relevant information can be incorporated into market prices and that market transactions constitute sufficient means for communicating such information – highly dubious assumptions, as we have seen.

Fifth, the Coasean system of bribes can be tantamount to an invitation to corruption, as when the Aborigines in the Kakadu Conservation Zone in Australia are asked how much they would require for the use of their burial grounds for mineral exploration (or, in the case of the Mohawks at Oka near Montreal, to permit construction of a golf course).[14]

One could dismiss Coase as simply a crank were it not for the regard in which he is held in neoclassical and certain policy-making circles. George Stigler, likewise a Nobel Laureate, thought so highly of Coase's environmentalist contribution that he afforded the so-called Coase Theorem (a neologism, incidentally, for which Stigler proudly assumed credit) a full chapter, suitably entitled 'Eureka,' in his slender autobiography.[15] Indeed, Coase's Nobel Prize in 1991 was based largely on the work just described.[16] And the Coasean approach remains influential, infusing such policy approaches as tradeable carbon rights and trade settlement provisions.[17]

Case Study: Ethyl Inc. v. Canada

The Coasean principle of compensation for not polluting is applied increasingly in trade treaties. Under Chapter 11 of the North America Free Trade Agreement (NAFTA), for example, private investors and corporations can sue NAFTA-signatory governments in special tribunals for recompense for government policies or actions that investors believe violate their new rights under NAFTA.[18] Two of these new rights are

1. *Compensation for direct and indirect expropriation.* Article 1110 entitles foreign investors to compensation from NAFTA governments for both direct expropriation (nationalization) and for actions deemed to be 'tantamount to' expropriation.
2. *No performance requirements.* Article 1106 prohibits domestic content rules, regulations concerning environmental conduct, or directions to ensure that local economies benefit from an investment by a corporation from a NAFTA country.[19]

The first case brought under NAFTA Chapter 11 was *Ethyl Inc. v. Canada.*[20] In the 1950s, the Ethyl Corporation replaced lead, finally admitted to be a health hazard after decades of use, with MMT (methylcyclopentadienyl manganese tricarbonyl) as an additive for gasoline. MMT, however, contains manganese – a known human neurotoxin. In 1977, therefore, both the state of California and the U.S. Environmental Protection Agency (EPA) prohibited the addition of MMT to gasoline in their jurisdictions, and by 1995 'all developed countries' except Canada had banned the use of MMT as a gasoline additive.[21] Although the detrimental health hazards of airborne MMT from automobile exhausts had not been definitively proven, by the precautionary principle – namely, 'in cases where there is a risk to public health or the environment, but the current data is insufficient to fully quantify or assess that risk, government has a right and a responsibility to err on the side of safety'[22] – the bans were justified. Canada, however, continued to import MMT from the Ethyl plant in the United States, the chemical's only point of manufacture. Finally, in 1995 and again in 1996, the Canadian government introduced bills to disallow both the importation and the interprovincial transport of MMT. In addition to the health concerns described above, the government was cognizant that automobile manufacturers recommended that MMT not be added to gasoline as they alleged the product could damage catalytic converters and other pollution-control devices. Finally, MMT was believed to contribute to the build-up of greenhouse gases.

Even as the prospective import ban was being debated in Parliament, however, Ethyl Corporation announced it would seek recompense under NAFTA's Chapter 11 if the legislation was enacted. Nonetheless, Parliament passed the bill in April 1997, and Ethyl immediately filed a NAFTA 'investor-to-state' claim for $251 million, claiming *inter alia* that the ban was tantamount to an expropriation of assets. Receiving an unfavourable initial ruling from the United Nations Commission for

International Trade and Law, Canada withdrew its ban on MMT in 1998, paid Ethyl Corporation $13 million for legal fees and damages, and released a statement for use in Ethyl Corp's advertising that 'current scientific information' did not demonstrate MMT's toxicity or that MMT impairs functioning of automotive diagnostic systems.[23]

It is apparent that by entitling corporations to sue for damages arising from legislated attempts to curb environmental degradation, the NAFTA treaty fulfils at least two elements of the Coase Theorem. First, Ethyl Corp exemplifies the capacity of corporations to intimidate legislatures, just as the Coase Theorem opens possibilities for extortion. Before the bill banning importation of MMT had even been enacted, Ethyl announced it would sue. As Friends of the Earth remarks, such threats can have 'a chilling effect on future public interest policies being considered by governments and [can] result in governments pre-emptively conceding and changing a policy to avoid a trade challenge – as Canada did in this instance.'[24]

Second, the NAFTA provision established the principle of 'pay the polluter,' an explicit feature of the Coase system. Whereas Coase alleged, however, that in perfectly functioning marketplaces it really does not matter which party – polluter or victim – the law supports, in the case study presented here we see that this is in fact at the heart of the issue. The policy of 'pay the polluter' severely constrains the capacity of governments to enact environmental legislation.

Case Study: Methanex

In June 1999, the Canadian company Methanex initiated a claim for compensation of nearly $1 billion under NAFTA's Chapter 11 from California as recompense for the state's phasing out of the gasoline additive MTBE (methyl tertiary butyl ether), suspected to be a 'carcinogen that renders water foul tasting and undrinkable when it leaks out of gas storage tanks.'[25] Numerous cities in California felt compelled to truck in water after ground water became contaminated. Methanex is a producer of methanol, which it sells to companies that manufacture MTBE.[26] It claimed before the tribunal that phasing out MTBE would adversely affect its sales of methanol, and that it should be compensated for an action that was tantamount to an expropriation. As part of its defence brief, the State of California declared: 'If [Methanex's claim is] accepted by this Tribunal, no NAFTA Party could carry out its most fundamental governmental functions unless it were prepared to pay for each and every economic impact occasioned by doing so. The NAFTA Parties never intended the NAFTA to bring about such a radical change in the way they function, and Methanex cannot show otherwise.'[27] Hearings were held before the tribunal in June 2004, but no decision had been issued at the time this book was prepared.

Environmental Economics Today

A COASEAN CONTEMPORARY

Today's environmental economists follow very much in the footsteps of Coase and/or Pigou. Ian Willis is one such who typifies the Coasean approach. He opens his *Economics and the Environment* by acknowledging the inspiration he received from F.A. Hayek's classic paper 'The Use of Knowledge in Society.'[28] Willis suggests that the level of complexity Hayek dealt with, however, is dwarfed once economy-ecosystem interactions are taken into account.[29] Given this added complexity, Willis advises, prices become even more eminently suited for coordinating human interactions.[30]

Difficulties begin, however, with Willis's very definition of an 'environmental problem.' 'Environmental problems occur,' he writes, 'when some people are unhappy with other people's use of the natural environment, because it imposes harms on them to which they have not consented.'[31] As he notes, this definition implies that the focus of any analysis and the policy recommendations that ensue are on harms for which there is no prior consent, a position resonating completely with Coase. Environmental problems for Willis, then, do not include human-ecosystem interactions that damage the environment but of which humans are unaware; nor do they include environmental harms of which humans are aware but to which they accord little importance; nor do they even include all environmental degradations of which humans are cognizant and over which they are distressed. 'Environmental problems' for Willis are confined to those for which no bargain has been struck between those inflicting the damage and those upon whom it is inflicted. 'Scarce resources mean that harms to others are unavoidable,' Willis explains; hence, 'the issue is not whether such harms occur but whether they are subject to prior community agreement.' On that basis Willis concludes that environmental problems 'involve a lack of social coordination or consensus between resource users and those harmed,'[32] thereby deftly setting up prices, whether market based or adjusted, as the preferred 'solutions' to 'environmental problems.'

Referring specifically to both Chernobyl and *Exxon Valdez*, Willis writes: 'Commonly, although not always, [environmental problems are due to] the absence or distortion of signals about and incentives to respond to other people's concerns over the environment.'[33] Well, yes. One suspects that the nuclear reactors at Chernobyl, for instance, would never have detonated were the explosions somehow contingent upon the prior consent of the victims located in various countries of the world.

Willis acknowledges that neither economists nor ecologists fully understand the consequences of present-day policies and economic decisions on the capacity of ecosystems to renew and perpetuate themselves. He declares, correctly: 'Neither economists nor ecologists know enough about combined economic-environmental systems to understand all the future consequences of today's resource use ... There are so many possible interactions within and between the economy and the environment over space and time that it is simply impossible to know the future outcomes of today's use of the environment.'[34] One might have thought that in being aware of the radical uncertainty confronting economists, ecologists, and by implication average citizens, Willis would have abandoned price-based and market-based 'solutions'; given radical uncertainty, 'correct' prices are both impossible to estimate and will not result from the commodification of pollution. Willis, however, takes the exact opposite tack. Incredibly, he declares: 'If economic-environmental systems are so complex that it is impossible to know what actions will promote sustainability, the signalling and incentive system itself may be the best indicator of sustainability – of ability to adapt to changing economic and environmental circumstances.'[35] This is, shall we say, peculiar advice, given that the very same system of signals and incentives mired us in our present environmental morass in the first place.

Willis agrees with Coase that in a world of exclusive property rights, zero transactions costs, and perfect knowledge, markets and prices are sufficient to eliminate *all* environmental problems,[36] or, more accurately, those falling within Willis's/Coase's truncated definition. Given the theory, and despite the radical uncertainty, Willis's 'preferred' policy response to real-world environmental problems is, wherever possible, to 'find ways of lowering cost, technological and organizational barriers to exclusion.'[37] 'Barriers to exclusion' are defined by the author as factors that preclude the delineation and enforcement of private property rights. Property rights, of course, are a requirement for market prices as exchange transactions cannot take place in their absence, and as we have seen it is Willis's view that in market prices lies humanity's best hope for environmental well-being.

Scientific/technological advances, he continues, give rise to new ways of forging desirable exclusions ('the introduction of barbed wire greatly reduced the costs of excluding other people's livestock from grazing land ... the introduction of devices that can scramble and decode television signals has created a market for pay television programming'),[38] thereby permitting market exchanges and market prices to penetrate areas from which they had previously been precluded due to the impossibility of enforcing exclusive claims. This trend in technology, Willis asserts, is highly desirable as market exchanges can increasingly provide the incentives and signals necessary to coordinate production and consumption of non-collective goods.

For cases where exclusive ownership remains impossible, he advises, policy makers must decide among (a) doing nothing, (b) introducing direct controls, and (c) creating marketable permits and taxes. These are the only options that Willis presents. He argues that marketable permits and taxes are preferable to direct controls, as these operate through the marginal conditions of the individual producers and thereby affect the prices of items offered for sale. Moreover, marketable permits, unlike direct controls, make use of each 'polluter's private information about their individual MBP [marginal benefits of pollution] curves,'[39] and hence are a more cost-effective way of reducing pollution. Pollution taxes, likewise, 'enlist private information to achieve least cost emissions reductions.'[40] Willis advises that the size of the taxes and the cost of the permit allocations should reflect the costs in money terms of the harms experienced by victims[41] – not an easy amount to estimate. (More on this below.)

I turn now to Willis's account of human nature, which, like his faith in the efficacy of market prices even in the context of monumental uncertainty, predicates his entire analysis. Willis is in agreement with standard economic doctrine that human desires are 'effectively unbounded.'[42] 'In all known societies,' he declares, 'with desires unbounded, resources (natural, created and human) are inadequate to produce all the goods and services necessary to satisfy all human wants; this is the economist's definition of scarcity.'[43] Having proposed unlimited wants as endemic to societies of every time and place, he then turns to the variable nature of those wants: 'People's wants include privacy, clean air and water, preservation of flora, fauna and ecosystems and so on,'[44] he writes. Unfortunately, rather than ask how such ecologically friendly 'wants' can attain higher priority, which would be to pose a deeply ecological question, the author merely repeats the standard neoclassical position of *De Gustibus non est disputandum*: 'How these wants are weighted relative to wants for powerful cars or hamburgers,' he declares, 'is determined by communities' ethical norms and the values which result from those norms, not by the economist, who takes people's likes and dislikes as given.'[45] Of course, no one has suggested that economists 'determine' people's hierarchy of desires; but economists' acceptance of that hierarchy as sacrosanct, and as being the base criterion for all economic policy – despite possibly disastrous environmental consequences – is one of the reasons for declaring environmental economics, as currently constituted, extremely anti-environmental.

From the perspective of a culture of ecology, human wants are not simply given; they are, rather, the heart of the matter. Nor is it simply a question of the finiteness vs infinite expansibility of wants that is at issue; it is also very much the composition of wants that, as the author remarks, is a function in part at least of the 'communities' ethical norms.' These 'norms' through human history have varied immensely from community to community, as anthropologists (and advertisers) well know, although in the age of global media one suspects a homogenization to be under way. But that is not to say that through concerted effort wants cannot be made more environmentally sound, and that the doctrine of 'unbounded desires' cannot be reined in as well.

To illustrate by just one example how important community norms are in individual want formation, consider the North American indigenous peoples of the West Coast. According to Houghton Mifflin's *Encyclopedia of North American Indians*:

> Throughout native North America, gift giving is a central feature of social life. In the Pacific Northwest of the United States and British Columbia in Canada, this tradition is known as the *potlatch*. Within the tribal groups of these areas, individuals hosting a potlatch give away most, if not all, of their wealth and material goods to show goodwill to the rest of the tribal members and to maintain their social status. Tribes that traditionally practice the potlatch include the Haidas, Kwakiutls, Makahs, Nootkas, Tlingits, and Tsimshians. Gifts often included blankets, pelts, furs, weapons, and slaves during the nineteenth century, and jewelry, money, and appliances in the twentieth.
>
> The potlatch was central to the maintenance of tribal hierarchy, even as

it allowed a certain social fluidity for individuals who could amass enough material wealth to take part in the ritual ...

When Canadian law prohibited the potlatch in 1884, tribes in British Columbia lost a central and unifying ceremony. Their despair was mirrored by the tribes of the Pacific Northwest when the U.S. government outlawed the potlatch in the early part of the twentieth century. With the passage of the Indian Reorganization Act of 1934 in the United States and the Canadian Indian Act of 1951, the potlatch was resumed legally. It remains a central feature of Pacific Northwest Indian life today.[46]

CONTEMPORARY PIGOUVIANS

The essential difference between Coase and Pigou, it will be recalled, is that the former expressed faith in unadjusted market prices to resolve environmental problems provided that property rights are adequately delineated so as to enfold 'externalities' within the ambit of markets, whereas the latter contended that market prices need to be 'adjusted' through taxes and/or subsidies to resolve environmental issues. What the two theorists share in common, however, is an avowed faith in the efficacy of prices to resolve environmental issues, qualifying each as a forerunner of neoclassical environmental economics. In this section I explore contemporary exponents of the Pigouvian position, which invariably entails as a first step estimating the costs or benefits of an externality in order to determine how large the tax or subsidy should be.

Advocates of 'cost-benefit' analyses contend that to make rational, non-arbitrary decisions regarding environmental services, some common measuring unit must be applied to make comparisons. According to Pearce et al., for example, 'Physical accounts are useful in answering ecological questions of interest and in linking environment to economy ... However, physical accounts are limited because they lack a common unit of measurement and it is not possible to gauge their importance relative to each other and non-environmental goods and services.'[47] Consistent with Alfred Marshall's famous dictum, contemporary advocates of cost-benefit analysis propose that in money one finds just such a universal measure. In an oft-cited piece,[48] Robert Costanza and associates endeavoured to apply the money measure to *all* of 'nature's services.' A forest, for example, renders such 'services' as soil retention, waste storage, soil formation, and habitat provisioning, among many others. The total figure Costanza and associates came up with for 'nature's services' was U.S.$33 trillion annually, about twice the world's GDP for 1997.

Costanza's study is, of course, fully consonant with the approach to environment and externalities recommended by neoclassical economists, namely, enfolding as much of nature as possible into the ambit of the price system. Indeed, the authors write: 'If ecosystem services were actually paid for, in terms of their value contribution to the global economy, the global price system would be very different from what it is today.'[49]

While Costanza's approach is certainly of interest insofar as it calls attention to a range of ecosystem interactions usually disregarded by environmental economists, it is nonetheless quite misguided in presuming that monetary value can meaningfully be ascribed to these 'services.' Costanza et al. err, in brief, in presuming that ecosystem interactions can and should be conceptualized as subsets of the economy. The authors declare: 'Ecosystem services provide an important portion of the total contribution to human welfare on this planet; we must begin to give the natural capital stock that produces these services adequate weight in the decision-making process.'[50] The authors, in brief, fail utterly to recognize that there would be no 'contribution to human welfare' without 'ecosystem services.' Without the earth's 'services,' no humans would exist to impute value to anything.

Let us turn next to *The Measurement of Environmental and Resource Values* by environmental economist A. Myrick Freeman III. This is an award-winning tome published in 2003 by Resources for the Future.[51] The book sets out to 'provide an introduction and overview of the principal methods and techniques of resource valuation.'[52] Through its quantitative techniques the author intends to enable policy-makers to come up with well-reasoned answers to the following types of questions:

- Is the diversion of resources mandated by the US Congress to improve air and water quality worth the cost?
- Are the restrictions on development in ecologically sensitive areas such as Arctic National Wildlife Refuge worth the costs they impose on society in reduced availability of and higher prices for energy and minerals?
- What degree of reduction in greenhouse gas emissions is warranted by the benefits of slowing or preventing global warming?[53]

The underlying premise of the book is as follows:

Natural resources, such as forests and commercially exploitable fisheries, and environmental attributes, such as air quality, are valuable assets in that they yield flows of services to people. Public policies and the actions of indi-

> viduals and firms can lead to changes in the flows of these services, thereby creating benefits and costs. Because of externalities and the common-property and public-good characteristics of at least some of these services, market forces can be relied on neither to guide them to their most highly valued uses nor to reveal prices that reflect their true social values.[54]

Freeman, then, is much less sanguine than Coase or Willis regarding the capacity of market prices to resolve environmental issues. However, he does not forsake pricing as a key to alleviating environmental problems, qualifying him as an 'environmental economist' in the tradition of Pigou. Freeman explores 'shadow pricing' as an aid to centralized decision making regarding large-scale projects. To reach a determination on environment related issues, Freeman writes, the analyst needs to ascertain the 'true' monetary value of the 'services' that nature provides as a first step toward deriving the value of the natural resource asset in question. The economic value of an environmental resource such as a forest is, according to Freeman, 'the sum of the discounted present values of the flows of all of the services' it yields.[55] (Among the 'services' yielded by a forest, according to Robert Costanza, are climate regulation, water regulation, water supply, soil erosion control, soil formation, nutrient cycling, waste treatment, biological control, food production, raw materials, genetic resources, recreation, and cultural services.)[56] The 'quantity' of these 'services' over time needs to be estimated, then a money value ascribed to each; these money amounts must then be discounted (by a 'suitable' rate of interest, whatever that means), and the 'present values' of all the services aggregated to arrive at the estimated value of the forest as an economic asset.

The foregoing, of course, begs the question of exactly how each of the 'services' is to be imputed with a monetary value. Freeman provides a discussion on the meaning of value to an economist: 'In economics, the goal is increased human well-being. The economic theory of value is based on the ability of things to satisfy human needs and wants or to increase the well-being or utility of individuals. The economic value of something is a measure of its contribution to human well-being. The economic value of resource-environment systems resides in the contributions that the ecosystem functions and services make to human well-being.'[57] Once more the persistence of anthropocentrism in environmental economics is apparent.

Freeman next notes there are broadly two (and, I hasten to add, methodologically individualist and anthropocentric) expressions of value. One, 'willingness to pay' (WTP), is 'the maximum sum of money the individual would be willing to pay rather than do without an increase in some good such as an environmental amenity.' The second, 'willingness to accept compensation' (WTA), is 'the minimum sum of money the individual would require to voluntarily forgo an improvement that otherwise would be experienced.'[58] Freeman's implicit indebtedness to Coase is quite clear.

According to Freeman, moreover, there are also two basic methods of measuring value, whether WTP or WTA. One is to observe the actual behaviour of consumers in the marketplace in terms of the types of substitutions they make in their everyday activities (a method termed 'revealed preferences') and to infer on the basis of these observations the value of the services of a natural asset. The other is to ask people what they would hypothetically pay for, or accept in lieu of, some benefit (the 'stated preferences' method).[59] In this latter regard, a voluminous, technical literature has arisen on the merits of various forms of questionnaires, modes of questioning, and interpretation (for example, 'contingent valuation methods');[60] these need not detain us here since the very premise of evaluating nature's resources on the basis of commodity substitutions is the far more basic, and problematic, issue.

Freeman himself remarks, however, on yet further complexity inherent to the proposed method. While a given policy may well increase the present value of one or some 'services,' it may also decrease the flow of others.[61] To be complete, therefore, it would appear that nothing short of a total modelling of the world as an ecosystem (with the human economy as a component) is required, and values (prices) imputed to all components as they interact. The impossibility of accomplishing such a task is what persuaded Willis to rely on market prices as the best available proxy for social benefits and costs. The distance between Willis and Freeman, then – both environmental economists – is cavernous indeed.

But let us return to the basic strategy of imputing value to nature's assets on the basis of 'consumers'' willingness to make substitutions, the premise underlying both WTP and WTA. Some of the deficiencies of this approach I have noted previously in chapter 2. Vatn and Bromley, however, make a highly significant additional point: 'individual preferences are context relative.' Hence, there is 'a fundamental problem [of] which of many "contexts" is pertinent to any particular choice problem.' They continue: 'In essence, individuals are both consumers and citizens and environmental choices uniquely span both domains.'[62] Neoclassical economists by definition, of course, cast people in the individualistic mode of hedonistic consumers, and neglect or efface people's capacity to make disinterested decisions as citizens.

For John Ralston Saul, perhaps the most significant falsity spread by 'elites' today is denial of the existence of a 'public' or 'common good,' which is to say a subject matter for the citizenry. Elites do this, he writes, on the one hand by largely disregarding (or neglecting even to mention) the common or public good, and on the other by continually promoting its opposite – self-interest. Seldom, he writes, do elites encourage the citizenry to adopt a 'disinterested' perspective from which to contemplate the larger well-being of society as a whole.[63] What Saul states regarding elites is certainly true of neoclassical environmental economists.

Environmental economists' penchant of asking people how much they value nature's essential 'services' is deficient in another important way as well. As people normally do not have to pay for these 'services,' they never enter people's cost calculations. (What value would the reader ascribe to the soil-retaining 'services' of a nearby forest, for example? Is this not a ludicrous question?) By contrast, many market-based items are heavily promoted and consumers continuously have to make monetary decisions on these. The very method of valuation chosen by environmental economists, then, is extremely biased toward favouring increased consumption of private goods and services, as opposed to conservation and preservation of natural assets.

An alternative, of course, is to afford citizens-in-community an opportunity to arrive collectively, and through processes of debate, discussion, and education, at a consensus concerning the valuations of nature's 'assets' and 'services.'

One further serious flaw to the cost-benefit methodology as forwarded by neoclassicists such as Freeman concerns the discounting into the present of future costs and benefits. Once a money value has been assigned to the flow of environmental services over time, these amounts must be discounted to arrive at an estimate of present value. One level of debate concerns what the discount rate should be. The more basic issue, however, is the fact that future generations – those who will actually experience the consequences of today's decisions – are rendered voiceless by the procedure.

Ecological Economics

For most ecological economists, the price solutions proffered by neoclassical environmental economists are quite inadequate and often perverse. Ecological economist Robin Grove-White remarks: 'Economic theory has provided – indeed continues to provide – the underpinning for many environmentally destructive practices.'[64] Ecological economics differs from environmental economics, therefore, in the first instance, by contending that pricing as a solution to environmental problems is at best inadequate, if not indeed perverse. Ecological economists, moreover, have reformulated what is taken to be the economic problem. Whereas mainstream economists concentrate primarily on efficient allocation of resources and on maximizing economic growth, ecological economists focus fundamentally on the issue of scale – on how big is too big.[65] However, as noted by Daly, by insisting that there are limits to growth, ecological economists necessarily, even if but inadvertently, become closely embroiled in issues of wealth distribution: 'As long as the economy is growing, we can always offer to the poor the future prospect of a slice of a larger pie.' Daly continues: 'As soon as we call for an end to growth, this option is gone ... Thus distribution is of central importance to ecological economics.'[66]

Most fundamentally, however, ecological economics proposes a different initial postulate than does neoclassical economics generally and environmental economics in particular. For mainstream economists, the 'whole' is the human economy. Ecological economics, in contrast, insists that the human economy is but a component or subset 'of a larger enveloping and sustaining Whole – namely, the Earth, its atmosphere, and its ecosystems.' Moreover, 'that larger system is finite [and is] nongrowing.'[67]

I begin this discussion of ecological economics, an umbrella term used here to encompass the non-neoclassical approaches to environmental issues, of three forerunners: Kenneth Boulding, Nicholas Georgescu-Roegen, and Herman E. Daly.

Forerunners

KENNETH BOULDING

In 1966 Kenneth E. Boulding (1932–93), a former president of the American Economics Association, presented a seminal paper, 'The Economics of the "Coming Spaceship Earth,"' to an environmental conference in Washington, DC. In his paper – subsequently widely published – Boulding proposed that humans' image of their place in the world is rapidly changing, from the belief that we live in an open system, which he whimsically termed the 'cowboy economy,' to the belief that we live in a closed system, for which he coined the term the 'spaceman economy.'[68]

These metaphors, Boulding continued, are in opposition to one another. The 'cowboy economy' is emblematic of 'reckless, exploitative, romantic, and violent behavior.' In the cowboy economy, consumption and production are regarded as good things, and the success of the economy 'is measured by the amount of the throughput from the "factors of production."'[69] The greater the flow of throughputs (inputs of factors of production, outputs of goods and services), the better the economy's performance. In the 'spaceman economy,' by contrast, the earth is likened to 'a single spaceship, without unlimited reserves of anything, either for extraction or for pollution.' According to the spaceship metaphor, 'throughput is ... to be minimized rather than maximized.' In the spaceman economy, moreover, 'what we are primarily concerned with is stock maintenance.'[70] Boulding then added, 'This idea that both production and consumption are bad things rather than good things is very strange to economists, who have been obsessed with the income-flow concepts to the exclusion, almost, of capital-stock concepts.'[71]

While Boulding's metaphor of 'Spaceship Earth' and his focus on the capital stock remains foreign to mainstream economists, even forty years later, they form the cornerstones for an emerging, insurgent ecological economics. Had these two notions been Boulding's only contributions to formulating an environmentally sound economics, he would still be honoured in the pantheon of forerunners to modern ecological economics.

Still in reference to his influential speech, 'Spaceship Earth,' however, Boulding introduced two other seminal ideas to economics discourse. One was *entropy*, the second law of thermodynamics, according to which order decreases, or randomness increases, as a result of any process; there is a tendency for states to become more probable, more chaotic, less ordered, less differentiated according to this second law. Entropy has been accepted by many ecological economists as basic to their field. The other revolutionary idea mentioned in 'Spaceship Earth' was to reformulate the factors of production. The two ideas are, as we will see, inextricably connected and, I would argue, fundamental to integrating economics and ecology in a manner consistent with a culture of ecology. I begin now with the latter idea.

In 'Spaceship Earth' but also in other texts – most significantly in his seminal book, *Ecodynamics: A New Theory of Societal Evolution* – Boulding proposed that land-labour-capital – the orthodox triad of factors of production – be replaced by information-matter-energy. For Boulding, production, 'whether of a chicken from an egg or of a house from a blueprint,' is a process whereby 'some kind of information or knowledge structure is able to direct energy toward the transportation, transformation, or rearrangement of materials into less probable structures than those existing at the start of the process.'[72] When a seed germinates in the ground, Boulding maintained, its informational structure (DNA) utilizes and directs stored energy to draw selectively upon nutrients or 'building materials' in the soil to produce its *phenotype* (the plant). Likewise for animals, *genomes* (that is, the total inherited genetic information) utilize energy and materials in directing processes of growth and development. Similarly, Boulding contended, a housing contractor studies a blueprint and from the knowledge or instructions embedded therein utilizes energy to assemble construction materials, which he or she then rearranges to produce a more complex or improbable structure than had existed previously. Boulding therefore also defined production as the realization of phenotypes from genotypes.

In justifying this proposal, Boulding merely stated: 'I am arguing that the classical economic taxonomy of factors of production into land, labor, and capital is ... too heterogeneous to be useful and that know-how, energy, and materials are a much more useful taxonomy in understanding productive processes.'[73] From the standpoint of a culture of ecology, however, what makes the new taxonomy so potentially useful is that it appears to correspond precisely with David Suzuki's depiction of ecology as the study of the 'pathways' through which matter, energy, and information circulate within ecosystems. We do indeed glimpse here the beginnings of an ecological economics.

Boulding attributed a tremendous role to information in evolutionary/developmental processes. He declared, for instance, that 'It is a powerful and accurate metaphor to see the whole evolutionary process from the beginning of the universe as a process in the increase of knowledge or the information structure.'[74] He even defined 'evolution' as 'a process of cumulative change of know-how.'[75]

Analogous to Paul Ehrlich's distinction between genetic and extragenetic information, Boulding distinguished between *biogenetic evolution* and *noogenetic evolution.* The former occurs when genetic information (or know-how) undergoes mutation, the mutant phenotype then being subject to selection processes in its environment. The latter occurs when knowledge transmitted from one generation to another undergoes change and becomes subject to cognitive social selection processes.[76]

Despite the huge role in social, cultural, and economic development/evolution that he accorded information (or know-how), Boulding did not treat it thoroughly or even consistently, and this undoubtedly explains the reluctance of ecological economists to pursue his suggested line of analysis. Below I critique Boulding's conception of information and propose a modification that could be incorporated into ecological economics. But before temporarily parting company with Boulding, I must acknowledge yet another set of his marvellous and seminal insights that helped inspire ecological economics.

For Boulding, organic species and human artefacts (which he termed 'social species') are components of *ecosystems*, defined as 'interacting populations of different species in which the birth and death rates of each population are a function of its own size and the size of the other populations with which it is in contact.'[77] Species, whether organic or social, occupy *niches*, defined as equilibrium populations of phenotypes in their ecosystems.[78] Social species are similar to organic species in the sense that both are 'selected' for occupancy of niches. Commodities, for instance, at any moment have a population or stock that increases through production and decreases through consumption, and, like biological species, they interact continuously, influencing each other's birth, growth, and death rates.

Modes of species' interaction for Boulding are various. Petroleum and automobiles, for example, are in continuous symbiotic interaction, whereas inter-city trains and buses tend to interact competitively. Social artefacts may also be competitive with organic species (e.g., automobiles with horses), or co-operative with them (e.g., chemical fertilizers with domesticated crops). Boulding also analysed predator-prey relations and host-parasite relations. Here again we see, in its incipiency, a new discipline integrating economics and ecology.

Boulding was a pioneer, and an inspiring one at that. Herman Daly, considered a co-founder of ecological economics, acknowledges his indebtedness to Kenneth Boulding as one of the teachers of his generation from whom he learned the most. The other was Nicholas Georgescu-Roegen.[79]

NICHOLAS GEORGESCU-ROEGEN

Like Boulding, Nicholas Georgescu-Roegen (1906–94) was well respected within mainstream economic circles before veering into environment-related analyses in about 1966. His life's work is often divided into two parts. In the first, he made contributions to neoclassical consumer and production theory and on growth modelling; in the second, he endeavoured to incorporate entropy into economic models, a rather subversive exercise estranging him from the economics mainstream. 'Only economists,' Georgescu-Roegen once wrote, 'still put the cart before the horse by claiming that the growing turmoil of mankind can be eliminated if prices are right. The truth is that only if our values are right will prices also be so.'[80]

In his introductory essays to *Analytical Economics* (1966), Georgescu-Roegen set out to establish that 'the economic process as a whole is not a mechanical phenomenon.'[81] He began by recounting the origin of the first two laws of thermodynamics: Sadi Carnot in 1824 had observed that heat always moves from hotter to colder bodies and that only a fraction of heat energy can be transformed into work; since 'the [Newtonian] laws of mechanics cannot account for a unidirectional movement, ' Georgescu-Roegen continued, a 'new branch of physics using nonmechanical explanations had to be created.'[82] The result was thermodynamics, with two laws formulated by Rudolf Clausius in 1865:

> *The energy of the universe remains constant* [law of conservation]
>
> *The entropy of the universe at all times moves toward a maximum* [law of entropy].[83]

Updating the second law from Clausius's formulation, Georgescu-Roegen noted the entropy law is now applied to matter as well as energy; he summarized: 'As physicists put it in nontechnical terms, *In nature there is a constant tendency for order to turn into disorder.*'[84]

The entropy law, Georgescu-Roegen continued, is 'strictly an evolutionary law with a clearly defined time's arrow.' Indeed Clausius coined the word 'entropy' from a Greek word meaning 'transformation.'[85] Incorporation of the idea of entropy into economics discourse transforms economics from a mechanistic science of static equilibrium into an evolutionary science. 'Only in thermodynamics,' Georgescu-Roegen explained, 'of all branches of physics [are] laws functions of *T* [that is, history, or the flow of time through the observer's consciousness].'[86] In the rest of physics, time, denoted by *t*, means duration as measured by a mechanical clock, and this *t* can have both a positive and a negative sign.[87] The invocation of physics is important because, as Mirowski argued (and as Georgescu-Roegen well knew),[88] neoclassical economics is closely related to classic physics.[89] As we saw in chapter 2, one reason for declaring neoclassical economics to be anti-environmental is the doctrine of reversible or unlimited bidirectional substitutions, whereas life processes, Georgescu-Roegen insisted, are irreversible: 'The idea that the life process can be reversed seems so utterly absurd to almost every human mind that it does not appear even as a myth in religion or folklore. The millenary evidence that life goes always in only one direction suffices as proof of the irreversibility of life for the ordinary mind but not for science [or, evidently, for neoclassical economics].'[90]

Georgescu-Roegen drew out further economic implications from entropy, including the following. First, 'Thermodynamics ... explains why the things that are useful have also an economic value – not to be confused with price ... The amount of low entropy within our environment (at least) decreases continuously and inevitably, and ... a given amount of low entropy can be used by us only once ... [It is not] possible, say, to burn the same piece of coal over and over again *ad infinitum.*'[91]

Second, 'From the purely physical point of view, the economic process is entropic: it neither creates nor consumes matter or energy, but only transforms low into high entropy.'[92] In *The Entropy Law and the Economic Process,* Georgescu-Roegen made the same point in starker terms: 'The product of the economic process is waste [pollution].'[93]

Third, and most significantly, 'there can be no doubt about it: any use of the natural resources for the satisfaction of nonvital needs means a smaller quantity of life in the future; if we understand well the problem, the best use of our iron resources is to produce plows or harrows as they are needed, not Rolls Royces, not even agricultural tractors.'[94] As Alain Alcouffe, Sylvie Ferrari, and Horst Hanusch summarize, for Georgescu-Roegen 'only negative growth can save a world governed by the entropy law.'[95] Robert L. Nadeau summarizes Georgescu-Roegen's contributions as follows: 'The writings of Georgescu-Roegen are well known and appreciated by Ecological Economists, but there are, to my knowledge, no discussions of his work in standard textbooks on mainstream economics.'[96]

HERMAN E. DALY

Herman Daly, too, was a forerunner of ecological economics, in the sense that he first proposed a 'steady state economy' in 1968,[97] two decades before ecological economics became an organized movement.[98] That plea was enlarged upon in his 1977 book, *Steady State Economics.* Daly also co-founded with Robert Costanza in 1989 the journal *Ecological Economics,* and in the same year he published with John C. Cobb what may be regarded as the foundational text, *For the Common Good.* Since that time he has authored, co-authored, and co-edited a series of books on ecological economics, including *Beyond Growth: The Economics of Sustainable Development,*[99] *Natural Capital and Human Economic Survival,*[100] *An Introduction to Ecological Economics,*[101] and *Ecological Economics and the Ecology of Economics: Essays in Criticism,*[102] and most recently (with Joshua Farley), *Ecological Economics: Principles and Applications,*[103] an undergraduate textbook, which I review at the close of this chapter.

Ecological Economics Today

Ecological economics became a formal movement in the late 1980s, near the end of Kenneth Boulding's life. It has been aptly termed 'a transdisciplinary field of study.'[104] According to Jeroen van den Bergh, 'EE integrates elements of economics, ecology, thermodynamics, ethics, and a range of other natural and social sciences to provide an integrated and biophysical perspective on environment-economy interactions.'[105] It is, of course, in the concluding section of a single chapter impossible to canvass thoroughly such a huge field, although some of that breadth will already be evident from the discussion of forerunners. However, I will in the following pages reference a few outstanding works in the field.

MALTE FABER, REINER MANSTETTEN, AND JOHN PROOPS, ECOLOGICAL ECONOMICS: CONCEPTS AND METHODS

According to these authors, phenomena such as the thinning of the ozone layer, pollution, habitat destruction, and species extinctions, 'although very important, reflect only the *external* [i.e., manifest] aspects of the environmental crisis.'[106] For them, the human predicament runs far deeper: it concerns the very 'dynamics of modern society.' Only by comprehending the roots of these dynamics, they claim, will we arrive at helpful responses to environmental problems; otherwise, our responses will themselves be 'infected ... by the dynamic which produces such problems.'[107] (By implication, the authors might agree that by proposing to extend the reach of markets and prices, environmental economists are 'infecting' their responses to environmental problems with the very contaminants that gave rise to the problems in the first place.)

Faber, Manstetten, and Proops define ecological economics as 'studies [investigating] how ecosystems and economic activity interrelate,'[108] a definition that clearly fits that of environmental economics too. What distinguishes the two camps, then, is not divergence in definitions, but differences concerning the range of factors that are deemed fixed and/ or outside the proper realm of their respective discourses.

For Faber et al. ecological economics is an evolutionary, dialectical science that deals not simply with 'interactions between humans and the natural world,' but acknowledges as well that these interactions are themselves 'ever evolving as the very interactions impact upon the ecosystem and alter it, and as perceptions of the environment also change.'[109] They add: 'One could say that Ecological Economics seeks to understand the human position in the world, where that world is being simultaneously created and destroyed by humans.'[110]

For ecological economics, according to the authors, the *unit of evolution* is 'the entire set of interacting economic agents and their institutions and artefacts.'[111] That being said, it is also to be remarked that in practice even ecological economists seldom explore changes in the full panoply of cultural artefacts or engage in textual interpretation ('discourse analysis' or 'cultural studies') of those artefacts; this self-imposed limitation goes a long way toward differentiating ecological economics from what I refer to here as a culture of ecology. Implicit in the culture of ecology is the critique that much of our symbolizing, not just mainstream economics discourse, has a direct, and often negative, impact on the environment. That being said, ecological economics certainly constitutes an important component of a culture of ecology.

In addressing the evolution of economic systems, Faber et al. distinguish between *phenotypic evolution*, by which they mean changes that incline an economy toward equilibrium, and *genotypic evolution*, which entails changes in tastes, techniques, and economic institutions that transform the nature of the economy itself.[112] The former, phenotypic evolution, is typically the domain of neoclassical economics; the latter, genotypic evolution, is quite beyond neoclassicism's pale.

In the inanimate ('physical') world, the authors note, genotypic evolution has all but ceased (perhaps they would agree, however, that radioactive decay remains one manifestation of genotypic evolution in the physical sphere); hence the focus there is on phenotypic evolution, which is often described quite adequately by mechanical laws (e.g., laws of motion, of gravity, of magnetic attraction, and so forth). The stability of the potentialities of physical systems, they write, has allowed physics to become an accurately predictive science.[113]

Genotypic evolution persists, of course, in the biological sphere, but here species evolution as guided by genetic mutations in the context of natural selection is quite slow. Moreover (as noted by Arthur Koestler[114] among others), genotypic evolutionary theory makes no predictions, only after-the-fact explanations. In contrast, predictions are often a part of biospheric phenotypic evolution, for instance, the behaviour of Pavlov's dogs.

The authors pronounce that the genotypic evolution of economic *systems* can be quite rapid,[115] making economic predictions unreliable and mathematical modelling hazardous. Neoclassical economics, and by implication environmental economics, then, is quite misguided in patterning itself on physics, as it presumes that final equilibrium outcomes can be predicted on the basis of knowledge of existing states. One of the main variables leading to genotypic change in economies is shifting tastes and preferences, which environmental economists insist are not to be disputed or their causes even inquired into, but which in contrast ecological economists take to be the heart of the matter.

A related question these ecological economists ask is 'What *attitude* has led humankind to the continued endangering of nature and thus of its livelihood?' Faber et al. propose that the driving force has been 'the attempt to create a human world which is closed against the influence of uncontrollable nature'[116] – a position with which ecologist Rachel Carson, as we saw, would wholeheartedly agree. For Faber et al., ecological economics must entail an investigation into this drive, to be undertaken within the evolutionary framework of novelty, openness, and uncertainty.[117]

The authors, however, optimistically affirm that the environmental crisis consists not just of dangers, but also of opportunities: 'It offers us the chance to transcend those concepts and attitudes which block us from access to more openness, and thus to the true fullness of life.'[118] They suggest the cardinal rule for economic/environmental policy should be that 'economic activities are acceptable only to the extent that they do not destroy the health (the capacity for self-organising activity) of the larger ecological system within which the economy operates'[119] – a fundamental departure, to be sure, from environmental economics as well as from its offspring, sustainable development, as interpreted by the business and government mainstream, both of which premise their doctrines on human valuations of environmental impacts.

Recalling Georgescu-Roegen, Faber et al. also afford a central place in their analysis to entropy, writing that the entropy law informs us of 'the restrictions of the way we live in our world.'[120] They conclude: 'We believe the entropy concept to be fundamental to Ecological Economics; it gives insights into economy-environment interactions which are not otherwise available,' adding that 'The main strength of the entropy concept lies not in analytically *solving* problems, but in *detecting* problems and giving insights into their solution.'[121]

Finally, the authors propose that there needs to be developed 'a new language and a set of concepts to allow us to formulate the problem of economy-environment interactions ... All these concepts will allow us to go directly from the ecological sphere to the economic one, and vice versa. If we succeed in this endeavour, this will enable us to use one language to speak on problems of both economy and ecology.'[122]

LESTER R. BROWN, ECO-ECONOMY

Lester R. Brown, founder and former president of the Worldwatch Institute and currently president of the Earth Policy Institute, based in Washington, DC, provides a practical agenda for approaching an 'environmentally sustainable economy,' or an 'eco-economy.'[123] According to Brown, at present there is 'no shared vision even within the environmental community, much less in society at large.' His purpose in writing *Eco-Economy* was to 'outline the vision,'[124] admitting, however, that a conversion 'is a monumental undertaking.'[125] Indeed, he asserts, the conceptual shift required for this 'Environmental Revolution' is comparable to that of the Copernican revolution.[126]

An eco-economy, according to Brown, entails phasing out certain old industries ('sunset industries'), restructuring some existing ones, and creating new ones ('eco-economy industries'). Industries to be phased out include coal mining, oil pumping, nuclear power generation, clearcut logging, the making of disposable products, and automobile manufacturing. Industries that need to grow include fish farming, bicycle manufacturing, wind farm construction, wind turbine manufacturing, hydrogen generation, fuel cell manufacturing, solar cell manufacturing, light rail construction, and tree planting.[127] An eco-economy, according to Brown, will require increased numbers in the following professions: wind meteorologists, family planning midwives, foresters, hydrologists, recycling engineers, aquacultural veterinarians, ecological economists, geothermal geologists, environmental architects, bicycle mechanics, and wind turbine engineers.[128] The last half of Brown's book essentially enlarges on the foregoing.

BRIAN MILANI, DESIGNING THE GREEN ECONOMY

Brian Milani is a former carpenter and builder who for about a decade has been active with the Coalition for a Green Economy in Toronto. In his book *Designing the Green Economy*, Milani proposes 'eco-design' as an umbrella term for means of moving toward a 'green economy.' 'Ecological design,' he writes, is 'a process of making human and ecosystem regeneration both the *means* and the *ends* of economic development.'[129] One aspect of a 'green service economy' that resonates with earlier material in this book, is to 'dethrone' money as 'the goal of the economy': 'Just like matter, [money] is a means and not an end, and just like matter, its open-ended accumulation is a force destructive to both society and nature.'[130]

More generally, however, Milani proposes that 'design' entails recognizing the importance of culture in economic life. Examples include restructuring human organization to let, so far as possible, nature do the work within natural processes and modelling human organization on the ecosystem.

Here are six principles Milani forwards that convey the idea of a green economy:

1. *The primacy of use-value, intrinsic value and quality.* Milani here is implicitly hearkening back to Aristotle in denigrating exchange value due to its stimulation of accumulation. Rather, he remarks, the focus should be on the end uses or satisfactions, and on various means to satisfy these. Once products are recognized as *means,* he explains, 'we can creatively minimize the matter and energy embodied in them.'[131]
2. *Following natural flows.* A green economy requires that political and ecological boundaries coincide more closely with ecosystem boundaries. Society is to become 'more bioregional.'[132]
3. *Waste equals food.* Human industrial processes need to conform more closely to the biospheric principle that in nature there is no waste: 'every process output is an input for some other process.'[133] Conforming to this principle means substituting as byproducts nutrients in place of toxins.
4. *Appropriate scale/linked scale.* Even the smallest activities, Milani notes, may have larger impacts. A green economy will recognize and account for this and integrate regenerative processes across multiple scales.
5. *Diversity.* Health and stability seem to depend on diversity, and a green economy will account for this.
6. *Localism.* For flexibility and resilience, local observation, participation, and control form important components of a green economy.

COLIN HINES, LOCALIZATION: A GLOBAL MANIFESTO

Colin Hines, former head of Greenpeace International's Economics

Unit and a Fellow of the International Forum on Globalization, enlarges on point 6 above. In *Localization: A Global Manifesto,* he proposes that for a sustainable ecosystem, as well as for democracy and authentic culture, there must be a sustained resistance to globalization. He writes: 'The global commandment that every nation must contort its economy to outcompete every other country's is an economic, social and environmental nonsense. It is a beggar-your-neighbour act of economic warfare.'[134] Among other detriments, according to Hines, globalization is environmentally destructive. Phasing back globalization and increasing local and regional production, he adds, will be environmentally beneficial, for the following reasons.

First, competition from countries with low or negligible environmental regulations would be minimized, reducing pressure on other countries to conform to the lowest common denominator. Hines notes that 'developed countries that used to be in the vanguard of environmental protection, such as Germany and the United States, are now putting the needs of being competitive before any "green" transformation of their economies.'[135] Sometimes relaxation of environmental regulations is actually forced on countries by the World Trade Organization (WTO). For example, Hines reports that in 1996 the WTO ruled in favour of Venezuela and Brazil, who had opposed provisions in the U.S. Clean Air Act as discriminating against their polluting refineries; in May 1997, the U.S. Environmental Protection Agency announced that the Clean Air Act would be amended to conform with the WTO ruling.[136] There are many similar cases on record.

Second, polluting industries would have less incentive to move to those parts of the world where pollution standards are the most lax. The Maquiladoras 'free trade zone' in Mexico is but one of many infamous examples of regions that have experienced industrialization by being lax in environmental and other standards.[137]

Third, 'relocalization' would reduce long distance transportation and concomitant energy use and pollution.

Fourth, with localization, any adverse environmental impact from production would be experienced locally where ownership and control reside; thereby the potential for improved standards of operations is increased.

Fifth, due to the present global division of production, environmental conditions have worsened dramatically in many parts of the world as 'small farmers have had to make way for intensive agriculture for exports.' As well, 'wood and fish exports are increasingly destroying forests and collapsing fisheries.'[138] The alternative, namely, that as much as possible be produced within a nation or region, would go some distance in rectifying these ills.

HERMAN E. DALY AND JOSHUA FARLEY, ECOLOGICAL ECONOMICS: PRINCIPLES AND APPLICATIONS

In 2004 Herman Daly and co-author Joshua Farley published *Ecological Economics,* which mediates the chasm between neoclassical environmental economics and ecological economics. Through this text, Daly seems to be attempting to bring ecological economics more into the mainstream. Altogether, the book is a formidable undertaking. Read selectively, it could constitute a mainstream intermediate textbook in both microeconomics and macroeconomics; read as a whole, it provides both a nuanced introduction to ecological economics and convincing arguments as to why neoclassicism should be considered, at most, a specialized subset of a more holistic ecological economics.

Part II convincingly sets out the fundamental postulates that define ecological economics and distinguish it from neoclassicism – namely, that the human economy is but a subset of a larger, finite ecosystem and that the law of entropy pertains to the human economy. Part III surveys thoroughly neoclassical marginalist approaches to resource allocation, and then proceeds to address 'market failure.' The analysis in this part is neoclassical insofar as marginalist techniques and monetary representations form a core of the discussion. It differs from mainstream neoclassical analyses in claiming that market failure is the rule rather than the exception.

Part IV reviews and critiques mainstream macroeconomics. Particularly telling is Daly and Farley's denial that Gross National Product (GNP) is an adequate indicator of well-being. For one thing, standard measures of GNP and growth in GNP do not subtract certain costs (pollution, commuting, stress, lost leisure, breakdown of community, and so on) entailed in the production of GNP. Nor is depletion of natural capital factored in. Moreover, GNP addresses but one aspect of well-being, namely, personal consumption, but is silent on a plethora of other needs such as physical and mental health, self-esteem, friendships, family, skills, peace of mind, and so on.

The authors devote a chapter to money. Money, they argue, is the one thing that does not obey the laws of thermodynamics. Money can be created and destroyed.[139] And this property of money, they conclude, gives rise to all sorts of environmental ills.

In Part V, the authors dispute the relevance of the economic theory of comparative advantage for an era with international mobility of capital; in today's world, capital seeks absolute advantage, not comparative or relative advantage, meaning that some countries may well face deterioration in their economies from globalization. Indeed, they note that one manifest consequence of globalization has been increased disparities in income, both within and among nations.[140] Furthermore, pursuit of freer markets weakens the capacity of nation states to enact environmental and social welfare measures. The authors also raise the issue of the appropriate scale of the economy relative to the ecosystem.

The final section concerns policy. The authors suggest that ecological economics has three overarching policy goals: sustainable scale, just distribution, and efficient allocation of resources.[141] Separate chapters on various policy approaches to these three major goals close the book.

Ecological Economics is a unique contribution to the economics/ecological economics literatures. For the uninitiated it provides an introduction to mainstream microeconomic and macroeconomic thought. It also critiques this thought based on the presumptions of ecological economics. The book is less radical in tone and substance than much of Daly's previous work. There is much less talk about a 'steady state' economy, for instance, and instead more talk about a sustainable scale, which we may or may not have reached. There is less discussion of the inherent deficiencies of markets and prices, and more about allowing them to allocate resources in certain spheres. The authors are explicit that policy-makers must approach an economic system as they find it, and hence make incremental changes only. They write: 'Even though our goal may be far from the present state of the world, the latter remains our starting point. We never start from a blank slate. Present institutions must be reshaped and transformed, not abolished. This imposes a certain gradualism. Even though gradualism is often a euphemism for doing nothing, it is nevertheless a principle that must be respected.'[142]

In keeping with gradualism, readers of *Ecological Economics* are not encouraged to sense the urgency that characterizes much of environmentalist literature. And by patiently explaining the logic of standard neoclassical models, albeit always with an ensuing critique, the authors may inadvertently lend support to neoclassical economics. For example, while arguing that in certain circumstances direct regulation (outright bans, emission standards, and so forth) may be suitable, the authors maintain that direct regulation does not satisfy the 'marginal conditions' (marginal cost equals marginal revenue) for efficient allocation; therefore, they recommend Pigouvian taxes and subsidies – environmental economics policies![143] On the other hand, they are much less enamoured with the prospect of pricing non-market goods and services so as to bring them into the ambit of market activity.[144]

Daly and Farley's book is of monumental importance to the ecological economics movement and to a culture of ecology. It can be regarded as an introduction to ecological economics for economists trained in the neoclassical tradition. It is a bridge between environmental economics and a more radical ecological economics – an ecological economics to which Daly has contributed substantially in previous volumes.

As noted in chapter 1, ecological economics comprises a heterogeneous assortment of positions and modes of analysis. At its best, it is clearly distinguished from environmental economics through its holism, its insistence that the human economy is a subset of a finite and non-growing ecosystem, its refusal to consider price strategies as adequate to resolve environmental issues, its penchant for proposing that human economies conform to ecosystem principles, its consideration and incorporation of entropy into its analysis, and its understanding that events are not reversible. An evolving ecological economics will be an important component of a culture of ecology.

6 Information, Entropy, and Infinite Earth

In this brief chapter, I will take two ideas – the notion of an 'information economy/network society' and Boulding's proposal that information constitutes a component of a new triad of factors of production – and relate them to the contention that through information, knowledge, and technology the earth becomes essentially an infinite resource, meaning that over the long term there are no 'limits to growth.' Brundtland, the World Bank, Royal Dutch Shell, and others, it will be recalled from chapter 1, interpret 'sustainable development' as 'sustaining economic growth.' This must mean that they view human ingenuity as being capable, over the long term, of recombining the earth's elements in ways that mitigate or obviate the needs for conservation and for constraining consumption and production.[1] However, if human knowledge and ingenuity are in fact constrained, then the earth too will prove to be finite, and the proponents of an infinite earth are making suicidal policy recommendations.

The claim that human knowledge can indefinitely expand the earth's resources could be assessed in various ways. One way would be historical, and indeed in previous chapters we surveyed present indicators of environmental degradation ensuing from previous applications of human ingenuity to the earth's crust; much more, obviously, can be done from an historical perspective.[2] The challenge to this historical approach is always, however, the argument that matters are changing or have changed to such an extent that history no longer is reliable as an indicator of future trends. Alvin Toffler is but one of many who gained fame by staking out that position.[3] The present chapter largely eschews a historical approach, valuable though that is, in favour of investigating further two key categories: 'information' and 'entropy.'

Information Economy/Network Society and 'Convergence'

The term 'information society,' first used in 1967 in Japan,[4] became ubiquitous in the decades following to indicate what many considered to be a sharp break with the industrial past. Foundational were the writings of economist Fritz Machlup and sociologist Daniel Bell. Machlup's 1962 book, *The Production and Distribution of Knowledge in the United States*,[5] was seminal in conceiving information and/or knowledge production, processing, and distribution as important economic activities. Machlup's work was extended by Marc Porat, who in 1977 pronounced that by 1967 the United States had become an 'information economy'; Porat estimated that the information sector, in that year, accounted for about 46 per cent of U.S. GNP.[6]

Even more influential, though, was Bell, who invented the term 'post-industrial society.' Bell proposed that for pre-industrial societies the major resource is land and the major output food and other agricultural products; for industrial societies the key resource is machines or capital, and the key outputs are factory-produced items; but for modern, post-industrial societies, he averred, the key resource is knowledge or information, and the characteristic outputs are symbolic.[7]

Early discourses on post-industrial or the information society,[8] like those of Machlup and Bell, were accompanied and indeed inspired by technological developments. Computing began to spread into everyday life in the early to mid-1960s. As noted by Simon Nora and Alain Minc, until then computers remained bulky (several cubic metres in size), expensive, fragile, and accessible only by a relatively few skilled technicians versed in machine language. This 'pre-historic age of data processing' ended in 1965, when IBM introduced the first computers with integrated circuits in place of transistors – improving performance, lowering price, decreasing size, and increasing reliability.[9] Today, of course, the personal computer is omnipresent, at least in the rich North – an indispensable household appliance for millions of families. Because of computerization, analogue encoding and transmissions are increasingly giving way to digital or binary encoding and transmissions – the language of computers.

Claude Shannon and Warren Weaver were among the early theorists of digital communication, developing in 1949 the 'mathematical theory of communication.' They denoted the 'quantity' of information as the number of binary digits ('bits') needed to specify any given selection from a field of possibilities.[10] The digitization of communication as we understand the term today, however, certainly surpasses Shannon and Weaver's modest expectations. Any and all information that could previously be transmitted electronically can now be transformed for purposes of transmission into sequences of binary (on-off) charges or impulses. This digitization of communication is the technical basis of 'convergence,' the term used to summarize the blurring of industry or sector boundaries in the communication field.

According to the Organization for Economic Cooperation and Development (OECD), *convergence* comprises technical, functional, and corporate dimensions.[11] *Technical convergence* means that increasingly a single mode of transmission (e.g., a coaxial or fibre-optical cable) transmits simultaneously diverse information services such as voice, text, data, sound, and/or image. Technical convergence also means that the same pattern of bits can be carried over many different pathways (e.g., satellite, optical fibre, coaxial cable, twisted copper pair wire, radio frequencies). *Functional convergence,* sometimes also referred to as multimedia, points to hybrid services that combine voice, data, text, and/or image. Electronic encyclopedias, for example, combine text, video, and sound. While closely allied to technical convergence, functional convergence is nonetheless distinct insofar as this latter term emphasizes services and products as opposed to carriage or modes of transmission. Finally, *corporate convergence* refers to mergers, amalgamations, and diversifications whereby media organizations come to operate across previously distinct industry boundaries.

More recently, the term 'network society,' derived particularly from writings by Manuel Castells, has come into prominence. According to Castells, 'The network society ... is made up of networks of production, power and experience, which construct a culture of virtuality in the global flows [of information] that transcend time and space.'[12] Network society discourses differ from post-industrial and information economy discourses through their emphasis on the ubiquity of networks, that is, the connectivity and interdependence of all those forming 'nodes.' However, the network society also replays the major theme of both the post-industrial and information economy discourses, namely, that 'the basis of economic life has shifted dramatically, not from capitalism to some other system, but rather from an economy driven by resource extraction and industrial manufacturing to one driven by the circulation and application of knowledge.'[13] Digitized networks allow economies and societies, according to Castells, to operate on a global basis as flows of digitized information easily transcend time and space, creating in the process a 'culture of virtuality.'

De-Materializing 'Information'

Katherine Hayles attributes to Shannon and Weaver the conceptualization, common today, of information 'as an entity distinct from the substrates [or media] carrying it.'[14] If Shannon and Weaver provided the theory for thus conceptualizing information, however, convergence in its three aspects provides the apparent manifestation – and hence is even more convincing. Hayles also proposed that from Shannon and Weaver's formulation, it 'was a small step to think of information as a kind of bodiless fluid that could flow between different substrates without loss of meaning or form.'[15]

At the very time Shannon and Weaver were purporting to measure information by counting the number of binary digits, other theorists were indeed 'de-materializing' information along the lines noted by Hayles. In *The Human Use of Human Beings* (1950), for instance, cyberneticist Norbert Wiener (1894–1964), a former professor of Claude Shannon,[16] maintained that organisms can be viewed, metaphorically, as *messages.* 'To describe an organism,' he explained, 'we do not try to specify each molecule in it, and catalogue it bit by bit, but rather to answer certain questions about it which reveal its pattern.'[17] Organisms, including human organisms, for Wiener, are *patterns,* which is to say *recurring forms*; only secondarily are they material. In an elegant, almost rhapsodic passage, Wiener described how much more important, or at least fundamental, pattern is than matter:

> Life is an island here and now in a dying world. The process by which we living beings resist the general stream of corruption and decay is known as *homeostasis* ... It is the pattern maintained by this homeostasis which is the touchstone of our personal identity. Our tissues change as we live: the food we eat and the air we breathe become flesh of our flesh and bone of our bone, and the momentary elements of our flesh and bone pass out of our body every day with our excreta. We are but whirlpools in a river of ever-flowing water. We are not stuff that abides, but patterns that perpetuate themselves.[18]

Kenneth Boulding, a contemporary of Wiener, went even further. He downplayed the material aspect of information to such an extent that he proposed that 'information' is unconstrained by the laws of physics – and in particular by the first two laws of thermodynamics. As noted previously, the first law (the law of conservation) asserts that matter-energy can neither be created nor destroyed. The second (the law of entropy) maintains that matter-energy in isolated systems continually degrades into less complicated (i.e., less differentiated) states.[19] (Isolated systems are defined as those that do not exchange matter or energy with their surroundings; the trajectory for isolated systems, according to this second law, is toward homogeneity, and eventually total randomness or heat death – the absence of differentiation or structure).[20] Because of what he (at times) saw as its inherent 'immateriality,' Boulding claimed that information/knowledge is not subject to these two laws.

Regarding the law of conservation, he maintained that information/knowledge alone is what can really increase, making it 'primal' to evolutionary processes:

> The through-put of information in an organization involves a 'teaching' or structuring process which does not follow any strict law of conservation even though there may be limitations imposed upon it. When a teacher instructs a class, at the end of the hour presumably the students know more and the teacher does not know any less. In this sense the teaching process is utterly unlike the process of exchange which is the basis of the law of conservation. In exchange, what one gives up another acquires; what one gains another loses. In teaching this is not so. What the student gains the teacher does not lose. Indeed, in the teaching process, as every teacher knows, the teacher gains as well as the student. In this phenomenon we find the key to the mystery of life.[21]

And again, the same thought, expressed twenty years later: 'Knowledge ... is the field within which evolution takes place. It is the only thing that can really change, the only thing that is not conserved.'[22] A further implication of the purported capacity of information/knowledge to defy or transcend the law of conservation (if true) is the inapplicability of the law of entropy. In fact, Boulding saw information as a force countering entropy.

Anthropologist Gregory Bateson (1904–80) likewise contributed mightily to the growing conception of information as disembodied. Bateson defined information as 'a difference which make a difference': a difference in the world, as between chalk and a blackboard, he maintained, becomes represented by a second corresponding difference in the mind. But difference, Bateson insisted, 'being of the nature of relationship, is not located in time or in space. We say the white spot is 'there,' in the middle of the blackboard, but the difference between the spot and the blackboard is not 'there.' It is not the spot; it is not the blackboard; it is not the space between the board and the chalk ... difference does not have location.'[23]

Yet another eminent scholar who celebrated the purported immateriality of information was Ithiel de Sola Pool. In his last major text, Pool declared, 'In a world of scarce resources, thought is pleasingly abundant; like air, it is a free good ... Communication, in short, is one of the good things in life that can be had without straining the world's scarce resources. In communication we are very far from the limits of growth.'[24]

In a widely read and influential essay, as a final example, John Perry Barlow proposed that internet 'space' is fundamentally different from the material territories governed by nation states: 'Cyberspace consists of transactions, relationships, and thought itself, arrayed like a standing wave in the web of our communications. Ours is a world that is both everywhere and nowhere, but it is not where bodies live. We are creating a world that all may enter without privilege or prejudice accorded by race, economic power, military force, or station of birth. We are creating a world where anyone, anywhere may express his or her beliefs, no matter how singular, without fear of being coerced into silence or conformity.'[25]

These are just a few of many possible citations. They gain added importance once it is realized that the (often implicit) premise that economic growth can continue forever through applications of human ingenuity to the earth's crust is contingent on information/knowledge being immaterial.

Information as Matter or Energy In-Form

It is amazing in this 'information age,' how recalcitrant theorists are to define 'information.' Marc Porat, for instance, who inherited Machlup's mantle as the foremost authority on macroeconomic analyses of the information sector, in his seminal work declared: 'Information is by nature a heterogeneous commodity';[26] and 'There is no single definition of information that embraces all aspects of the primary sector,'[27] and further, 'Information cannot be collapsed into one sector – like mining – but rather the production, processing, and distribution of information goods and services should be thought of as an *activity*.'[28]

In a similar vein, economist Beth Allen wrote: 'The preceding argument that various types of information may be available in the economy suggests immediately that we should treat information as a *differentiated commodity*.'[29] Other economists have proposed that information is what reduces uncertainty[30] – again, information being what it *does* with no description as to what it *is*. 'Information' according to this consequence-based conception does not exist objectively in and of itself so as to be countable; it exists only in particular contexts, and with regard to the state of ignorance or uncertainty of whatever particular person is being considered at the time.

In order to better comprehend the relation between information/knowledge/know-how on the one hand, and entropy on the other, I turn to physicist Carl Friedrich von Weizsäcker. According to von Weizsäcker, information is the shape or pattern of matter or energy perceptible to the senses.[31] There are three elements to von Weizsäcker's conceptualization of information: matter or energy (the 'substrate' or medium); the shape or pattern (what Boulding and Wiener emphasized), and perception. Forms that cannot be, or are not, perceived, von Weizsäcker implies, cannot constitute information.

But that is not quite enough. Forms or patterns must not only be perceived through the senses; they must also be recognized, or at least have meanings imputed to them, by those sensing them. Information, then, I would add, is not just form or pattern encoded onto a substrate and perceived by the senses, but also requires interpretation, which is to say, the form is part of a pre-existing code; this additional qualification seems quite in accord with von Weizsäcker's intent. Boulding's difficulty concerning the inapplicability of physical laws to information related primarily to his omission of this last requirement: he seemed to forget that when delivering his lectures by encoding the air, message recipients needed to work at decoding the condensations and rarefactions. Without recipients to process the sound waves, there is no 'in-forming.'

Physicist Hans Christian von Baeyer strikes a similar note in a more recent text: '[Information] is the strange, comprehensible stuff that flows out of a tangible object, be it an atom, a DNA molecule, a book or a piano, and after a complex series of transformations involving the senses, lodges in the conscious brain. Information mediates between the material and the abstract, between the real and the ideal.'[32] I would, however, part company with von Baeyer by including the shape of the tangible object as a component of information, and not focus on 'stuff that flows.'

Rather powerful support for these ideas is provided by neoclassical economist, Kenneth Arrow, who wrote: 'Let us now turn to the costs of information, that is, to the inputs needed for the installation and operation of information channels. First and most important, the individual himself is an input, indeed the chief input if quantification is at all meaningful here, into any of his information channels. Immediately or ultimately, the information must enter his brain through his sensory organs, and both brain and senses are limited in capacity. Information may be accumulated in files, but must be retrieved to be of use in decision-making.' Arrow continues by remarking that each individual must make 'an adequate investment of time and effort to be able to distinguish one signal from another; learning a foreign language is an obvious example of what I have in mind; the subsequent ability to receive signals in French requires this initial investment.'[33]

However, like many others, Arrow is not always consistent in his treatment of information, falling on occasion into undue materialism, as in the following extract: 'One of the most interesting economic characteristics of information is that its cost is independent of the scale on which it is used. A given *piece of information* costs the same to acquire, whether the decision to be based on it is large or small.'[34] But information, according to his previous argument, is not a 'piece' at all, and the costs entailed depend, among other things, on the number of recipients and the investments they have made or will need to make to decode the shape or forms.

Boulding, of course, acknowledged, that matter-energy *is* subject to the two laws of thermodynamics. Moreover, he knew that information relates to the forms or patterns assumed by matter or energy.[35] And he was aware that entropy is defined as the lessening of differentiation (i.e., loss of complexity of form). However, despite all this, he was not able to see that information is inextricably connected to the laws of thermodynamics.

Boulding also missed the essential point explained so well by Arrow: moving meaning onto a human mind entails work, and hence is entropic. While Boulding and his students, as he remarked, assuredly departed his lectures much enriched, all continued to produce entropy simply by living and learning – and, of course, by eventually dying.[36]

Since information is not simply form, but matter-in-form, which is decoded or to which meanings are ascribed, similar stimuli (patterns, forms), but not the same information, can be in many places at the same time. True, many people may share the same language, or code, or broadly culture, and hence they may interpret a particular 'form' in more or less the same way. But this does not gainsay the fact that each individual must work upon the stimulus to extract/impute meaning, and that individuals expend energy (even if but to remain alive) to do this.

Information has often been mistakenly described as a 'public good.' Public goods are defined as items whose use or enjoyment by one does not detract from use by others (examples being biodiversity, sanitation, sunlight). In fact, however, it is not information that is the public good, but the shapes/forms or stimuli that receivers sense and then process. This may seem like a fine point, but when the applicability of the first and second laws of thermodynamics is being called into question, fine points are called for. Since information/knowledge does not exist without (a) a material carrier and (b) people to process the forms or patterns, it follows that information/knowledge is indeed subject to the first and second laws of thermodynamics; information/knowledge, consequently, is not unconstrained or infinite.

Other Considerations

There is a second error in the position of those who propagate the doctrine of an infinite earth through unconstrained knowledge/information. They seem to think that all knowledge is wise, that it necessarily supports and increases the possibilities of life. Experience should teach us otherwise. If this were the case, we would not be facing the environmental crises described in chapter 1.

There are many reasons for the entropic thrust of much human knowledge in our era. One is the culture of militarism. The military and defence budget of the United States was set at $379 billion for 2002.[37] Military technology, naturally, is designed to destroy, to increase entropy.

Even more to the point is the nature of scientific knowledge itself. Western science is fundamentally reductive: it breaks systems down into subsystems, and subsystems into components, and components into parts; and it looks for linear, one-to-one causal relations among these. It often views nature in mechanistic terms, through the metaphor of the machine – a perspective quite at odds with the concept of the holistic ecosystem that is so fundamental to environmentalism. Thus, science lauded the technology of DDT as an effective pesticide, remaining oblivious for years to the wider environmental and health repercussions.

From general systems theory we learn that systems and subsystems are bound together through complex and intricate pathways that cannot be understood unless the larger picture is always borne in mind. The ecosystem concept implies that individual subsystems and components depend upon and interact with one another to survive, grow, and change. As systems theorist Brent Ruben has declared, 'The complexity and intricacy of pathways and interconnections necessary to even maintain these systems are impossible to enumerate, and difficult even to conceive of.'[38]

This book has addressed a further factor that challenges the mainstream economists' position that growth in knowledge is all that is required to extricate humanity from the environmental morass: large portions of technological change and knowledge development are guided by the price system. As discussed in chapter 2, the system of money, markets, and prices is immensely biased in the direction of ecological collapse.

By and large our experience to date with applications of human knowledge ('technologies') to the earth's crust has indeed been entropic – as the litany of environmental indictors reviewed in chapter 1 demonstrates. The best explanation for why neoclassical theorists have chosen to ignore this simple fact probably lies in their propensity to themselves respond to the incentives of the price system in formulating their theories.

There is yet another aspect to the error made by propagators of the doctrine of infinite earth through the purported infinite expansibility of knowledge/information. Jane Jacobs proposed three principles of development, of which the third is key to the present argument.[39] Her first principle is that *differentiation emerges from generality.* Her second is that *differentiations become generalities from which further differentiations emerge.*[40] Her third principle is that *development depends on co-developments,* which she explained as follows: 'I mean that development can't usefully be thought of as a "line," or even as a collection of open-ended lines. It operates as a web of interdependent co-developments. No co-development web, no development.'[41] She further proposed that economies and ecosystems are similar inasmuch as both follow, indeed are governed by, these three principles.

We see from the foregoing how the error of unconstrained information/knowledge could easily arise. 'Differentiation proceeds from previous generalities' could be applied as follows: new information/

knowledge derives from previous information/knowledge. On account of their steadfast anthropocentrism, however, advocates of infinite Earth through unconstrained knowledge/information do not recognize the third principle, the necessity of co-evolution, particularly of economies with ecosystems. There is a vast amount of genetic 'information' in natural ecosystems, but due to the encroachment of economies on ecosystems, that 'information' is in steady decline through extinctions. Growth in human knowledge and in applications of human knowledge are constrained by co-evolutionary developments in ecosystems. Previously we called this biodiversity. Unless accommodations are made by adhering to principles of ecology in our economic lives, human knowledge/information too will ultimately decline.

The Revised Triad

Finally, in light of the foregoing, let's reconsider Boulding's proposal to reconstitute the basic factors of production: from the triad of *land-labour-capital*, to *matter-energy-information/knowledge.*[42] According to Boulding, land, labour and capital are too 'imprecise,' whereas *material, energy, and information/knowledge* are more 'universal.'

As we just saw, however, there is a problem with Boulding's conceptualization of information. Our dispute with Boulding is that the shapes and patterns assumed by matter or energy need to be 'read' or interpreted before they constitute 'information,' meaning that information exists neither as pure, Platonic, disembodied shapes or patterns, nor as material objects 'out there'; information entails application of a 'code.' Hence, I would reformulate Boulding's triad as *matter-energy-form plus code.*

That qualification aside, what Boulding's proposal accomplishes, from an ecological perspective, is to extend the notion of production *to all nature,* rather than confining it, as it is with the land-labour-capital triad, to activities that pass through markets. Labour as a factor of production is by definition human effort that is recompensed through salaries or wages. Land as a factor of production in the economic paradigm is owned and compensated through rent. And capital is what earns interest or profit. These three compensations, when totalled, give national income in the system of accounts.

By contrast, energy as a factor of production does not necessarily pass through markets; indeed, only a minuscule portion does. Energy comprises not just human work, or even oil, gas, and electricity, but also wind, nuclear, water, biotic and solar power, and for most of this no monetary representation is attached and no market exchanges are possible. Similarly, whereas the notion of land as a factor of production denotes a commodity that receives rent, materials encompass much more, comprising also the vast array of elements ranging from rainfall and oxygen to nitrogen and phosphorous that circulate through the biosphere in the absence of price or commodity exchange. By accepting the Boulding paradigm, revised as suggested above, we would be well on our way to an ecological economics that truly integrates economics and ecology in a manner more conducive to biospheric well-being.

E.F. Schumacher once remarked that humans tend not to value what they have not themselves made;[43] land-labour-capital proffered by economists as the basic factors of production illustrates the truth of Schumacher's remark. Recasting the productive triad as matter-energy-form/code would induce us to reconsider thoroughly our modes of valuation, and this could not but help us progress toward the goal of achieving a more ecologically sound culture.

Conclusion

A culture of ecology is a culture that is in tune with its ecosystem. Culture is made up of the world of symbols (stories, discourses, rituals) and the world of activity (institutions, technologies, markets, production). There is an interdependence between these two worlds, and the flow of influence is not one way. Certainly our thoughts, beliefs, theories, knowledge, superstitions, and habits of mind help determine our actions, but our actions have consequences for our surroundings, and changes to our physical environs affect our discursive lives. How we 'read' the material world affects our actions upon it. Different readings, or decodings, are not only possible but inevitable. But from an environmentalist perspective not all codes and decodings are equal. One of the most pernicious of current codes, I have argued, is mainstream or neoclassical economics.

Neoclassical economics is, in large measure, a theory of prices and of the price system. It is not the only theory of money and prices, but it is certainly the pre-eminent theory, and a justificatory one at that since it proposes that 'correct' prices are sufficient to achieve Pareto optimality. A large part of the problem with neoclassical economics, I would propose, is that it theorizes uncritically or apologetically a technology, namely, money, that is inherently anti-environmental; I developed several arguments in support of that assertion in chapter 2 and also in chapter 5.

For this conclusion, instead of recapitulating arguments favouring ecological economics over environmental economics, I propose to look again at money, as it seems to be the root of the problem, and in particular at ways in which its use can be reduced.

It has been argued that neoclassicists' understanding or interpretation of human nature arose with the monetarization of life. Recall

Aristotle's warning that money would cause individuals to focus on accumulation as opposed to civic service, and that both Adam Smith and Karl Marx proposed that production based on 'value in exchange' differs fundamentally from production premised on 'value in use.' Money permits accumulation far beyond one's present capacities to use. If the pecuniary culture is indeed fundamental to the transformation of human nature into what neoclassical economists now understand it to be, then the pecuniary component of our economy and culture needs to be reduced.

One way of circumscribing the role of money, as Aristotle recommended, is by increasing self-sufficiency – whether at the level of the family, the city, the region, the province, or the country. The division of labour, which underlies commodity exchange, as writers as diverse as Adam Smith and Karl Marx have noted, takes a severe human toll. It also, however, imposes a heavy environmental toll because of the speed-up of production and the decline in responsibility for environmental outcomes. Likewise, global divisions of production heighten the predominance of the price system, with even further deleterious environmental impacts. Being tied into a world economy means that nations give priority to their place in that economy and take steps to increase trade, often despite adverse consequences for local conditions. Like curtailing consumption, increasing self-sufficiency is much easier said than done, but the beginnings are already evident in the anti-globalization movement.

Another way of phasing back money is by increasing the relative importance of public or common property. One expeditious step would be to expand significantly national and provincial parks and municipal green spaces – areas in which ecosystem interactions would be allowed to proceed with minimal human interference; this policy would explicitly recognize that ecosystems envelop economies, not the reverse. Nearly a century and a half ago, Henry David Thoreau recommended that each town 'should have a park, or rather a primitive forest, of five hundred or a thousand acres, where a stick should never be cut for fuel, a common possession forever, for instruction and recreation.'[1] Likewise, ecosystem theorist Eugene Odum proposed that 'the landscape needs to be compartmentalized (i.e., "zoned") to provide a safe balance between productive and protective ecosystems; restrictions on the use of land and water are our only practical means of avoiding overpopulation, or overexploitation of resources, or both.'[2] The announcement by the World Wildlife Fund of Canada on 1 December 2003 that 600 million hectares of Canada's boreal forest will be protected through a coalition of eleven groups – including Suncor Energy, three forestry companies, the Innu in Labrador, Deh Cho Dene in the Northwest Territories, Kaska Dene in the Yukon and British Columbia, and Poplar River First Nation in Manitoba – is immensely heartening.[3] The companies and First Nations groups that have joined the agreement, known as the Boreal Forest Conservation Framework, control a sixth of the 21.3 billion acres of Canadian boreal forests, and they will press others to join. Their objective is to preserve 50 per cent of the forests in their pristine state, and to develop the other 50 per cent in an ecologically sustainable way. If successful in this, the expanded agreement will cover roughly one-quarter of the planet's remaining intact forests. It is delightful to conclude this book on such a heartening note.

In opposition to proposals such as these for phasing back the ambit of money and prices, some might point to the 'tragedy of the commons,' an insight and doctrine often ascribed to Garett Hardin.[4] According to Hardin, the tragedy of the commons is manifest in two ways – when we take things from the environment, and when we put things back into it. Regarding the first, he asks us to picture a pasture open to all (a commons). Each herdsman, he proposes, will try to keep as many cattle as possible on the commons, and each will continue adding cattle until 'the day of reckoning' – the time when the capacity of the pasture is exceeded. Hardin explains 'the tragedy' this way: Whereas a herdsman individually receives the full proceeds from selling each individual animal, the cost experienced by him from the overgrazing caused by an additional animal is spread among all herdsmen using the commons. The 'rational herdsman,' therefore, will increase his herd irrespective of the consequences for the pasture as a whole. Hardin summarizes: 'Each man is locked into a system that compels him to increase his herd without limit – in a world that is limited. Ruin is the destination toward which all men rush, each pursuing his own interest in a society that believes in the freedom of the commons. Freedom in a commons brings ruin to all.'[5] The same dilemma, according to Hardin, applies to pollution, that is, when we put things back into the commons. He writes: 'We are locked into a system of "fouling our own nest,"' through pollution – whether sewage, chemicals, radioactivity, or heat – 'so long as we behave only as independent, rational, free enterprisers.'[6]

Hardin then declares that 'the tragedy of the commons as a food basket is averted by private property, or something formally like it,' but adds pessimistically that no such easy solution exists for pollution: '... the air and waters surrounding us cannot readily be fenced, and so the tragedy of the commons as a cesspool must be prevented by different means, by coercive laws or taxing devices.'[7] In other words, Hardin's 'solution' of privatization applies only to resource extraction, not to effluent disposal. Reading Hardin, however, one would conclude that the last thing he would recommend for environmental well-being is to extend the commons.[8]

But Hardin can be critiqued. For one thing, as noted by Daly and Farley, Hardin is not really referring to a 'commons' at all; 'common property is property for which a community, not an individual, controls the property rights ... In many cases, communities have developed institutions that prevent individuals within the community from overexploiting the resource, and there is no problem with the "tragedy of the commons." A better term, therefore, is the "tragedy of open access regimes" or simply "the open access problem."'[9] Even in the case of open access regimes, however, the 'tragedy' stems from inconsistent patterns of ownership, not from the absence of private property. If the cows, too, were communally owned, the 'tragedy' would disappear, even in the absence of an explicit rule limiting the number of cattle, and concomitantly monetary exchanges would be reduced. In the case of pollution, the problem again arises not on account of the public nature of air and water, which is what they are intrinsically, but because, as Hardin notes, the ethic of individual maximization is inculcated into people's hearts and minds through private property; this ethic would only become more deeply entrenched were the commons to be further enfolded into the private property system for purposes of resource extraction, as recommended by Hardin. In societies in which common ownership is the norm (as has been the case with many indigenous peoples), the ethic of preserving the commons for the benefit of the seventh generation has taken on an importance that escapes we who live in the monetarized West. Since the basic elements that sustain life (air, earth, water, biodiversity) are inextricably in the commons, it makes sense to conform our system of property and our economy to that reality. As a general principle, an economy should conform to ecological principles, for at least two reasons: First, it is the economy, not ecological principles that humans can control. Second, the economy is contingent on the environment, not the reverse.

In 1948, the year of his death, forester and conservationist Aldo Leopold wrote a landmark essay entitled 'A Land Ethic,'[10] which remains as pertinent today as when it was published. There, Leopold lamented that Western society lacked 'a land ethic.' All ethics, he declared, have a common premise: that each individual is a member of a community of interdependent parts. He defined ethic generally as 'a limitation on freedom of action in the struggle for existence.' As an individual-in-community, he continued, reminiscent of the questions raised by Rabbi Hillel and quoted at the outset of this book, everyone lives a contradiction, or dialectic: on the one hand, people's instincts may prompt them to compete for a place in that community; on the other, their ethics prompt them to co-operate. Leopold then advised that a land ethic is distinguishable from ethics generally only because it 'enlarges the boundaries of the community to include soils, waters, plants, and animals, or collectively "the land."' Adhering to a land ethic, Leopold observed, 'changes the role of Homo sapiens from conqueror of the land community to plain member and citizen of it.'

What is suggested here is that Leopold was far closer to an environmentally sound mode of valuation than Garett Hardin, the utilitarians, and modern-day environmental economists. Indeed, as Leopold saw it, the environmental problem was that in the absence of a land ethic, the human-land relation remained strictly economic, 'entailing privileges but no obligations.'

Ecological economics at present remains a marginalized, heterodox approach to environmental well-being. It is dwarfed in terms of influence by neoclassical economics generally and by 'environmental economics' in particular. Yet, one cannot help but feel that as the environment continues to deteriorate under the sway of the price system, ecological economics will grow and develop to eventually supplant neoclassicism. If and when that happens, we will as a culture and society have progressed monumentally toward a culture of ecology.

Neoclassical economics is certainly not the only anti-environmental discourse in our moribund culture, monumentally influential though it is. Nor are the business/governmental/consumerist practices neoclassicism 'justifies' the only factors degrading the environment, significant though these are. In the years to come, I would hope that others, too, would continue this current project by addressing critically other discursive systems and their related practices, in the hope that sooner rather than later we may shift direction and begin to approach a culture of ecology.

As David Suzuki remarked, 'It's a matter of survival.'

Glossary

Biomagnification Accumulations of toxic substances passing up the food chain in ever-increasing concentrations.

Biotic community (biocoenosis) An association of various living organisms within a particular geographic location forming an integrated community.

Bhopal The world's worst industrial accident occurred on 2 December 1984 at Bhopal, India, when a chemical release from a Union Carbide pesticide plant caused at least 6,500 deaths and an estimated 20,000 to 50,000 serious injuries.

Brundtland Report This 1987 report of the United Nations World Commission on Environment and Development (Brundtland Commission), entitled *Our Common Future*, proposed 'sustainable development' as the means of alleviating world poverty in a world beset by environmental degradation.

Carrying capacity The absolute limit of the earth's capacity to sustain the human population. Although no definitive estimate exists for the earth's carrying capacity, the concept persists in the ecological literature; it is virtually absent from mainstream economics. What *is* crystal clear is that civilizations in the past – for example, those of the Tigris and Euphrates valleys, Easter Island, the Mayan and Anasazi civilizations – exceeded the carrying capacity of their local environments.

Chernobyl In April 1986 the world's worst nuclear power accident occurred at Chernobyl in the former USSR. More than 30 people died immediately, and 135,000 were evacuated. Nuclear fallout extended far beyond the USSR into the Netherlands, Belgium, Great Britain, the Balkans, Austria, eastern and southern Switzerland, parts of southern Germany, and Scandinavia.

Chrematistike (Chrematistics) According to Aristotle, the mere acquisition of goods and wealth.

Classical economics Adam Smith, Karl Marx, and other of the classical economists proposed a labour theory of value, an insatiability to human wants, and (Marx excepted) the efficacy of the price system to allocate resources. This was an anthropocentric and methodologically individualist mode of analysis. It was replaced by neoclassical economics about 1890 as the predominant mode of economic analysis.

Coase theorem Named for neoclassical economist Ronald Coase. The theorem claims that in 'purely competitive' economies with no 'transactions costs,' market forces will maximize production value by internalizing externalities irrespective of how the law assigns legal liability. The Coase Theorem is subject to many criticisms.

Co-development or *co-evolution* The principle that nothing evolves or develops in isolation. In particular, economic development depends on ecosystem development – an argument against continued exponential economic growth.

Collective or *public goods* A good or service that is not used up when enjoyed by an individual. Examples include parks, public health and sanitation, aesthetically pleasing architecture, and biodiversity. Market-driven economies are characterized by an undersupply of collective goods because, by definition, there can or should be no exclusive proprietary rights to public goods.

Consumer sovereignty The guiding principle of neoclassical economics. The task of economic policy, according to neoclassicism, is to organize the economy in such a way that it will satisfy so far as possible 'autonomous,' pre-existing, undisputed, and 'sovereign' tastes and preferences.

Convergence The blurring of industry or sector boundaries in the communications field, often attributed to the digitization of information (i.e., computer communications).

Culture of ecology A system of symbolization and praxis largely conforming to principles of ecology. To attain a culture of ecology, a radical transformation in our thinking and discourse about the economy and environment is required.

Dialectic Tension between opposites. Dialectical logic presumes that the irreducible unit of analysis is the relation, not the thing. A dialectical approach is inconsistent with methodological individualism and linear analysis.

Digitization The transformation of messages into a binary code. The Morse code (dots and dashes) was an early mode of digitization. Today's digitized messages consist of a series of on-off electrostatic charges or impulses. Digitization is at the heart of the network society and convergence.

Division of labour or *specialization* According to Adam Smith, specialization increases the output of each worker and is the major source of increases in the wealth of nations, and hence is much to be desired, despite severely deleterious consequences to workers.

Ecological economics An evolutionary, dialectical science that deals not only with interactions between humans and the natural world, but also acknowledges that these interactions are themselves evolving as they affect the ecosystem and alter it, and because perceptions of the environment change. For ecological economics, the unit of analysis is the entire set of interacting economic agents, their institutions, and their artefacts.

Entropy The second law of thermodynamics states (according to one formulation) that a degradation of energy from a concentrated form to a dispersed form always accompanies an energy transformation. In another formulation, the amount of free energy (energy capable of doing mechanical work) decreases continually in an isolated system (a system in which neither matter nor energy can enter or escape).

Environmental economics A non-dialectical science dealing with interactions between humans and the natural world, it applies mainstream economic principles and modes of analysis to environmental concerns. Ecology becomes, in effect, a branch of neoclassical economics. The main recommendation of 'environmental economists' is to subject, as far as possible, human-environment interactions to market forces and to price indicators.

Eudaimonia Aristotle described the ultimate end, or the 'good,' of human existence as happiness and relegated all other 'goods' to being merely means (or instruments) to that end. For Aristotle, then, *eudaimonia* was an intrinsic value.

External economies Defined by Alfred Marshall as cost savings per unit of production accruing to a firm as a result of increases in industry-wide production. A precursor to the neoclassical economics concept of externalities.

Externalities Discrepancies between individual economic interests and those of the community; costs or benefits that are not considered by the persons engaging in a transaction.

Exxon Valdez On 24 March 1989, the tanker *Exxon Valdez* spilled nearly 11 million gallons of oil into the waters of Prince William Sound.

Holism The view that the whole is the fundamental unit of analysis and, furthermore, that components in interaction produce systems that have properties beyond those that can be ascertained by merely aggregating the parts. Holism is the opposite of methodological individualism. The holism of ecology, in contrast to the methodological individualism of neoclassical economics, is inherent in the very notion of an ecosystem. Ecology emphasizes relations among entities, whereas economics tends to focus on entities themselves, whether through the theory of the firm, the theory of production, or the theory of the consumer.

Incremental principle Perhaps the most striking trait differentiating neoclassical economics from its precursors. For maximization, the marginal or incremental cost or disutility must just approach the revenues or benefit to be gleaned from an increment of activity.

Infinite Earth The belief or doctrine that the earth can sustain high rates of economic growth indefinitely. This doctrine is often 'justified' by the view that applications of human knowledge (technology) are unconstrained.

Information The shape or pattern that matter or energy assumes and to which meanings are imputed by those sensing the shape or pattern.

Information economy (Machlup, Porat). An economy in which the production and sale of information or knowledge is a leading economic activity. According to Daniel Bell, 'Post-industrial society' (his term for an information economy or information society) is the third stage in societal/economic evolution, the first two being agriculture/resource extraction and manufacturing.

Intrinsic relation For Arne Naess, an intrinsic relation is one so basic that, in its absence, the system's components are no longer the same things. Methodological individualism is blind to intrinsic relations.

Institutional and evolutionary economics Founders include Thorstein Veblen, John R. Commons, and Clarence Ayres. According to this school of economics, institutions are taken to be the irreducible unit of analysis; neoclassicism, by contrast, proposes the individual as the basic unit of analysis. Institutions include commonly held patterns of behaviour and habits of thought that are associated with people interacting in groups or larger collectives. Examples of institutional units of analysis include money, organizations, property rights, and norms and conventions.

Isolated system A system in which no matter or energy can enter or exit. The law of entropy eventually causes such a system to become totally random.

Just price According to Aristotle, the midpoint between the lowest price a seller would accept and the highest amount a buyer would pay. In the Middle Ages, the just price barely allowed individuals to purchase the goods required to maintain their positions in the social hierarchy.

Kyoto protocol The first global agreement establishing binding targets for cutting greenhouse gas emissions. In 1997 representatives of 160 countries gathered at Kyoto, Japan, and signed the protocol.

Labour theory of value A principal feature of the classical economics of Adam Smith, Karl Marx, and others. Commodities attain their value from the amount of labour that went into their fabrication. Decidedly an anti-environmental theory of value as nature's goods, which entail no human fabrication, are by implication worthless.

Law of conservation The first law of thermodynamics, which maintains that matter-energy can be neither created nor destroyed.

Localization The opposite of globalization. The position that ecological well-being is improved by greater local and regional self-sufficiency.

Methodological individualism The view that the part or the individual is the unit of analysis; wholes are deemed to be no more than aggregations of the parts. This view typifies mainstream economic approaches.

Neoclassical economics Mainstream economics in the West since about 1900. It abandoned a labour theory of value, proposing instead that value stems ultimately from people's wants, tastes, and preferences, which are deemed to be 'sovereign.' It is characterized also by the marginal principle for maximization (equating marginal or incremental benefits and costs). With neoclassicism, economics became largely a logical-mathematical-deductive science. The radical anthropocentrism of neoclassical economics is shown by its insistence that there is no intrinsic value, only relative value, and that market price, based in part on market demand, is an adequate indicator of value.

Neoclassical triad Land, labour, and capital as the basic factors of production. Each of these factors passes through markets and hence commands a price.

Network society A term denoting the ubiquity of digitized networks for information management and retrieval; a society in which networks constitute a basic form of human organization and relationship.

Oeconomica (economics) For Aristotle, the entire field of household (and community) management.

Pareto optimality A criterion of efficiency or maximization proffered by neoclassical economics. A situation in which no one can be made better off without at least one person becoming worse off. Pareto optimality has little to do with distributive justice, as even an economy in which a single person has all the wealth satisfies the Pareto criterion of 'optimality.'

'Perfect' competition A cornerstone of the neoclassical economic model. The assumptions of this competitive environment include many small sellers of homogeneous products, none possessing market power, perfect information and knowledge, no price rigidities, no transactions costs, no externalities, no public goods.

Physiocrats Led by François Quesnay in France during the 1760s, the Physiocrats proposed a land theory of value. They maintained that all economic activity (and all value) depends ultimately on agriculture and natural resources.

Political economy The investigation of institutional, financial, political, and other pressures that shape production and distribution. For political economists, the media's ideological function, for example, can only be understood when the media are recognized as consisting of power sites within the larger political-economic system.

Postindustrial society (Daniel Bell) The contention that the production, distribution, and sale of information (symbols) has superseded in importance both agriculture and manufacturing.

Postmodernism The plurality of contemporary knowledge leads to a devaluation of knowledge. The contention that knowledge is more often a product power relations than a reflection of truth. The denial of grand narratives or all-encompassing world views, such as Marxism, liberalism, or scientism.

Potlatch Ceremonial gift giving by aboriginal peoples of the West Coast of North America.

Price system A system of information/communication denoting the relative exchange values as set forth in money terms. Prices are 'biased' transmitters of information; some of the anti-environmental biases are the principle of unconstrained, bi-directional substitutions, shortened time horizon and present-mindedness, the notion of continuous exponential growth, the bias toward the exchange of private goods, and the doctrine of quid pro quo.

Principle of natural selection (Darwin) Also known as the 'survival of the fittest,' the principle proposes that traits enabling phenotypes to live to reproduce will be carried forward into future generations.

Principle of population (Thomas Malthus) The theory that population growth tends to outpace growth in the food supply, giving rise to such 'natural checks' on population as war, famine, disease, and pestilence. Through education and 'moral restraint,' Malthus argued in later editions of his book, people can perhaps avoid or mitigate these natural checks. Malthus anticipated Darwin's principle of natural selection.

Public goods Benefits that are not used up for others when enjoyed by one. Examples include sanitation and biodiversity. Since there is no exclusion for public goods, there can be no market for them either.

Quid pro quo An exchange of equivalences; the view that what I give to you must be worth at least what you give to me. A society functioning exclusively by quid pro quo will engage solely in commodity exchange/barter relations.

Shadow price A price computed for purposes of cost-benefit analysis to incorporate more of the social costs and benefits than market prices.

Signified A key component of the semiotics of Ferdinand de Saussure. The mental image induced by a signifier.

Signifier A key component of the semiotics of Ferdinand de Saussure. The physical presence of a 'sign,' that is, an object that points to something other than itself.

Steady state economy Zero economic growth.

Sustainable development A polysemous term coined by the United Nations World Commission on Environment and Development (Brundtland Commission). Brundtland defined sustainable development as comprising policies and activities that meet the needs of the present without sacrificing the capacity of future generations to meet their needs. Today, sustainable development is widely cited by industry and government as signifying economic growth that can be maintained into the indefinite future. For some environmental groups, however, economies must cut back on present rates of resource use as they have already exceeded sustainable levels of activity, as proven by such environmental indicators as species extinctions.

Threshold A point of no return, a place where bidirectional substitutions are no longer possible. Events have finality once a threshold is crossed. An example is the reduction in the population of a species to the point where extinction becomes inevitable.

Notes

1. Sustainable Development vs Sustainable Ecosystem

1 The Bretton Woods Conference established the International Monetary Fund (IMF), and the International Bank for Reconstruction and Development (World Bank). See Yale Law School, 'Bretton Woods Agreements,' http://www.yale.edu/lawweb/avalon/decade/decad047.htm.

2 Quoted in Robert L. Nadeau, *The Wealth of Nature: How Mainstream Economics Has Failed the Environment* (New York: Columbia University Press, 2003), 78.

3 Gilbert Rist, *The History of Development: From Western Origins to Global Faith* (London: Zed Books, 1997), 71.

4 President Truman, Inaugural Address 1949, as quoted in ibid., 71–2.

5 See Mark Sagoff, 'Do We Consume Too Much?' *Atlantic Monthly*, June 1997, 80–96; Julian Simon, *The Ultimate Resource II* (Princeton, NJ: Princeton University Press, 1998), http://www.africa2000.com/RNDX/chapter003.html; Bjorn Lomborg, *The Skeptical Environmentalist* (Cambridge: Cambridge University Press, 2001); Terry L. Anderson and Donald R. Leal, *Free Market Environmentalism*, rev. ed. (New York: St Martin's Press, 2001).

6 Darin Barney, *Prometheus Wired: The Hope for Democracy in the Age of Network Technology* (Vancouver: UBC Press, 2000), 19.

7 Michael Carley and Ian Christie, *Managing Sustainable Development*, rev. ed. (London: Eathscan, 2000), vii.

8 World Commission on Environment and Development (Brundtland Commission), *Our Common Future* (Oxford: Oxford University Press, 1987), 8. Although the term, 'sustainable development' is new, the concept is not. It echoes the thought of early American conservationists such as Theodore Roosevelt in the late 19th and early 20th centuries. Regarding forestry, for example, Roosevelt declared: 'Wise forest protection does not mean the

withdrawal of forest resources, whether of wood, water, or grass, from contributing their full share to the welfare of the people, but, on the contrary, gives the assurance of larger and more certain supplies. The fundamental idea of forestry is the perpetuation of forests by use. Forest protection is not an end in itself; it is a means to increase and sustain the resources of our country and the industries which depend upon them.' Theodore Roosevelt, 'Conservation, Protection, Reclamation, and Irrigation,' Excerpt from State Papers as Governor and President 1899–1909. in Lisa M. Benton and John Rennie Short, eds., *Environmental Discourse and Practice: A Reader* (Oxford: Blackwell, 2000), 111.

9 Brundtland Commission, *Our Common Future,* 1.

10 Ibid., 213.

11 Jim MacNeill, 'Strategies for Sustainable Development,' *Scientific American* 261, no. 3 (1989): 154–65; quoted in Robert Goodland, 'The Case the World Has Reached Limits,' in *Population, Technology, and Lifestyle,* ed. Robert Goodland, Herman E. Daly and Dalah El Serafy (Washington, DC: Island Press, 1992), 4.

12 Brundtland Commission, *Our Common Future,* 1.

13 Ibid., 213.

14 Royal Dutch Shell, *People, Planet and Profits: The Shell Report 2001,* 8; available at http://www.shell.com/static/royal-en/ downloads/shell_report_ 2001.pdf.

15 Ibid. In 2003, Friends of the Earth issued a press release entitled 'Shell Record Profits at Expense of People and Planet.' http://www.foe.co.uk/ resource/press_releases/shell_record_profits _at_ex.html.

16 International Petroleum Industry Environmental Conservation Association, International Association of Oil and Gas Producers (OGP), *Industry as a Partner for Sustainable Development,* 2002, http://www.uneptie.org/outreach/ wssd/contributions/sector_reports /sectors/oil-gas/oil-gas.htm.

17 Herman E. Daly, *Beyond Growth: The Economics of Sustainable Development* (Boston: Beacon Press, 1996), 5. Daly is referencing the bank's 1992 World Development Report, entitled *Development and the Environment.*

18 World Bank, *Sustainable Development in a Dynamic World: Transforming Institutions, Growth and Quality of Life,* World Development Report 2003, 184, http://econ.worldbank.org/wds/wdr/2003/.

19 Ibid., 184.

20 Ibid., 196.

21 Canada, 'Departmental/Agency Strategies: Industry Canada,' 2002, http://www.sdinfo.gc.ca/federal_sd_resources/strategies_display_e.cfm? id=18.

22 Canada, 'Departmental/Agency Strategies: Environment Canada,' http://www.sdinfo.gc.ca/federal_sd_resources/strategies_display_e .cfm?id=13.

23 Alanna Mitchell, 'An Environment Minister of Another Colour,' *Globe and Mail*, 12 October, 2004, A7.

24 Friends of the Earth, 'Tomorrow's World,' 1997, http://www.foe.co.uk/campaigns/sustainable_development/publicatio ns/tworld/tw-in-10.html.

25 Friends of the Earth, 'Shell Record Profits.'

26 Lester R. Brown, *Eco-Economy: Building an Economy for the Earth* (New York: Norton, 2001), 77.

27 Ibid., 4.

28 Goodland, 'The Case the World Has Reached Limits,' 3–22.

29 Daly, *Beyond Growth*, 9

30 Ibid., 28.

31 Herman Daly, *Steady-State Economics*, 2nd ed. (Washington, DC: Island Press, 1991), p. 75.

32 Greenpeace, 'We Must Stop the War on the Planet,' Earth Summit 2002, http://archive.greenpeace.org/earthsummit/background.html.

33 World Business Council for Sustainable Development and Greenpeace International, 'Climate Change and the Kyoto Protocol,' 2002, http://www.environment.gov.za/sustdev/jowsco/paraEvents/ClimateChange.html.

34 World Business Council for Sustainable Development, 'About the WBCSD,' 2005, http://www.wbcsd.org/templates/TemplateWBCSD1/layout.asp?type=p&M enuld=NjA&doOpen=1&ClickMenu=Lef.

35 Lisa M. Benton and John Rennie Short, 'The Early Environmental Movement,' in *Environmental Discourse and Practice: A Reader*, ed. by Lisa M. Benton and John Rennie Short (Oxford: Blackwell, 2000), 91.

36 Ibid., 106.

37 Gifford Pinchot, *Breaking New Ground* (1905); as quoted in Donald Worster, *Nature's Economy: A History of Ecological Ideas*, 2nd ed. (Cambridge: Cambridge University Press, 1994), 266.

38 Worster, *Nature's Economy*, 257–65.

39 Mark Neuzil and William Kovarik, *Mass Media & Environmental Conflict: America's Green Crusades* (Thousand Oaks, CA: Sage, 1996), xi.

40 Al Gore, Introduction to *Silent Spring*, by Rachel Carson (New York: Houghton Mifflin, 1994), xv.

41 Worster, *Nature's Economy*, 122.

42 Alex MacGillivray, *Rachel Carson's* Silent Spring (Hauppauge, NY: Barron's, 2004), 6.

43 This book, published in 1952, was on the *New York Times* bestseller list for eighty-six weeks.

44 Andrew Goudie, *The Human Impact on the Natural Environment*, 5th ed. (Cambridge, MA: MIT Press, 2000), 123.
45 Online Ethics Center for Engineering and Science at Case Western Reserve University, 'Rachel Carson's Story,' http://onlineethics.org/moral/carson/main.html.
46 Rachel Carson, *Silent Spring* (1962; New York: Houghton Mifflin, 1994), 1.
47 Ibid., 3.
48 Ibid., 104.
49 Ibid., 187–8.
50 Ibid., 188.
51 Ibid., 189. Emphasis added.
52 Sharon Beder, *Global Spin: The Corporate Assault on Environmentalism* (White River Junction, VT: Chelsea Green, 1998), 108.
53 Online Ethics Center, 'Rachel Carson's Story.'
54 Natural Resources Defense Council, 'The Bush Administration's Slash & Burn Environmental Budget,' 2001, http://www.nrdc.org/legislation/abudget03.asp.
55 Gore, Introduction to Carson, *Silent Spring*, xvi–xvii.
56 Protagoras is credited with declaring, 'Man is the measure of all things.'
57 Carson, *Silent Spring*, 297.
58 Emphasis added. The complete text of the declaration may be found at http://www.tufts.edu/departments/fletcher/multi/texts/STOCKHOLM-DECL.txt.
59 Emphasis added. United Nations, 'Stockholm Declaration on the Human Environment,' adopted 16 June 1972, http://www.unesco.org/iau/sd/stockholm.html.
60 Brundtland Commission, *Our Common Future*, 4.
61 See note 8.
62 Canada, National Round Table on the Environment and the Economy, 'Who We Are,' n.d., http://www.nrtee-trnee.ca/eng/overview/What-we-do_e.htm.
63 Ibid.
64 Canada, 'Sustainable Development Information Systems,' http://www.sdinfo.gc.ca/main_e.cfm.
65 Ibid.
66 United Nations, Johannesburg Summit 2002, 'With a Sense of Urgency, Johannesburg Summit Sets an Action Agenda,' 3 September 2002, http://www.johannesburgsummit.org/html/whats_new/feature_story38. htm.
67 Donella H. Meadows, 'Changing the World through the Informationsphere,' in *Media and the Environment*, ed. Craig L. LaMay and Everette E. Dennis (Washington, DC: Island Press, 1991), 72.

68 Sagoff, 'Do We Consume Too Much?'
69 Simon, *Ultimate Resource II*, chpts. 3, 4.
70 Lomborg, *Skeptical Environmentalist*; and Anderson and Leal, *Free Market Environmentalism.* In January 2003 the Danish Committees on Scientific Dishonesty declared that Lomborg's research falls 'within the concept of scientific dishonesty' and is 'clearly contrary to the standards of good scientific practice.' Matthew Nisbet, 'The Skeptical Environmentalist: A Case Study in the Manufacture of News,' 2003, http://www.csicop.org/scienceandmedia/environmentalist/.
71 Clive Ponting, *A Green History of the World: The Environment and the Collapse of Great Civilizations* (New York: Penguin, 1991), 175.
72 Quoted in ibid., 168.
73 United Nations Environment Programme, *Global Environment Outlook 3: Past, Present and Future Perspectives* (London: Earthscan, 2002), 121.
74 Bruce Coblentz, 'Vulnerability to Extinction,' n.d., http://www.orst.edu/instruct/fw251/notebook/extinction.html.
75 World Conservation Union, 'Species Extinction,' 2004; http://www.google.ca/search?q=cache:blLpxtqATZUJ:www.iucn.org/wss d/files/media%2520brief/mb_species.pdf+IUCN+Extinction+media+Brie f&hl=en.
76 Gary Gardner, 'The Challenge for Johannesburg: Creating a More Secure World,' in The World Watch Institute, *State of the World 2002: Special World Summit Edition*, ed. Christopher Flavin et al., 8 (New York: Norton, 2002).
77 David Suzuki with Amanda McConnell, *The Sacred Balance* (Vancouver: Grey-Stone Books, 1997), 124.
78 Sagoff, 'Do We Consume Too Much?'
79 UN Environment Programme, *Global Environment Outlook 3*, 64.
80 Ibid., 62.
81 Ibid., 64.
82 Seth Dunn and Christopher Flavin, 'Moving the Climate Change Agenda Forward,' in World Watch Institute, *State of the World 2002: Special World Summit Edition*, ed. Christopher Flavin et al. (New York: Norton, 2002), 26.
83 Ibid., 28.
84 Anne Platt McGinn, 'Reducing Our Toxic Burden,' in World Watch Institute, *State of the World 2002* (New York: Norton, 2002), 77.
85 United Nations, *Global Challenge, Global Opportunity 2002*, reported in Steven Chase, 'UN Delivers Stern Warning Over Water Use,' *Globe and Mail*, 14 August 2002, A9.
86 Wallace Immen, 'Thick Blanket of Smog Considered Health Threat,' *Globe and Mail*, 14 August 2002, A14.
87 McGinn, 'Reducing Our Toxic Burden,' 78.

88 United States Department of Health and Human Services, Centers for Disease Control and Prevention, *Second National Report on Human Exposure to Environmental Chemicals,* January 2003, http://www.cdc.gov/exposurereport/.
89 CDC, Media Relations, 'CDC Telebriefing Transcript,' 31 January 2003, http://www.cdc.gov/od/oc/media/transcripts/t030131.htm.
90 Pesticide Action Network North America, 'Chemical Trespass: Pesticides in Our Bodies and Corporate Accountability,' May 2004, http://www.panna.org/campaigns/docsTrespass/chemicalTrespass2004. dv.html
91 Environmental Defence and the Canadian Environmental Law Association (Pollution Watch), *Shattering the Myth of Pollution Progress in Canada: A National Report,* December 2004, http://www.pollutionwatch.org/pub/natreport2004.jsp.
92 Centre for Atmospheric Science, 'The Ozone Hole Tour: Part 1, The History Behind the Ozone Hole,' n.d., http://www.atm.ch.cam.ac.uk/tour/part1.html.
93 McGinn, 'Reducing Our Toxic Burden,' 97.
94 UN Environment Programme, *Global Environment Outlook 3,* 212.
95 Ibid.
96 Michelle L. Bell, Aidan McDermott, Scott L. Zeger, Jonathan M. Samet, and Francesca Dominici, 'Ozone and Short-term Mortality in 95 US Urban Communities, 1987–2000,' *Journal of the American Medical Association,* 292, no. 19 (2004): 2372–9, http://jama.ama-assn.org/cgi/reprint/292/19/2372.
97 Ibid., 2376.
98 Herman E. Daly and John C. Cobb, Jr, *For the Common Good: Redirecting the Economy toward Community, the Environment and a Sustainable Future* (Boston: Beacon Press, 1989), 21.
99 'So far as is desirable' is an important qualification. As Simon explains, 'The problem of pollution for economists is like the problem of collecting a city's garbage: do we want to pay for daily collection, or collection twice a week, or just once a week? With environmental pollution as with garbage, a rational answer depends upon the cost of cleanup as well as our tastes for cleanliness.' He adds, 'And as our society becomes richer, we can afford and are prepared to pay for more cleanliness.' Simon, *Ultimate Resource II,* ch. 15.
100 Peter Söderbaum, *Ecological Economics* (London: Earthscan, 2000), 20.
101 Norgaard writes that, on the one hand, 'Ecological Economists prefer a people-in-nature world over a people-above-nature world; similarly, we prefer a people-in-society world over an individuals-above-society world.'

Unfortunately, he then erases these fine sentiments by declaring, 'Since Ecological Economists use many of the models of neoclassical economics, it is not the models that distinguish us.' See Richard B. Norgaard, 'Passion and Ecological Economics: Towards a Richer Coevolution of Value Systems and Environmental Systems,' in *New Dimensions in Ecological Economics: Integrated Approaches to People and Nature,* ed. Stephen Dovers, David I. Stern, and Michael D. Young (Cheltenham, UK: Edward Elgar, 2003), 29. As developed in this book, however, neoclassical models through their championing of commodity exchange and the price system inextricably position people above nature, and through their methodological individualism position individuals above society.

102 Once the biological drives have been satisfied, von Bertalanffy claimed, it is the values and ideals of the symbol system that govern people's actions, and it is in that sense that the symbolic universe of religious, aesthetic, scientific, and ethical values controls behaviour. Ludwig von Bertalanffy, *A Systems View of Man,* ed. Paul A. LaViolette (Boulder, CO: Westview Press, 1981), 17 (emphasis added).

103 Meadows, 'Changing the World,' 74.

104 See generally Stuart Ewen, *PR! A Social History of Spin* (New York: Basic, 1996).

105 The statement is ascribed to Protagoras, indicating that this position had a certain currency well before the Renaissance.

106 Noam Chomsky and Edward S. Herman, *Manufacturing Consent* (New York: Pantheon Books, 1988).

107 Walter Lippmann, *Public Opinion* (New York: Free Press, 1922).

2. Economics and Ecology as Discourses

1 Northrop Frye, 'The Language of Poetry,' excerpt from *Anatomy of Criticism* (1957), reprinted in *Explorations in Communication,* ed. Edmund Carpenter and Marshall McLuhan (Boston: Beacon Press, 1960), 44.

2 Lisa M. Benton and John Rennie Short, *Environmental Discourse and Practice* (Oxford: Blackwell, 1999), 1.

3 Donald Worster, *Nature's Economy: A History of Ecological Ideas,* 2nd ed. (Cambridge: Cambridge University Press, 1994), x.

4 Geoffrey Hodgson, 'Economics, Environmental Policy and the Transcendence of Utilitarianism,' in *Valuing Nature?: Economics, Ethics and Environment,* ed. John Foster (London: Routledge, 1997), 49.

5 The first use of the term has been attributed to Xenophon, about 365 BC.

6 Adam Smith, *The Wealth of Nations,* Book IV, introduction, ed. Edwin Cannon (1766; New York: Modern Library, 1937), 397.

7 Lionel Robbins, *An Essay on the Nature and Significance of Economic Science*, 2nd ed. (London: Macmillan, 1935), 15.
8 Milton Friedman, *Price Theory: A Provisional Text*, rev. ed. (Chicago: Aldine, 1962), 6.
9 Alfred Marshall, *Principles of Economics: An Introductory Volume*, 8th ed. (London: Macmillan, 1947), 14; first edition published in 1890.
10 Ibid.
11 Ibid., 14–15.
12 Ernst Haeckel, 'Ueber Entwickelungsang und Aufgabe der Zoologie,' *JenAische Zeitschrift fur Medicin und Naturwissenschaft V* (1870), 365; cited in *The Cultural Ecology of a Chinese Village*, by James D. Clarkson (Chicago: University of Chicago Press, 1968), 1, n. 1.
13 Christopher Beltway, *Environmental Philosophy: Reason, Nature and Human Concern* (Montreal & Kingston: McGill-Queen's University Press, 2001), 8. The same definition is provided by Frank Benjamin Golley in *A History of the Ecosystem Concept in Ecology: More than the Sum of the Parts* (New Haven, CT: Yale University Press, 1993), 6.
14 Golley, *Ecosystem Concept in Ecology*, 168.
15 Eugene Odum, *Fundamentals of Ecology*, 3rd ed. (Philadelphia: W.B. Saunders, 1971), 8.
16 Peter Knudstson and David Suzuki, *Wisdom of the Elders* (Toronto: Stoddart, 1992), 43.
17 David Suzuki with Amanda McConnell, *The Sacred Balance: Rediscovering Our Place in Nature* (Vancouver: GreyStone Books, 1997), 198. He asks, 'Is the visible solidity the only "real" part [of a tree], or does it exist as a process, relationship, connection as well? ... A tree we might say, is not so much a thing as a rhythm of exchange, or perhaps a centre of organizational forces' (p. 199).
18 Knudstson and Suzuki, *Wisdom of the Elders*, 45.
19 Ibid.
20 Odum, *Fundamentals of Ecology*, 37.
21 Jacob Oser, *The Evolution of Economic Thought* (New York: Harcourt, Brace & World, 1963), 29. See also Joseph Schumpeter, *History of Economic Analysis*, ed. Elizabeth Boody Schumpeter (New York: Oxford University Press, 1954), 223–43.
22 To be sure, the classical economists were more subtle. In his *Contribution to the Critique of Political Economy*, for example, Marx acknowledged, 'It would be wrong to say that labour which produces use-values is the only source of the wealth produced by it, that is of material wealth. Since labour is an activity which adapts material for some purpose or other, it needs material as a prerequisite. Different use-values contain very different proportions of labour

and natural products, but use-value always comprises a natural element.' And again: 'The level of the productivity of labour, which is predetermined in manufacturing industry, depends in agriculture and extractive industry also upon unpredictable natural conditions. The same quantity of labour will result in a larger or smaller output of various metals – depending on the relative abundance of the deposits of these metals in the earth's crust. The same amount of labour may yield two bushels of wheat in a favourable season, and perhaps only one bushel in an unfavourable season. Scarcity or abundance brought about by natural circumstances seems in this case to determine the exchange-value of commodities, because it determines the productivity of the specific concrete labour which is bound up with the natural conditions.' None of this is to negate, however, the essential proposition that labour is the source of value, and without labour there is no value – a most anthropocentric, anti-environmental position. Karl Marx, 'Part 1: The Commodity,' *A Contribution to the Critique of Political Economy*, 1859, http://www.marxists.org/archive/marx/works/1859/critique-pol-economy/ch01.htm.

23 John Anton, 'Aristotle and Theophrastus on Ecology,' in *Philosophy and Ecology*, vol. 1, ed. Konstantine Boudouris and Kostas Kalimtzis, 15–27 (Athens: Iona, 1999). See also Michael Lahanas, 'Theophrastus of Eresos: Father of Botany and Ecology,' October 2004, http://www.mlahanas.de/Greeks/Theophrast.htm. Aristotle, for example, advanced the humus theory of plant nutrition and the eternal recycling of elements. See Gerhard Wiegleb, 'Lecture Notes on the History of Ecology and Nature Conservation' (Cottbus, Germany: Brandenburg Technical University, 2000), 29, http://www.tu-cottbus.de/BTU/Fak4/AllgOeko/erm/erm1.htm.

24 Worster, *Nature's Economy*, 5.

25 Ibid., 7.

26 Gerhard Wiegleb lists the following as Linnaeus's contributions to ecology: floristics, vegetation geography, mire science, lake science, indicator plants, succession, food chains, experimental ecology, dispersal ecology, balance of nature as a scientific theory and not as a divine plan. See G. Wiegleb, 'Lecture Notes,' 15, 16.

27 Worster, *Nature's Economy*, 32. The phrase 'economy of nature' was first used in 1658 by Sir Kenelm Digby in proposing a 'natural science compatible with religion,' Worster, 37.

28 Jan Oosthoek, 'Environmental History: Between Science and Philosophy,' 2001, http://forth.stir.ac.uk/~kjw01/philosophy.html.

29 Quoted in Worster, *Nature's Economy*, 37.

30 Wiegleb, 'Lecture Notes,' 16.

31 Worster, *Nature's Economy*, 39.

32 Wiegleb, 'Lecture Notes,' 16.

33 Quoted in Lisbet Koerner, *Linnaeus: Nature and Nation* (Cambridge, MA: Harvard University Press, 1999), 2.

34 Ibid., 95.

35 Adam Smith, *Essays on Philosophical Subjects*, ed. W.P.D. Wightman and J.C. Bryce, vol. 3 of *The Glasgow Edition of the Works and Correspondence of Adam Smith* (Indianapolis, IN: Liberty Fund, 1982); http://oll.libertyfund.org/Texts/LFBooks/Smith0232/GlasgowEdition/PhilosophicalSubjects/0141-04_Bk.html#lf0141.4.

36 Henry David Thoreau, *Walden and Other Writings by Henry David Thoreau*, ed. Joseph Wood Krutch (New York: Bantam Books, 1962). *Walden* first published in 1854.

37 The others most often cited are, of course, Adam Smith and David Ricardo.

38 Thomas Robert Malthus, *An Essay on the Principle of Population; Or, A View of its Past and Present Effects on Human Happiness; With an Inquiry Into Our Prospects Respecting the Future Removal or Mitigation of the Evils Which It Occasions*, ed. Donald Winch (1803; Cambridge: Cambridge University Press, 1992), 23.

39 Charles Darwin, *On The Origin of the Species By Means of Natural Selection, Or The Preservation of Favoured Races in the Struggle For Life*, ed. Morse Peckham (1859; Philadelphia: University of Pennsylvania Press, 1959), 147.

40 R.M. Young, 'Malthus and the Evolutionists: The Common Context of Biological and Social Theory,' *Past and Present* 43 (1969): 116.

41 Charles Darwin, *Origin of the Species* (1859; London: J.M. Dent & Sons, 1972), 463.

42 William Graham Sumner, *Social Darwinism: Selected Essays of William Graham Sumner*, ed. Stow Persons (Englewood Cliffs, NJ: Prentice-Hall, 1963), 17.

43 The 'Darwinian view,' as expressed in the writings of Thomas Huxley, Spencer, Sumner and others, can be regarded as something of a caricature of Darwin's own position, which was at once more subtle and contradictory. See note 44.

44 Worster makes the point that Darwin was narrowly construed. Whereas *On the Origin of the Species* undoubtedly focuses on the individual organisms' struggle for survival, *The Descent of Man* emphasizes that all species are bound together through common ancestry, declaring even that nature is held together essentially through 'mutual love and sympathy.' Nonetheless, the damage had been done with *Origin of the Species*, and in the writings of popularizers like Thomas Huxley and Herbert Spencer, as well as in the public's mind, Darwin became associated almost exclusively with the competitive struggle for survival. See Worster, *Nature's Economy*, 182.

45 Tansley used the term to denote all organisms in a given area plus their relationship to the inorganic environment. Alfred George Tansley, 'The Use and Abuse of Vegetational Concepts and Terms,' *Ecology*, 16, no. 3 (1935): 284–307; see also Golley, *Ecosystem Concept in Ecology*, 8 ff.
46 Tansley, 'Vegetational Concepts and Terms,' 284–307.
47 Worster, *Nature's Economy*, 302.
48 Odum, *Fundamentals of Ecology*, 36.
49 Ibid., 22.
50 Odum defined mutualism as growth and survival of two populations being dependent upon one another. Ibid., 211.
51 Ibid., 510–16.
52 Worster, *Nature's Economy*, 392.
53 Thomas Söderqvist, *The Ecologists: From Merry Naturalists to Saviours of the Nation: A Sociologically Informed Narrative Survey of the Ecologization of Sweden, 1895–1975* (Stockholm: Almqvist and Wiksell International, 1986); quoted in Worster, *Nature's Economy*, 413.
54 See Golley, *Ecosystem Concept in Ecology*.
55 Brent D. Ruben, 'General Systems Theory,' in *Approaches to Human Communication*, Richard W. Budd and Brent D. Ruben (Rochelle Park, NJ: Hayden Book Company, 1972), 124.
56 Worster, *Nature's Economy*, 173.
57 World Commission on Environment and Development (Brundtland Commission), *Our Common Future* (New York: Oxford University Press, 1987), 37.
58 Ibid.
59 Many works could be cited here. Two of the most famous are Hayek's *The Road to Serfdom* and Milton and Rose Friedman's *Free to Choose*.
60 Jeremy Bentham, 'An Introduction to the Principles of Morals and Legislation'; quoted in Wesley C. Mitchell, *Types of Economic Theory*, vol. 1, ed. Joseph Dorfman (New York: Kelley, 1967), 203.
61 C.B. Macpherson, *Democratic Theory: Essays in Retrieval* (Oxford: Clarendon Press, 1973), 63.
62 Herman E. Daly and John B. Cobb Jr, *For the Common Good: Redirecting the Economy Toward Community, the Environment and a Sustainable Future* (Boston: Beacon Press, 1989), 145–6.
63 Arild Vatn and Daniel W. Bromley, 'Choices without Prices without Apologies,' in *The Handbook of Environmental Economics*, ed. Daniel W. Bromley (Oxford: Blackwell, 1995), 3.
64 George Stigler and Gary Becker, 'De Gustibus Non Est Disputandum,' *American Economic Review* 67, no. 2 (1977): 75–90.
65 Mark Sagoff, 'Do We Consume Too Much?' *Atlantic Monthly*, June 1997, 80–

96; available at http:// www.puaf.umd.edu/faculty/papers/sagoff/consume.pdf. Sagoff here quotes E.O. Wilson, *The Diversity of Life* Cambridge, MA: Harvard University Press, 1992), 345.

66 'Word IQ,' n.d., http://www.wordiq.com/definition/Efficiency_%28economics%29.

67 F.A. Hayek, 'The Use of Knowledge in Society,' *American Economic Review* 35, no. 4 (September 1945): 519.

68 Ibid., 520.

69 Ibid., 525.

70 Ibid., 526.

71 Ibid., 527.

72 Kenneth Arrow, 'The Economics of Information,' in *The Computer-Age: A Twenty-Year View*, ed. Michael Dertouzos and Joel Moses (Cambridge, Massachusetts: MIT Press, 1979), 313–14. Emphasis added.

73 Kenneth Arrow, *The Limits of Organization* (New York: Norton, 1974).

74 See, for example, Sagoff, 'Do We Consume Too Much?' and Julian Simon, *The Ultimate Resource II* (Princeton: Princeton University Press, 1998), http://www.africa2000.com/RNDX/chapter003.html.

75 Sagoff, 'Do We Consume Too Much?'

76 Ibid.

77 Simon, *Ultimate Resource II.*

78 Harold Barnett and Chandler Morse, *Scarcity and Growth: The Economics of Natural Resource Availability* (Baltimore: Johns Hopkins University Press, 1963), 10.

79 Ibid., 10, 11.

80 They explained further that 'Nature's input should now be conceived as *units of mass and energy*, not acres and tons. Now the problem is more one of manipulating the available store of iron, magnesium, aluminum, carbon, hydrogen, and oxygen atoms, even electrons. This has major economic significance' (ibid., 238; emphasis added).

81 They explained that 'The Conservationists' premise that the economic heritage will shrink in value unless natural resources are "conserved," is wrong for a progressive world. The opposite is true. In the United States, for example, the economic magnitude of the estate each generation passes on – the income per capita the next generation enjoys – has been approximately double that which it received, over the period for which data exist. Resource reservation to protect the interest of future generations is therefore unnecessary.' Ibid., 247–8.

82 Harold A. Innis, *The Bias of Communication* (Toronto: University of Toronto Press, 1951).

83 According to neoclassical founder William Stanley Jevons, 'In commerce bygones are forever bygones and we are always starting clear at each moment, judging the value of things with a view to future utility. Industry is essentially prospective not retrospective.' William Stanley Jevons, *The Theory of Political Economy*, 3rd ed. (London: Macmillan, 1888), 164.

84 Herman Daly, *Steady-State Economics*, 2nd ed. (Washington, DC: Island Press, 1991).

85 M. King Hubbert, 'Exponential Growth as a Transient Phenomenon in Human History,' in *Societal Issues, Scientific Viewpoints*, ed. Margaret A. Strom (New York: American Institute of Physics, 1987), 75–84; reprinted in *Valuing the Earth: Economics, Ecology, Ethics*, ed. Herman Daly and Kenneth Townsend (Cambridge, MA: MIT Press, 1993), 116.

86 Technically, this is known as 'operationalization in reverse.'

87 Arne Naess, 'The Shallow and the Deep, Long Range Ecology Movements: A Summary,' originally published in *Inquiry* Oslo, 16 (1973): 95–100. http://www.alamut.com/subj/ideologies/pessimism/Naess_deepEcology.html.

88 Daly and Cobb, *For the Common Good*, 113–14, 121.

89 John Kenneth Galbraith, *The New Industrial State* (Boston: Houghton Mifflin, 1967).

90 The work of Costanza, who endeavours to set a monetary value on ecosystem 'services,' is addressed in a subsequent chapter.

91 Simon, 'The Grand Theory,' ch. 4 of *Ultimate Resource II.*

92 Andrew Goudie, *The Human Impact On the Natural Environment*, 5th ed. (Cambridge, MA: MIT Press, 2000), 152.

93 'Bioeconomists' reduce the study of ecosystem interactions to mere flows of energy and matter.

94 The organisms within an ecosystem constitute a *biocoenosis*, and their inanimate environment is called a *habitat*. The totality of all ecosystems on earth is the *biosphere.*

95 Odum, *Fundamentals of Ecology*, 8.

96 Ibid.

97 Worster, *Nature's Economy*, 302.

98 See Brent Ruben, 'General Systems Theory,' in *Approaches to Human Communication*, ed. Richard Budd and Brent Ruben (Rochelle Park, NJ: Hayden, 1972), ch. 7.

99 Peter Sengbusch, 'What Is an Ecosystem?' University of Hamburg, Ecology Online, 2003, http://www.biologie.uni-hamburg.de/b-online/e54/54a.htm.

100 Paul R. Ehrlich, *Human Natures: Genes, Cultures, and the Human Prospect*

(Washington, DC: Island Press, 2000), 45; see also Golley, *Ecosystem Concept in Ecology.*

101 UN, Convention on Biological Diversity, 'Sustaining Life on Earth: How the Convention on Biological Diversity Promotes Nature and Human Well-Being,' n.d., http://www.biodiv.org/doc/publications/guide.asp.

102 Suzuki with McConnell, *Sacred Balance,* 124.

103 Ibid., 124–6.

104 Ehrlich, *Human Natures,* 61.

105 Jane Jacobs, *The Nature of Economies* (Toronto: Random House Canada, 2000), 19.

106 John Phillips, 'The Biotic Community,' *Journal of Ecology* 19 (1931): 20; as quoted in Golley, *Ecosystem Concept in Ecology,* 12.

107 Worster, *Nature's Economy,* 302.

108 Charles Elton, *Animal Ecology* (1927), cited in Peter J. Bowler, *The Environmental Sciences* (New York: Norton, 1992), 529.

109 Odum, *Fundamentals of Ecology,* 8.

110 Suzuki with McConnell, *Sacred Balance,* 130.

111 Alfred Russel Wallace, *Contributions to the Theory of Natural Selection: A Series of Essays* (1870; New York: AMS Press, 1973), 314.

112 Ibid.

113 Ehrlich, *Human Natures,* 63.

114 Ibid., 64.

115 Multinational Monitor Online, *From Stewards to Shareholders,* 1993. http://multinsationalmonitor.org/hyper/issues/1993/03/mm0393-09.html.

116 Alfred, Lord Tennyson, *In Memoriam A.H.H.,* 1850, 56, 3.

117 Guy Murchie, *The Seven Mysteries Of Life, An Exploration in Science & Philosophy* (Boston: Houghton Mifflin, 1978).

118 Ibid., 475.

119 Naess, 'Shallow and Deep.'

120 Ibid.

121 David Frisby, preface to the 2nd ed. of Georg Simmel, *The Philosophy of Money,* ed. David Frisby (London: Routledge: 1990), xxvii.

122 Matthias Ruth, *Integrating Economics, Ecology and Thermodynamics* (Dordrecht: Kluwer Academic Publishers, 1993), 48.

123 Nicholas Georgescu-Roegen, *The Entropy Law and the Economic Process* (Cambridge, MA: Harvard University Press, 1971), 129.

124 The distinctions made here are between *isolated systems,* for which there are no throughputs, whether of matter or energy; *closed systems,* where there is no throughput of matter, but for which energy throughputs exist; and *open*

systems, where matter and energy are taken in from outside and degraded forms thereof expelled from the system.

125 Odum, *Fundamentals of Ecology,* 37.

126 Ruth, *Integrating Economics, Ecology and Thermodynamics,* 49.

127 Herman Daly and Joshua Farley, *Ecological Economics: Principles and Applications* (Washington, DC: Island Press, 2004), 70.

128 Hubbert, 'Exponential Growth,' 116. See also Hubbert, 'M. King Hubbert on Growth,' Testimony before The Subcommittee on the Environment of the Committee on Interior and Insular Affairs House of Representatives, 6 June 1974, http://www.technocracy.org/articles/hub-gro.html.

129 Ehrlich, *Human Natures,* 321.

130 Clive Ponting, *A Green History of the World: The Environment and the Collapse of Great Civilizations* (New York: Penguin, 1991), 7.

131 See Worster, *Nature's Economy,* 301–10.

132 Odum, *Fundamentals of Ecology,* 5–6

133 Golley, 194, 205.

134 Jacobs, *The Nature of Economies,* 10.

3. Ancient Syntheses

1 Lynn White Jr, 'The Historical Roots of Our Ecological Crisis,' *Science* 155, no. (10 March 1967): 1203–7, reprinted in *This Sacred Earth: Religion, Nature, Environment,* ed. Roger S. Gottlieb (New York: Routledge, 1996), 184–93. Also available at http://www.geocities.com/Yosemite/Falls/6185/lynwqhite.htm.

2 Eugene C. Hargrove, *The Foundations of Environmental Ethics* (Englewood Cliffs, NJ: Prentice Hall, 1989), 33.

3 John Passmore, *Man's Responsibility for Nature: Ecological Problems and Western Traditions* (New York: Scribner's, 1974). See also David E. Cooper, 'John Passmore,' in *Fifty Key Thinkers on the Environment,* ed. Joy A. Palmer (London: Routledge, 2001), 216–21.

4 Hargrove, *Foundations of Environmental Ethics,* 33.

5 Ibid., ch. 1.

6 David Suzuki with Amanda McConnell, *The Sacred Balance: Rediscovering Our Place in Nature* (Vancouver: Greystone Books, 1997), 191.

7 Quoted in W.C. Dampier, *A History of Science and Its Relation with Philosophy and Religion,* 4th ed. (Cambridge: Cambridge University Press, 1961), 23–4.

8 Ibid., Dampier, *History of Science,* 29.

9 Timothy McDermott, introduction, to *Selected Philosophical Writings,* by

Thomas Aquinas, ed. and trans. Timothy McDermott (Oxford: Oxford University Press, 1993), xiv.

10 G. Wiegleb, 'Lecture Notes on the History of Ecology and Nature Conservation,' 2000, 8, http://www.tu-cottbus.de/BTU/Fak4/AllgOeko/erm/erm1.htm.

11 Ibid., 8.

12 Aristotle, *The Politics*, Book I, viii, trans. T.A. Sinclair, rev. Trevor J. Saunders (London: Penguin, 1981), 79.

13 Aristotle, *De Anima*, Book I, ch 2, trans. J.A. Smith, in *Introduction to Aristotle*, 2nd, rev. ed., ed. Richard McKeon (Chicago: University of Chicago Press, 1973), 1260.

14 Aristotle, *Politics*, Book I, v, 68.

15 George Boger, 'Aristotle on the Intention and Extension of Person and the Focal Concern of Environmental Philosophy,' in *Philosophy and Ecology: Greek Philosophy and the Environment*, ed. Konstantine Boudouris and Kostas Kalimtzis (Athens: International Center for Greek Philosophy and Culture, 1999), 42–3.

16 Jeremy Bentham, 'An Introduction to the Principles of Morals and Legislation,' extracted in Wesley C. Mitchell, *Types of Economic Theory*, Vol. 1, ed. Joseph Dorfman (New York: Kelley, 1967), 203.

17 According to the translator, E.S. Forester, however, neither of the two books of *Oeconomica* can be regarded as the work of Aristotle alone; the first book, for instance, contains elements derived from Xenophon. See E.S. Forester, preface to *Oeconomica*, in *The Works of Aristotle*, vol. 10, trans. W.D. Ross (London: Oxford University Press, 1921), 1343.

18 Aristotle, *The Nicomachean Ethics*, trans. David Ross, rev. J.L. Ackrill and J.O. Urmson (Oxford: Oxford University Press, 1998), Book 5, 1, 107.

19 Ibid., 110.

20 Ibid., 108.

21 Ibid., 112.

22 Ibid., 115.

23 'There will, then, be reciprocity when the terms have been equated so that as farmer is to shoemaker, the amount of the shoemaker's work is to that of the farmer's work for which it exchanges.' Ibid., 5, 119.

24 For example, the virtuous mean between cowardice and rashness is courage; between selfishness and prodigality, liberality. Most moral virtues, Aristotle maintained, are at the mean between two extremes, which due to their extremity may be considered vices. See Aristotle, *Nicomachean Ethics*. Book 2, ch. 8.

25 Aristotle, *Politics*, Book 1, 4, 64–5, and Book 1, viii x, 75–87. Daly and Cobb

explain that 'Oikonomia differs from chrematistics in three ways. First, it takes the long-run rather than the short-run view. Second, it considers costs and benefits to the whole community, not just to the parties to the transaction. Third, it focuses on concrete use value and the limited accumulation thereof, rather than on abstract exchange value and its impetus toward unlimited accumulation.' Herman E. Daly and John Cobb, *For the Common Good: Redirecting the Economy toward Community, the Environment and a Sustainable Future* (Boston: Beacon Press, 1989), 139.

26 Aristotle, *Politics*, 87.

27 Ibid., Book 1, 9, 83.

28 Ibid., 87.

29 Aristotle, *Nicomachean Ethics*, Book V, 5, 119.

30 Aristotle, *Politics*, 83–4.

31 Ibid., 60.

32 Ibid., 59.

33 Ibid., 60.

34 Ibid.

35 Aristotle, *Ethica Nicomachea*, Book 1, trans. W.D. Ross, in *Introduction to Aristotle*, ed. Richard McKeon (Chicago: Unviersity of Chicago Press, 1973), 355. Aristotle continues: 'But some limit must be set to this; for if we extend our requirement to ancestors and descendents and friends' friends we are in for an infinite series.'

36 Aristotle, *The Metaphysics*, trans. Hugh Lawson-Tancred (London: Penguin, 1998), 115.

37 John Anton, 'Aristotle and Theophrastus on Ecology,' in *Philosophy and Ecology*, vol. 1, ed. Konstantine Boudouris and Kostas Kalimtzis (Athens: Ionia Publications, 1999), 17.

38 Ibid., 18.

39 Ibid., 19.

40 White Jr, 'Our Ecological Crisis,' 184–93.

41 Clive Ponting, *A Green History of the World: The Environment and the Collapse of Great Civilizations* (New York: Penguin Books, 1991).

42 William Leiss, *The Domination of Nature* (1972; Montreal & Kingston: McGill-Queen's University Press, 1994).

43 Donald Worster, *Nature's Economy: A History of Ecological Ideas*, 2nd ed. (Cambridge: Cambridge University Press, 1994).

44 White, 'Our Ecological Crisis,' 189.

45 Ibid.

46 Ibid.

47 Actually this depiction of the pagan conception of time is oversimplified.

According to Mircea Eliade, who spent considerable time contemplating these matters, for religious people of all types there have been two conceptions of time: sacred time, whereby through ritual sacred events recur, and profane time, an 'ordinary temporal duration in which acts without religious meaning have their setting.' See Mircea Eliade, *The Sacred and the Profane: The Nature of Religion*, trans. Willard R. Trask (New York: Harcourt Brace Jovanovich, 1959), 68.

48 Jeremy Cohen, *'Be Fertile and Increase, Fill the Earth and Master It,' The Ancient and Medieval Career of a Biblical Text* (Ithaca: Cornell University Press, 1989), 5.

49 J. Philip Wogaman, 'Theological Perspective on Economics,' in *Morality of the Market*, ed. Walter Block, Geoffrey Brennan, and Kenneth Elzinga (Vancouver, BC: The Fraser Institute, 1985), 41.

50 Philippe Crabbé, 'Biblical and Ancient Greek Thought about Natural Resources and the Environment and the Latter's Continuity in the Economic Literature Up to the Physiocrats,' in *Philosophy and Ecology*, vol. 1, ed. Konstantine Boudouris and Kostas Kalimtzis (Athens: Ionia Publications, 1999), 54.

51 Wogaman, 'Theological Perspective on Economics,' 41.

52 Meir Tamari, 'Judaism and the Market Mechanism,' in *Religion, Economics and Social Thought*, ed. Walter Block and Irving Hexham (Vancouver, BC: Fraser Institute, 1985), 393–421.

53 Robert Nisbet, *History of the Idea of Progress* (New York: Basic Books, 1980), 11.

54 Ibid., 12.

55 'Do not be anxious about your life, what you shall eat, nor about your body, what you shall put on. For life is more than food, and the body more than clothing ... Instead, seek [God's] kingdom, and these things shall be yours as well' (Luke 12:22–3, 31).

56 'You know that the rulers of the Gentiles lord it over them, and their great men exercise authority over them. It shall not be so among you: but whoever would be great among you must be your servant, and whoever would be first among you must be your slave; even as the Son of man came not to be served but to serve, and to give his life as a ransom for many' (Matthew 21:25–8).

57 Riches, avarice, and worldly gain, were personified as Mammon, a false god, in the New Testament.

58 Nisbet, *Idea of Progress*, 64–7.

59 Paul Johnson, *A History of Christianity* (New York: Atheneum, 1976), 122.

60 George Grant, *Time As History* (Toronto: CBC Learning Systems, 1969).

61 Paul Johnson explained the distinction well: 'The Jews, then, are unanimous in seeing history as a reflection of God's activity; the past was not a series of

haphazard events but unrolled remorselessly according to a divine plan which was also a blueprint and code of instructions for the future.' Johnson, *History of Christianity*, 10.

62 Toshio Kuwako, 'The Possibility of Environmental Discourse in Aristotle,' in *Philosophy and Ecology*, ed. Boudouris and Kalintzis, 113.

63 Johnson, *History of Christianity*, 76.

64 Ibid., 126.

65 Ibid.

66 McDermott, introduction, xiv.

67 Thomas Aquinas, *Summa Theologica*, extracted in Aquinas, *Selected Philosophical Writings*, 378–9.

68 Ibid.

69 Ibid., 378–9.

70 R.H. Tawney, *Religion and the Rise of Capitalism: A Historical Study* (1926; New York: Mentor, 1954), 25.

71 Ibid., 25.

72 Thomas Aquinas, *Summa Theologica*, cited in Bernard W. Dempsey, 'Just Price in a Functional Economy,' *American Economic Review*, 35 (1935): 471–86; reprinted in *Economic Thought: A Historical Anthology*, ed. James A. Gherity (New York: Random House, 1965), 4–23.

73 Herbert Heaton, *Economic History of Europe*, rev. ed. (New York: Harper and Row, 1948), 193.

74 Dempsey, 'Just Price in a Functional Economy,' 5.

75 Tawney, *Rise of Capitalism*, 43.

76 Heaton, *Economic History of Europe*, 191.

77 Tawney, *Rise of Capitalism*, 55.

78 Lewis Mumford, *The Pentagon of Power: The Myth of the Machine* (New York: Harcourt Brace Jovanovich, 1964), 7–8.

79 The start of the Protestant Reformation is often given the date of 31 October 1517, with Martin Luther on that day nailing his ninety-five theses to the door of Castle Church at Wittenberg; these theses, in Latin, opposed the sale of indulgences (release from temporal penalties for sin through the payment of money). Of course Luther had precursors, for example, John Wycliffe (1330–84), who a century and a half previous had attacked what he saw as corruption in the Church.

80 Max Weber, *The Protestant Ethic and the Spirit of Capitalism*, trans. Talcott Parsons (New York: Charles Scribner's, 1976), 40.

81 Ibid., 48–50.

82 Ibid., 51.

83 Ibid.

84 Ibid., 52.
85 Ibid. (emphasis added).
86 Jane Jacobs, *Systems of Survival: A Dialogue on the Moral Foundations of Commerce and Business* (New York: Vintage, 1992).
87 John Wesley, 'Causes of the Inefficacy of Christianity,' Sermon 16, Dublin, 1789, http://gbgm-umc.org/umhistory/wesley/sermons/serm-116.stm.

4. Shattering the Synthesis: Hobbes, Smith, and Neoclassicism

1 Peter Dickens, *Society & Nature: Changing Our Environment, Changing Ourselves* (Cambridge: Polity, 2004), 2.
2 Richard Tuck, introduction to *Leviathan*, by Thomas Hobbes, ed. Richard Tuck (Cambridge: Cambridge University Press, 1991), xl.
3 Jacob Bronowski and Bruce Mazlish, *The Western Intellectual Tradition: From Leonardo to Hegel* (New York: Harper & Row, 1960). The other influential book cited by Bronowski is *Two Treatises of Government* by John Locke (1690), which set out a defence of parliamentary government, as opposed to the defence of the monarchy and the absolutist state as endorsed by Hobbes.
4 Tuck, introduction to *Leviathan*, ix; see also C.B. Macpherson, introduction to *Leviathan*, by Thomas Hobbes (London: Penguin Books, 1968), 14.
5 Roger E. Backhouse, *The Ordinary Business of Life* (Princeton, NJ: Princeton University Press, 2002), 53.
6 Tuck, introduction to Hobbes, *Leviathan*.
7 Herbert Heaton, *Economic History of Europe*, rev. ed. (New York: Harper & Row, 1948), 309.
8 Karl Polyani, *The Great Transformation: The Political and Economic Origins of Our Time* (1944; Boston: Beacon Press, 1957), 178.
9 Heaton writes, 'The villein ... was a "customary tenant." Any arrangement, privilege, or obligation that had been accepted "since time whereof the memory of man runs not to the contrary" had thereby gained in his eyes the immutability of the hills and the right to continue unchanged. Its basis was not a document, but human memory.' Heaton, *Economic History of Europe*, 92.
10 E.P. Thompson, *The Making of the English Working Class* (Harmondsworth, UK: Pelican Books, 1968), 237.
11 Ibid., 237–8.
12 Maurice Dobb, *Studies in the Development of Capitalism*, rev. ed. (New York: International Publishers, 1963), 123–76.
13 Max Weber, *The Protestant Ethic and the Spiri of Capitalism* (1904–5; New York: Scribner's, 1958).

14 Heaton, *Economic History of Europe*, 219.

15 The mercantilist policy of imperialism proved to be exceedingly detrimental to the environment. Part and parcel of colonialism was both a commodification of nature and an ideology of 'taming the wilderness.' As Benton and Short note, with commodification, beaver pelts in the New World, for example, became valued according to their *exchange value* in international markets rather than their *use value* to indigenous hunters. With commodification, what 'had been a communal resource became a private appropriation, a source of individual wealth and individual aggrandizement.' Market forces and the system of relative prices supplanted sanctions and restrictions regarding overhunting, and for the first time native populations faced the prospect of hunger and starvation. Throughout the Americas native populations were decimated, whether through warfare, disease, or the anomie instigated by an economy based on individualism and intense commodification. For mercantilist writers and others sympathetic to their cause, such tragedies if lamentable were all but inevitable, and marked 'progress' in the sense of material gain, 'taming the wilderness,' and spreading 'civilization.' Lisa M. Benton and John Rennie Short, *Environmental Discourse and Practice* (Oxford: Blackwell, 1999), 29.

16 Wesley C. Mitchell, *Types of Economic Theory: From Mercantilism to Institutionalism*, vol. 1, ed. Joseph Dorfman (New York: Augustus M. Kelley Publishers, 1967), 104.

17 Ibid.

18 C.B. Macpherson, *The Political Theory of Possessive Individualism: Hobbes to Locke* (London: Oxford, 1962), 30.

19 'During the time men live without a common Power to keep them all in awe, they are in that condition which is called Warre; and such a Warre as is of every man, against every man.' Hobbes, *Leviathan*, ed. Richard Tuck (1651; Cambridge: Cambridge University Press, 1991), 185.

20 'So that in the nature of man, we find three principall causes of quarell. First, Competition; Secondly, Diffidence; Thirdly, Glory. The first maketh men invade for Gain; the second, for Safety; and the third, for Reputation. The first use Violence, to make themselves Masters of other men's persons, wives, children, and chattell; the second, to defend them; the third, for trifles.' Ibid., Hobbes, *Leviathan*, 88.

21 Ibid., 223.

22 Cf. Macpherson, *Possessive Individualism.*

23 Hobbes, *Leviathan*, 89.

24 Ibid., 188.

25 Ibid., 189.

26 Ibid., 190.
27 Ibid.
28 Ibid., 227.
29 Ibid., 202.
30 One of the early theorists of mercantilism, Thomas Mun, published *England's Treasure by Forraign Trade* in 1664, little more than a decade after Hobbes published *Leviathan*; on the continent, another name associated with mercantilism was Jean-Baptiste Colbert, who lived between 1619 and 1693. See Joseph Schumpeter, *History of Economic Analysis,* ed. Elizabeth Boody Schumpeter (New York: Oxford University Press, 1952), 196, 147.
31 Bronowski and Mazlish, *Western Intellectual Tradition,* 196.
32 Although he paid lip service to the medieval principle of final cause in terms of the Supreme Being, 'for all practical purposes,' Bronowski remarked, 'he put it to one side.' Ibid., 198.
33 Hobbes, *Leviathan,* 9.
34 Ibid., 15.
35 Ibid., 38.
36 Ibid., 39 (emphasis added).
37 Ibid., 151.
38 Ibid., 150.
39 Ibid., 152.
40 The following from Hobbes's *Leviathan,* 39, is particularly illuminating: 'But whatsoever is the object of any man's Appetite or Desire; that is it, which he for his part calleth *Good:* And the object of his Hate, and Aversion, *Evill;* And of his Contempt, *Vile* and *Inconsiderable.* For these words of Good, Evill, and Contemptible, are ever used with relation to the person that useth them: There being nothing simply and absolutely so; nor any common Rule of Good and Evill, to be taken from the nature of the objects themselves; but from the Person of the man (where there is no Common-Wealth;) or, (in a Common-wealth,) from the Person that representeth it; or from an Arbitrator or Judge, whom men disagreeing shall by consent set up, and make his sentence the Rule thereof.'
41 Ibid., 168–9.
42 Ibid., 197.
43 Ibid., 202.
44 'A Multitude of men, are made *One* Person, when they are by one man, or Person, Represented.' Ibid., 220.
45 Note how closely the following from Jeremy Bentham (1748–1832), classical political economist and father of utilitarianism, echoes Hobbes on Appetite and Aversion: 'Nature has placed mankind under the governance of two sov-

ereign masters, *pain* and *pleasure.* It is for them alone to point out what we ought to do, as well as to determine what we shall do. On the one hand the standard of right and wrong, on the other the chain of causes and effects, are fastened to their throne.' Jeremy Bentham, 'An Introduction to the Principles of Morals and Legislation,' 1798, quoted in Mitchell, *Types of Economic Theory*, 203.

46 Max Lerner, introduction to *The Wealth of Nations*, by Adam Smith (New York: Random House, 1937), v. Nor is Lerner alone. Wesley Mitchell, for example, declares that most histories of economic thought begin with Adam Smith, 'because his formulation was the earliest which exercised a potent influence upon the work of later times.' Mitchell, *Types of Economic Theory*, 48–9.

47 Bronowski and Mazlish, *Western Intellectual Tradition*, 342.

48 Backhouse, *Ordinary Business of Life*, 123; Warren J. Samuels, *The Classical Theory of Economic Policy* (Cleveland, OH: The World Publishing Company, 1966), 21–97; see also, D.D. Raphael and A.L. Macfie, introduction to *The Theory of Moral Sentiments*, by Adam Smith (Indianapolis, IN: Liberty Press, 1982), 21.

49 Warren J. Samuels, personal communication, 21 December 2003. See Smith's addition as preface to the sixth edition of *Moral Sentiments.*

50 Raphael and Macfie, introduction to *Moral Sentiments*, 21.

51 Smith, *Moral Sentiments*, ed. D.D. Raphael and A.L. Macfie (1759; Indianapolis, IN: Liberty Press, 1982), 10.

52 Ibid., 43.

53 Ibid., 317.

54 Raphael and Macfie, introduction to Smith, *Moral Sentiments*, 20.

55 It is a reversal, likewise, to the position of the mercantilists who preceded him and with whom he is usually contrasted. On one matter, however, Smith and the mercantilists were agreed: the primary job of the state is to create conditions favourable to increase in the material wealth of the nation.

56 Whereas Smith helped separate political economy from moral philosophy, a subsequent narrowing was the segregation of economics from political science, and this segregation is a major difference distinguishing classical Political Economy (as practised by Smith, Marx, Ricardo, Bentham, Malthus, and James Mill) from modern (neoclassical) economics.

57 Smith, *Moral Sentiments*, 25.

58 Smith was well aware of Hobbes's work, and addresses his position at 318–19 of *Moral Sentiments;* there is but one brief allusion to Hobbes in *Wealth of Nations* (at 31).

59 Ibid., Smith, *Moral Sentiments*, 9.

60 The competitive struggle for existence, an aspect of ecosystem relations, is addressed below.
61 Adam Smith, *The Wealth of Nations*, ed. Edwin Cannan (New York: Modern Library, Random House, 1937), 145.
62 Ibid., 423.
63 Ibid., 13–14.
64 Ibid., 4–5.
65 Ibid. As noted by Scott Gordon, Smith was not the first to point out the economic consequences of specialization; this was treated by both Plato and Aristotle. What Smith did, according to Gordon, was to take this old idea and use it 'as the launching pad for a general theory of social organization.' Scott Gordon, *The History and Philosophy of Social Science* (London: Routledge, 1994), 137.
66 Smith, *Wealth of Nations*, Book 5, Article II, 735. Emphasis added.
67 Ibid., 737.
68 Ibid., 734–5.
69 Ibid., 17.
70 Ibid.
71 Mitchell, *Types of Economic Theory*, 51.
72 Smith, *Wealth of Nations*, 17–21.
73 Ibid., 4–5.
74 Ibid., 22–9.
75 Ibid., 55.
76 Ibid.
77 Ibid., 58.
78 Ibid., 78–80.
79 Bronowski and Mazlish, *Western Intellectual Tradition*, 349.
80 See note 82 below.
81 Smith, *Wealth of Nations*, Book 5, introduction, 397.
82 We can speculate on the reasons for this narrowing. First, it can be argued, this was part of a trend in all branches of knowledge: as knowledge deepens, it becomes more specialized; hence economists left important matters to psychologists, political scientists, and sociologists, as they specialized in price theory and macroeconomic indicators. Second, there were 'errors' or confusions in classical political economy, particularly concerning value, and neoclassical economics is distinguishable from classical political economy in part for proposing a new theory of value (see below). Third, by abstracting from class relations and other institutional arrangements, neoclassical economics suited well the ideological or propaganda needs of groups with wealth and power.

83 Ben B. Seligman, *Main Currents in Modern Economics: Economic Thought since 1870* (New York: Free Press of Glencoe, 1962), 257.

84 William Stanley Jevons, *Theory of Political Economy*, 3, quoted in Seligman, *Modern Economics*, 260. Economics is not entirely univocal, there being even today, for example, a marginalized tributary, acknowledged in a few universities, known as *institutional economics*, which indeed endeavours to take into account the political, social, and cultural setting within which economic activities take place.

85 Charles Perring, *Economy and Environment: A Theoretical Essay on the Interdependence of Economic and Environmental Systems* (Cambridge: Cambridge University Press, 1987), 153.

86 Moreover, according to the maxim *De Gustibus non est disputandum*, tastes and preferences are not considered subjects for investigation by economists, hence ruling out culture, persuasion, influence, and the broader social setting as objects for economic enquiry.

87 Milton Friedman, 'The Social Responsibility of Business Is to Increase Its Profits,' *New York Times* (1970). Reprinted in *Contemporary Issues in Business Ethics*, ed. Joseph R. Desjardins and John J. McCall (Belmont, CA: Wadsworth, 1985), 21–5.

88 Milton Friedman, *Essays in Positive Economics* (Chicago: University of Chicago Press, 1953), chapter 1.

5. Environmental vs Ecological Economics

1 Robert E. Babe, 'The Political Economy of Information and Communication,' in *An Institutionalist Approach to Public Utilities Regulation*, ed. Warren J. Samuels and Edythe Miller (East Lansing: Michigan State University Press, 2002).

2 George Stigler, 'The Economics of Information,' *Journal of Political Economy* 69 (1961), reprinted in *The Organization of Industry* (Homewood, IL: Irwin, 1968): 171–90; and 'Information in the Labor Market,' *Journal of Political Economy* 70 (1962), reprinted in *Organization of Industry*, 191–207. For a critique see Robert E. Babe, *Communication and the Transformation of Economics* (Boulder, CO: Westview Press, 1995).

3 Robert E. Babe, 'Information and Communication.'

4 John Foster, 'Introduction: Environmental Value and the Scope of Economics,' in *Valuing Nature?: Economics, Ethics and Environment*, ed. John Foster (London: Routledge, 1997), 6.

5 Geoffrey Hodgson, 'Economics, Environmental Policy and the Transcendence of Utilitarianism,' in *Valuing Nature?*, 48.

6 Alfred Marshall, *Principles of Economics: An Introductory Volume*, 8th ed. (London: Macmillan, 1947), 266.

7 A.C. Pigou, *The Economics of Welfare*, 4th ed. (London: Macmillan, 1932), 131–5.

8 As Pigou put it, 'It is as idle to expect a well-planned town to result from the independent activities of isolated speculators as it would be to expect a satisfactory picture to results if each separate square inch were painted by an independent artist. No "invisible hand" can be relied on to produce a good arrangement of the whole from a combination of separate treatments of the parts. It is, therefore, necessary that an authority of wider reach should intervene and should tackle the collective problems of beauty, of air and of light, as those other collective problems of gas and water have been tackled.' Ibid., 195.

9 R.H. Coase, 'The Problem of Social Cost,' *Journal of Law and Economics* 3 (1960): 8.

10 Ibid., 42.

11 OECD, Nuclear Energy Agency, 'Chernobyl: Assessment of Radiological and Health Impacts, *2002 Update of Chernobyl: Ten Years On*,' ch. 2, http://www.nea.fr/html/rp/chernobyl/chernobyl.html.

12 Anthony C. Fisher and Frederick M. Peterson, 'The Environment in Economics: A Survey,' *Journal of Economic Literature* 14, no. 1 (1976): 1–33.

13 Coase, 'Social Cost,' 37. Coase drew a number of his examples from Pigou, but not, however, the one concerning the manure pile.

14 John O'Neill, 'Value Pluralism: Incommensurability and Institutions,' in *Valuing Nature?*, 79.

15 George Stigler, *Memoirs of an Unregulated Economist* (New York: Basic Books, 1988).

16 Coase also wrote one other very famous article, 'The Nature of the Firm,' *Economica* 4, no. 16 (1937): 386–405. It was largely on the basis of the two papers that he was awarded the Nobel Prize.

17 Barbara Rippel, 'Tradable CO_2 Emissions Permits: Problems with the "Perfect" Solution?' A study prepared for the National Consumer Coalition under the auspices of Consumer Alert, 25 November 1997; available at http://www.consumeralert.org/pubs/Study/ets.htm.

18 Friends of the Earth, Public Citizen, *NAFTA Chapter 11 Investor-to-State Cases: Bankrupting Democracy Lessons for Fast Track and the Free Trade Area of the Americas* (Washington, DC: Public Citizen's Global Trade Watch, 2001), 2–5, http://www.citizen.org/trade/nafta/CH_11/index.cfm.

19 Ibid.

20 *Ethyl Inc. v. Canada.* Reported at: http://government.cce.cornell.edu/doc/pdf/EthylAp.pdf.

21 Summary, *Ethyl Inc. v. Canada*, reported at ibid.

22 Friends of the Earth, *Bankrupting Democracy*, 10.

23 Ibid., 9.

24 Ibid., 10.

25 Public Citizen, 'The Ten Year Tack Record of the North American Free Trade Agreement Undermining Sovereignty and Democracy,' 2004, http://www.citizen.org/documents/NAFTA_10_democracy.pdf.

26 Melinda Steffen, 'Protectionism or Legitimate Regulation? A Hope for Clarity in the Murky Waters of Chapter Eleven's Expropriation Provisions,' n.d., http://www.kentlaw.edu/perritt/honorsscholars/steffen.html.

27 Quoted in Kathryn Fredericks, *Dispute Resolution in NAFTA's Investor-State Chapter: A Shift to Market-Dominated Governance*, Institute of Political Economy, Carleton University, May 2005, 62.

28 Ian Willis, *Economics and the Environment: A Signalling and Incentive Approach* (St Leonards, Australia: Allen and Unwin, 1997), viii.

29 Ibid., 51.

30 Ibid., viii.

31 Ibid., 5.

32 Ibid.

33 Ibid., 29.

34 Ibid., 56–7.

35 Ibid., 57.

36 Ibid., 72.

37 Ibid., 101.

38 Ibid., 82

39 Ibid., 216.

40 Ibid.

41 Ibid., 217.

42 Ibid., 18.

43 Ibid.

44 Ibid.

45 Ibid.

46 'Potlatch,' *Encyclopedia of North American Indians* (New York: Houghton Mifflin, n.d.), http://college.hmco.com/history/readerscomp/naind/html/na_030900_ potlatch.htm.

47 D. Pearce et al., *Blueprint for a Green Economy* (London: Earthscan Books, 1989), 115; cited in O'Neill, 'Value Pluralism.' 77.

48 Robert Costanza et al., 'The Value of the World's Ecosystem Services and

Natural Capital,' *Nature*, 387 (15 May 1997): 253–60, http://www.uvm.edu/giee/publications/Nature_Paper.pdf.

49 Ibid., 259.

50 Ibid.

51 The book won the Association of Environmental and Resource Economists prize for 'Publication of Enduring Quality' for 2002.

52 A. Myrick Freeman III, *The Measurement of Environmental and Resource Values* (Washington, DC: Resources for the Future, 2003), xxvii.

53 Ibid., 2.

54 Ibid.

55 Ibid., 3.

56 Costanza et al., 'Natural Capital,' 256.

57 Freeman, *Environmental and Resource Values*, 7.

58 Ibid., 9.

59 Ibid., 24–5.

60 Ibid., 24–6.

61 Ibid., 3.

62 Arild Vatn and Daniel W. Bromley, 'Choices without Prices without Apologies,' in *The Handbook of Environmental Economics*, ed. Daniel W. Bromley (Oxford: Blackwell, 1995), 17.

63 John Ralston Saul, *The Unconscious Civilization* (Toronto: Anansi, 1995), 99.

64 Robin Grove-White, 'The Environmental "Valuation" Controversy: Observations on its Recent History and Significance,' in *Valuing Nature?*, 21.

65 Herman Daly and Joshua Farley, *Ecological Economics: Principles and Applications* (Washington, DC: Island Press, 2004), 12.

66 Ibid.

67 Ibid., 15.

68 Kenneth E. Boulding, 'The Economics of the "Coming Spaceship Earth."' Paper presented at the Sixth Resources for the Future Forum on Environmental Quality in a Growing Economy, Washington, DC, 8 March 1966; published in Boulding, *Beyond Economics: Essays on Society, Religion and Ethics*, (Ann Arbor: Ann Arbor Paperbacks, University of Michigan Press, 1970), 281.

69 Ibid.

70 Ibid., 281, 282.

71 Ibid., 282.

72 Kenneth E. Boulding, *Ecodynamics: A New Theory of Societal Evolution* (Beverly Hills, CA: Sage Publications, 1978), 12, 34.

73 Ibid., 11.

74 Ibid., 33.

75 Kenneth E. Boulding, 'World Society: The Range of Possible Futures,' in *How Humans Adapt: A Biocultural Odyssey*, ed. Donald J. Ortner (Washington, DC: Smithsonian Press, 1983); reprinted in Kenneth E. Boulding and Elise Boulding, *The Future: Images and Processes* (Thousand Oaks, CA: Sage, 1995), 47.
76 Kenneth E. Boulding, 'The Limits to Societal Growth,' in *Societal Growth: Processes and Implications*, ed. Amos H. Hawley (New York: Free Press, 1979); reprinted in Boulding and Boulding, *The Future*, 27.
77 Kenneth E. Boulding, *The World as a Total System* (Newbury Park, CA: Sage, 1985), 23–4.
78 Boulding, 'Limits to Societal Growth,' 27.
79 Herman E. Daly, *Steady-State Economics*, 2nd ed. (Washington, DC: Island Press, 1991), xvi.
80 Quoted in John Gowdy and Susan Mesner, 'The Evolution of Georgescu-Roegen's Bioeconomics,' *Review of Social Economy* 56, no. 2 (1998): 136–56.
81 Nicholas Georgescu-Roegen, *Analytical Economics* (Cambridge, MA: Harvard University Press, 1966), 74. Ideas appearing in this introduction were expanded upon in his magnum opus, *The Entropy Law and the Economic Process* (Cambridge, MA: Harvard University Press, 1971).
82 Georgescu-Roegen, *Analytical Economics*, 68.
83 Ibid.
84 Ibid., 75.
85 Ibid., 68.
86 Ibid., 69.
87 Ibid., 72.
88 Ibid., 92–4.
89 Philip Mirowski, *More Heat Than Light: Economics as Social Physics, Physics as Nature's Economics* (Cambridge: Cambridge University Press, 1989).
90 Georgescu-Roegen, *Analytical Economics*, 83.
91 Ibid., 93–4.
92 Ibid., 97.
93 Georgescu-Roegen, *Entropy Law*, 19.
94 Ibid., 21.
95 Alain Alcouffe, Sylvie Ferrari, and Horst Hanusch, 'Marx, Schumpeter and Georgescu-Roegen: Three Conceptions of the Evolution of Economic Systems? Toulouse, France: Université des Sciences Sociales, February 2004, 15, http://www.univ-tlse1.fr/LIRHE/.
96 Robert L. Nadeau, *The Wealth of Nature: How Mainstream Economics Has Failed the Environment* (New York: Columbia University Press, 2003), 136.
97 Herman E. Daly, 'On Economics as a Life Science,' *Journal of Political Economy* 76 (1968): 392–406.

98 See Robert Costanza, 'The Early History of *Ecological Economics* and the International Society for Ecological Economics (ISEE),' April 2003, www.ecoeco.org/publica/encyc_entries/Costanza.doc. See also Jeroen C.J.M. van den Bergh of the Free University, Amsterdam, who writes: 'The International Society for Ecological Economics (ISEE) was founded by participants at a workshop in Barcelona in 1987, while its roots go back at least to a meeting on the integration of economics and ecology in Sweden in 1982 ... The journal *Ecological Economics* was founded in 1989 by R. Costanza and H.E. Daly, who are still its editor in-chief and associate editor, respectively. An early collection of articles aimed at defining Ecological Economics [by] Costanza and Daly [appeared in] 1987.' Jeroen C.J.M. van den Bergh, 'Ecological Economics: Themes, Approaches, and Differences with Environmental Economics,' Discussion Paper 00–080/3, Amsterdam: Tinbergen Institute, University of Amsterdam, 2000, note 1; http://www.tinbergen.nl/scripts/papers.pl?paper=00080.rdf.

99 Herman E. Daly, *Beyond Growth* (Boston: Beacon Press, 1996).

100 With Thomas Prugh, R. Costanza, J. Cumberland, R, Goodland, and R. Norgaard (Solomons, MD: ISEE Press, 1995).

101 With R. Costanza, J. Cumberland, R. Goodland, and R. Norgaard (Boca Raton, FL: St Lucie Press, 1997).

102 Herman E. Daly, *Ecological Economics* (Cheltenham, UK: Edward Elgar, 1999).

103 Herman E. Daly and Joshua Farley, *Ecological Economics: Principles and Applications* (Washington, DC: Island Press, 2004).

104 Peter Söderbaum, *Ecological Economics* (London: Earthscan, 2000), 19.

105 Van den Bergh, 'Ecological Economics,' 5.

106 Malte Faber, Reiner Manstetten, and John Proops, *Ecological Economics: Concepts and Methods* (Cheltenham, UK: Edward Elgar, 1996), 1.

107 Ibid., 2.

108 Ibid.

109 Ibid., 15.

110 Ibid.

111 Ibid., 155.

112 Ibid., 155–6.

113 Ibid., 159.

114 Arthur Koestler, *Janus: A Summing Up* (London: Pan Books, 1979).

115 Faber, Manstetten, and Proops, *Ecological Economics*, 156.

116 Ibid., 26.

117 Ibid.

118 Ibid., 35.
119 Ibid., 46.
120 Ibid., 116.
121 Ibid., 133–4. My emphasis.
122 Ibid., 169.
123 Lester R. Brown, *Eco-Economy: Building an Economy for the Earth* (Washington, DC: Norton, 2001).
124 Ibid., xv.
125 Ibid., 81.
126 Ibid., 93.
127 Ibid., 86–9.
128 Ibid., 91.
129 Brian Milani, *Designing the Green Economy: The Postindustrial Alternative to Corporate Globalization* (Lanham, MD: Rowman and Littlefield, 2000), 91. My emphasis.
130 Ibid., 92.
131 Ibid.
132 Ibid., 93.
133 Ibid.
134 Colin Hines, *Localization: A Global Manifesto* (London: Earthscan, 2000), vii.
135 Ibid., 154.
136 Ibid., 224.
137 See, for example, Environmental Health Coalition, 'Maquiladoras,' n.d., http://www.environmentalhealth.org/maquiladoras.html; and *Globalization at the Crossroads: Ten Years of NAFTA in the San Diego/Tijuana Border Region* (San Diego: Environmental Health Coalition, 2004), http://www.environmentalhealth.org/maquiladoras.html.
138 Hines, *Localization*, 154.
139 Daly and Farley, *Ecological Economics*, 255.
140 Ibid., 323.
141 Ibid., 360.
142 Ibid., 362.
143 Ibid., 376–9.
144 Ibid., 405–11.

6. Information, Entropy, and Infinite Earth

1 Harold Barnett and Chandler Morse, *Scarcity and Growth: The Economics of Natural Resource Availability* (Baltimore, MD: Johns Hopkins University Press,

1963); Mark Sagoff, 'Do We Consume Too Much?' *Atlantic Monthly*, June 1997, 80–96; http:// www.puaf.umd.edu/faculty/papers/sagoff/consume.pdf; Julian Simon, *The Ultimate Resource II: People, Materials and Environment* (Princeton, NJ: Princeton University Press, 1998), http://www.inform.umd.edu/EdRcs/Colleges/BMGT/.Faculty/JSimon/Ultimate-Resource; Bjorn Lomborg, *The Skeptical Environmentalist: Measuring the Real State of the World* (Cambridge: Cambridge University Press, 2001).

2 Clive Ponting, *A Green History of the World: The Environment and the Collapse of Great Civilizations* (New York Penguin Books, 1991); and Andrew Goudie, *The Human Impact on the Natural Environment*, 5th ed. (Cambridge, MA: MIT Press, 2000).

3 Alvin Toffler, *The Third Wave* (New York: William Morrow, 1980).

4 Manuel Castells and Martin Ince, *Conversations with Manuel Castells* (Cambridge: Polity, 2003), 73.

5 Fritz Machlup, *The Production and Distribution of Knowledge in the United States* (Princeton, NJ: Princeton University Press, 1961).

6 Marc Porat, *The Information Economy: Definition and Measurement*, Special Publication 77–12(1) (Washington, DC: Office of Telecommunication, U.S. Department of Commerce, 1977).

7 Daniel Bell, 'The Social Framework of the Information Society,' in *The Computer Age: A Twenty-Year View*, ed. M. Dertouzos and J. Moses (Cambridge, MA: MIT Press, 1979), 163–211.

8 See, for example, Frank Webster, *Theories of the Information Society* (New York: Routledge, 1995).

9 Simon Nora and Alain Minc, *The Computerization of Society* (Cambridge, MA: MIT Press, 1980), 14.

10 Claude E. Shannon and Warren Weaver, *The Mathematical Theory of Communication* (Urbana, IL: University of Illinois Press, 1949).

11 Canada, Industry Canada, *Convergence: Competition and Cooperation – Policy and Regulation Affecting Local Telephone and Cable Networks*, Report of the Co-chairs of the Local Networks Convergence Committee (Ottawa: Minister of Supply and Services, 1992), 40.

12 Manual Castells, *End of the Millennium* (Oxford: Blackwell, 1998), 370; as quoted by Darin Barney, *The Network Society* (London: Polity Press, 2004), 27.

13 Barney, *The Network Society*, 77.

14 N. Katherine Hayles, *How We Became Posthuman: Virtual Bodies in Cybernetics, Literature, and Informatics* (Chicago: University of Chicago Press, 1999), xi.

15 Ibid.

16 Armand Mattelart and Michele Mattelart, *Theories of Communication: A Short Introduction* (London: Sage, 1998), 50.

17 Norbert Wiener, *The Human Use of Human Beings: Cybernetics and Society* (1950; New York: Avon Books, 1967), 129.

18 Ibid., 130.

19 As an everyday example, suppose that a barrier separating rooms of different temperature is removed; the rooms will tend toward the same temperature – a loss of differentiation, which is to say an increase in entropy.

20 The earth, it should be added, is not an isolated system, since energy from the sun enters our atmosphere and heat is dissipated into the universe; nonetheless, through the greenhouse effect the planet is becoming more closed in the sense that less heat radiates into the universe. A further principle of entropy is that increased complexity (differentiation) in one location must be at the expense of decreased complexity elsewhere. Thus, for example, the increased differentiation of social life made possible by the use of solar energy must be 'paid for' by the loss of complexity (e.g., pollution caused by the combustion of carbon-based fuels, perhaps even species extinctions) elsewhere.

21 Kenneth Boulding, *The Image: Knowledge and Life in Society* (Ann Arbor: University of Michigan Press, 1956), 35.

22 Kenneth E. Boulding, *Ecodynamics: A New Theory of Societal Evolution* (Beverly Hills, CA: Sage, 1978), 224.

23 Gregory Bateson, *Mind and Nature: A Necessary Unity* (New York: Dutton, 1979), 99.

24 Ithiel de Sola Pool, *Technologies without Boundaries: On Telecommunications in a Global Age* (Cambridge, MA: Harvard University Press, 1990), 220.

25 John Percy Barlow, 'A Declaration of the Independence of Cyberspace,' 1996, http://www.eff.org/~barlow/Declaration-Final.html. Darin Barney notes that Barlow, co-founder of the Electronic Frontier Association, was formerly a songwriter for the Grateful Dead. Darin Barney, *Prometheus Wired: The Hope for Democracy in the Age of Network Technology* (Vancouver: UBC Press, 2000), 3.

26 Porat, *Information Economy,* 16.

27 Porat, *Information Economy.*

28 Ibid., 18.

29 Beth Allen, 'Information as an Economic Commodity,' *American Economic Review* 80, 2 (May, 1990): 269.

30 According to Kenneth Arrow, for instance, 'The meaning of information is precisely a reduction in uncertainty.' Likewise, information economist Charles Jonscher wrote: 'Demand for information arises because of the presence of uncertainty; without uncertainty there is no need for information.' See Kenneth Arrow, 'The Economics of Information,' in *The Computer-Age: A*

Twenty-Year View, ed. Michael Dertouzos and Joel Moses (Cambridge, MA: MIT Press, 1979), 307; and Charles Jonscher, 'Notes on Communication and Economic Theory,' in *Communication and Economic Development*, ed. D.M. Lamberton and M. Jussawalla (Elmsford, NY: Pergamon Press, 1982), 63. See also Robert E. Babe, 'The Place of Information in Economics,' in *Information and Communication in Economics*, ed. Robert E. Babe (Boston: Kluwer, 1994).

31 Von Weizsäcker writes that 'This "form" can refer to the form of all kinds of objects or events perceptible to the senses and capable of being shaped by man: the form of the printer's ink on paper, of chalk on the blackboard, of sound waves in air, of current flow in a wire, etc.' He adds that 'A cupboard, a tree are made of wood. Wood is their "matter" ... But the cupboard isn't simply wood, it is a wooden cupboard. "Cupboard" is what it is intrinsically; cupboard is its *eidos*, its form. But a cupboard must be made of something; a cupboard without matter is a mere thought abstracted from reality.' Carl Friedrich von Weizsäcker, *The Unity of Nature* (New York: Farrar, Straus, and Giroux, 1980), 38–9, 274.

32 Hans Christian von Baeyer, *Information: The New Language of Science* (Cambridge, MA: Harvard University Press, 2004), 17.

33 Kenneth Arrow, *Limits of Organization* (New York: Norton, 1974), 39.

34 Arrow, 'Economics of Information,' 310. My emphasis.

35 Boulding wrote: 'Matter matters. Without the right encodee [substrate or medium], encoding cannot take place. Biological evolution did not take place on the moon, and probably not on any other planet in the solar system, because of the absence of certain coding materials such as water or carbon compounds. Similarly energy matters because energy moves matter, transports it, transforms it, and rearranges it into encodeable forms. Energy can also encode information directly.' Boulding, *Ecodynamics*, 33–4.

36 Boulding admits that ultimately *applications* or concrete manifestations of information/knowledge may be constrained by matter/energy, but he nonetheless contends that information/knowledge per se is unconstrained. He writes: '[Knowledge] is the only thing that can really change, the only thing that is not conserved ... The realization of knowledge into things, organizations, and persons, of course, will be limited by the absence of energy or materials. Energy and materials, however, are limiting factors rather than creative factors. The increase in knowledge furthermore pushes back these limits continually as new energy and new materials are discovered, although there may be an ultimate limit to this process.' Ibid., 224–5.

37 BBC, 'Big Boost for US Military Spending,' 24 January 2002, http://news.bbc.co.uk/1/hi/world/americas/1778681.stm.

38 Brent D. Ruben, 'General Systems Theory,' in *Approaches to Human Communication*, ed. Richard W. Budd and Brent D. Ruben (Rochelle Park, NJ: Hayden Book Company, 1972), 134.
39 Jane Jacobs, *The Nature of Economies* (Toronto: Random House Canada, 2000), 16, 15.
40 Ibid., 17.
41 Ibid., 19.
42 Boulding, *Ecodynamics*, 13.
43 E.F. Schumacher, *Small Is Beautiful: Economics as if People Mattered* (London: Abacus, 1974), 11.

Conclusion

1 Henry David Thoreau, 'Huckleberries,' in *The Natural History Essays*, ed. Robert Sattelmeyer (Salt Lake City, UT: Peregrine Smith, 1980), 211–62, cited in Donald Worster, *Nature's Economy: A History of Ecological Ideas*, 2nd ed. (Cambridge: Cambridge University Press, 1994), 75.
2 Eugene Odum, *Fundamentals of Ecology*, 3rd ed. (Philadelphia: W.B. Saunders, 1971), 510.
3 Alanna Mitchell, 'Coalition Aims to Save Boreal Forest: Natives, Environmentalists, Industry Allied in Bid to Preserve Half of Country's Area,' *Globe and Mail*, 1 December 2003, 16.
4 Garett Hardin, 'The Tragedy of the Commons,' in *Valuing the Earth: Economics, Ecology, Ethics*, ed. Herman E. Daly and Kenneth N. Townsend. (Cambridge, MA: MIT Press, 1993), 127–43; first published in *Science* 162 (13, December 1968): 1243–8. Note, however, that Hardin's case differs from the foregoing. Thoreau did not envisage a 'commons' to be used for resource extraction; it was to be left alone. Co-signors of the Boreal Forest Conservation Framework did not envisage the land as a 'commons' bereft of ownership, and large portions were to remain in pristine condition. Nonetheless, Hardin's 'Tragedy of the Commons' is relevant to the discussion and is a support for those advocating private property and commodity exchange as a means of addressing environmental issues.
5 Hardin, 'Tragedy of the Commons,' 132.
6 Ibid., 133.
7 Ibid., 133–4.
8 In a subsequent essay, Hardin is even more insistent: 'Action is what we must have now that the world is overcrowded – action in the form of rejecting the commons as a distribution system. Failing that, a tragic end is our

fate.' Garrett Hardin, 'Second Thoughts on "The Tragedy of the Commons,"' in Daly and Townsend, eds., *Valuing the Earth*, 145.

9 Daly and Farley, *Ecological Economics*, 261.

10 Aldo Leopold, 'The Land Ethic,' *A Sand County Almanac* (Oxford: Oxford University Press, 2001); first published in 1948; available at: http://www.tipiglen.dircon.co.uk/landethic.html.

Bibliography

Books and Scholarly and Professional Articles

Allen, Beth. 'Information as an Economic Commodity.' *American Economic Review* 80, no. 2 (1990): 268–73.

Anderson, Terry L, and Donald R. Leal. *Free Market Environmentalism.* Rev. ed. New York: St Martin's Press, 2001.

Anton, John P. 'Aristotle and Theophrastus on Ecology.' In *Philosophy and Ecology*, vol. 1, edited by Konstantine Boudouris and Kostas Kalimtzis, 15–27. Athens: Iona Publications, 1999.

Aquinas, Thomas. *Summa Theologica.* In *Selected Philosophical Writings*, translated by Timothy McDermott. Oxford: Oxford University Press, 1993.

Aristotle. *De Anima.* In *Introduction to Aristotle*, edited by Richard McKeon, translated by J.A. Smith. 2nd ed., Chicago: University of Chicago Press, 1973.

– *The Metaphysics.* Translated by Hugh Lawson-Tancred. London: Penguin Books, 1998.

– *The Nicomachean Ethics.* Translated by David Ross. Revised by J.L. Ackrill and J.O. Urmson. Oxford: Oxford University Press, 1998.

– *The Politics.* Translated by T.A. Sinclair. Revised and re-presented by Trevor J. Saunders. London: Penguin Books, 1981.

Arrow, Kenneth. 'The Economics of Information.' In *The Computer-Age: A Twenty-Year View*, edited by Michael Dertouzos and Joel Moses, 306–17. Cambridge, MA: MIT Press, 1979.

– *The Limits of Organization.* New York: Norton, 1974.

Babe, Robert E. *Canadian Communication Thought: Ten Foundational Writers.* Toronto: University of Toronto Press, 2000.

– *Communication and the Transformation of Economics.* Boulder, CO: Westview Press, 1995.

– Foreword to *Automating Interaction.* by Myles Ruggles. Cresskill, NJ: Hampton Press, 2005.
– 'Innis, Saul, Suzuki.' *Topia*, Spring 2004, 11–20.
– 'The Political Economy of Information and Communication.' In *An Institutionalist Approach to Public Utilities Regulation*, edited by Warren J. Samuels and Edythe Miller, 99–126. East Lansing: Michigan State University Press, 2002.
– 'Understanding the Cultural Ecology Model.' In *Cultural Ecology: The Changing Dynamics of Communications*, edited by Danielle Cliche, 1–23. London: International Institute of Communication, 1997.
Backhouse, Roger E. *The Ordinary Business of Life.* Princeton, NJ: Princeton University Press, 2002.
Baeyer, Hans Christian von. *Information: The New Language of Science.* Cambridge, MA: Harvard, 2004
Barnett, Harold, and Chandler Morse. *Scarcity and Growth: The Economics of Natural Resource Availability.* Baltimore: Johns Hopkins University Press, 1963.
Barney, Darin. *The Network Society.* Cambridge: Polity, 2004.
– *Prometheus Wired: The Hope for Democracy in the Age of Network Technology.* Vancouver: University of British Columbia Press, 2000.
Bateson, Gregory. *Mind and Nature: A Necessary Unity.* New York: Dutton, 1979.
Beder, Sharon. *Global Spin: The Corporate Assault on Environmentalism.* White River Junction, VT: Chelsea Green, 1998.
Bell, Daniel. 'The Social Framework of the Information Society.' In *The Computer Age: A Twenty-Year View*, edited by M. Dertouzos and J. Moses, 163–211. Cambridge, MA: MIT Press, 1979.
Beltway, Christopher. *Environmental Philosophy: Reason, Nature and Human Concern.* Montreal & Kingston: McGill-Queen's University Press, 2001.
Benton, Lisa M., and John Rennie Short. *Environmental Discourse and Practice.* Oxford: Blackwell, 1999.
Bertalanffy, Ludwig von. *A Systems View of Man.* Edited by Paul A. LaViolette. Boulder, CO: Westview Press, 1981.
Boger, George. 'Aristotle on the Intention and Extension of Person and the Focal Concern of Environmental Philosophy.' In *Philosophy and Ecology: Greek Philosophy and the Environment*, edited by Konstantine Boudouris and Kostas Kalimtzis, Athens, 32–58. International Center for Greek Philosophy and Culture, 1999.
Boller, Peter F., Jr. *American Thought in Transition: The Impact of Evolutionary Naturalism 1865–1900.* Chicago: Rand McNally, 1969.
Boman, Mattias, Runar Brännlund, and Bengt Krisröm, eds. *Topics in Environmental Economics.* Boston: Kluwer, 1999.
Boudouris, Konstantine. 'The Moral, Political and Metaphysical Causes of the

Ecological Crisis.' In *Philosophy and Ecology: Greek Philosophy and the Environment*, vol. 2, edited by Konstantine Boudouris and Kostas Kalimtzis, 59–72. Athens: International Association for Greek Philosophy and Culture, 1999.

Boudouris, Konstantine, and Kostas Kalimtzis, eds. *Philosophy and Ecology: Greek Philosophy and the Environment*, vols. 1 and 2. Athens: International Association for Greek Philosophy and Culture, 1999.

Boulding, Elise, and Kenneth E. Boulding. *The Future: Images and Processes.* Thousand Oaks, CA: Sage, 1995.

Boulding, Kenneth E. *Ecodynamics: A New Theory of Societal Evolution.* Beverly Hills, CA: Sage, 1978.

– 'The Economics of the "Coming Spaceship Earth."' In *Beyond Economics: Essays on Society, Religion and Ethics*, 275–87. Ann Arbor: University of Michigan Press, 1970.

– *The Image: Knowledge and Life in Society.* Ann Arbor: University of Michigan Press, 1956.

– 'The Limits to Societal Growth.' In *Societal Growth: Processes and Implications*, edited by Amos H. Hawley, 1979. Reprinted in Boulding and Boulding, *The Future*, 26–38.

– *A Primer on Social Dynamics: History as Dialectics and Development*, New York: Free Press, 1970.

– *The Skills of the Economist*, Toronto: Clarke, Irwin, 1958.

– 'World Society: The Range of Possible Futures.' In *How Human Adapt: A Biocultural Odyssey*, edited by Donald J. Ortner. Washington, DC: Smithsonian Press, 1983. Reprinted in Kenneth E. Boulding and Elise Boulding, *The Future: Images and Processes*, 39–56. Thousand Oaks, CA: Sage, 1995.

Bowler, Peter J. *The Environmental Sciences.* New York: Norton, 1992.

Bronowski, Jacob, and Bruce Mazlish. *The Western Intellectual Tradition: From Leonardo to Hegel.* New York: Harper and Row, 1960.

Brown, Lester R. *Eco-Economy: Building an Economy for the Earth.* New York: Norton, 2001.

Canada, Industry Canada. *Convergence: Competition and Cooperation – Policy and Regulation Affecting Local Telephone and Cable Networks.* Report of the Co-chairs of the Local Networks Convergence Committee. Ottawa: Minister of Supply and Services, 1992.

Carley, Michael, and Ian Christie. *Managing Sustainable Development.* London: Earthscan Publications, 2000.

Carson, Rachel. *The Sense of Wonder.* 1965. New York: HarperCollins, 1998.

– *Silent Spring.* 1962. New York: Houghton Mifflin, 1994.

Castells, Manuel, and Martin Ince. *Conversations with Manuel Castells.* Cambridge: Polity, 2003.

Chomsky, Noam, and Edward S. Herman. *Manufacturing Consent.* New York: Pantheon Books, 1988.

Coase, Ronald. 'The Nature of the Firm.' *Economica* 4, no. 16 (1937): 386–405.

– 'The Problem of Social Cost.' *Journal of Law and Economics* 3 (1960): 1–44.

Cohen, Jeremy. *'Be Fertile and Increase, Fill the Earth and Master It.' The Ancient and Medieval Career of a Biblical Text.* Ithaca, NY: Cornell University Press, 1989.

Costanza, Robert, et al. 'The Value of the World's Ecosystem Services and Natural Capital.' *Nature,* May 1997, 253–60.

Crabbé, Philippe. 'Biblical and Ancient Greek Thought about Natural Resources and the Environment and the Latter's Continuity in the Economic Literature Up to the Physiocrats.' In *Philosophy and Ecology,* vol. 1, edited by Konstantine Boudouris and Kostas Kalimtzis, 51–69. Athens: Ionia Publications, 1999.

Daly, Herman E. *Beyond Growth: The Economics of Sustainable Development.* Boston: Beacon Press, 1996.

– 'On Economics as a Life Science.' *Journal of Political Economy* 76 (1968): 392–406.

– *Steady-State Economics,* 2nd ed. Washington, DC: Island Press, 1991.

Daly, Herman E., and John C. Cobb Jr. *For the Common Good: Redirecting the Economy toward Community, the Environment and a Sustainable Future.* Boston: Beacon Press, 1989.

Daly, Herman E., and Joshua Farley. *Ecological Economics: Principles and Applications.* Washington, DC: Island Press, 2004.

Daly, Herman E., and Kenneth N. Townsend, eds. *Valuing the Earth: Economics, Ecology, Ethics.* Cambridge, MA: MIT Press, 1993.

Dampier, W.C. *A History of Science and Its Relation with Philosophy and Religion,* 4th ed. Cambridge: Cambridge University Press, 1961.

Darwin, Charles. *On The Origin of the Species By Means of Natural Selection, Or The Preservation of Favoured Races in the Struggle For Life.* Edited by Morse Peckham. Philadelphia: University of Pennsylvania Press, 1959. First published 1859.

Dempsey, Bernard W. 'Just Price in a Functional Economy.' In *Economic Thought: A Historical Anthology,* edited by James A. Gherity, 4–23. New York: Random House, 1965.

Dickens, Peter. *Society & Nature: Changing Our Environment, Changing Ourselves.* Cambridge: Polity, 2004.

Dobb, Maurice. *Studies in the Development of Capitalism.* Rev. ed. New York: International Publishers, 1963.

Dunn, Seth, and Christopher Flavin. 'Moving the Climate Change Agenda Forward.' In World Watch Institute, *State of the World 2002: Special World Summit Edition,* edited by Christopher Flavin et al., 24–50. New York: Norton, 2002.

Ehrlich, Paul R. *Human Natures: Genes, Cultures, and the Human Prospect.* Washington, DC: Island Press, 2000.

Eliade, Mircea. *The Sacred & the Profane: The Nature of Religion.* Translated by Willard R. Trask. New York: Harcourt Brace Jovanovich, 1959.

Ewen Stuart. *PR! A Social History of Spin* (New York: Basic, 1996).

Faber, Malte, Reiner Manstetten, and John Proops. *Ecological Economics: Concepts and Methods,* Cheltenham, UK: Edward Elgar, 1996.

Fisher, Anthony C., and Frederick M. Peterson. 'The Environment in Economics: A Survey.' *Journal of Economic Literature* 14, no. 1 (1976): 1–33.

Forester, E.S. 'Preface' to *Oeconomica.* In *The Works of Aristotle,* vol. X, translated by W.D. Ross. London: Oxford University Press, 1921.

Foster, John. 'Introduction: Environmental Value and the Scope of Economics.' In *Valuing Nature?: Economics, Ethics and Environment,* 1–17. London: Routledge, 1997.

Franklin, Ursula. *The Real World of Technology*. CBC Massey Lectures Series. Toronto: CBC, 1990.

Fredericks, Kathryn. *Dispute Resolution in NAFTA's Investor State Chapter: A Shift to Market-Dominated Governance.* Institute of Political Economy, Carleton University: Ottawa, 2005.

Freeman, A. Myrick, III. *The Measurement of Environmental and Resource Values.* Washington, DC: Resources for the Future, 2003.

Friedman, Milton. *Price Theory: A Provisional Text,* rev. ed. Chicago: Aldine, 1962.

Friedman, Milton, and Rose Friedman. *Free to Choose: A Personal Statement,* New York: Harcourt Brace Jovanovich, 1980.

– 'The Social Responsibility of Business Is to Increase Its Profits.' *New York Times,* 1970. Reprinted in *Contemporary Issues in Business Ethics,* edited by Joseph R. Desjardins and John J. McCall 21–5. Belmont, CA: Wadsworth, 1985.

Frisby, David. Preface to *The Philosophy of Money,* by Georg Simmel, edited by David Frisby, 2nd ed., London: Routledge, 1990.

Frye, Northrop. *Anatomy of Criticism: Four Essays.* 1957. Reprint, Princeton, NJ: Princeton University Press, 1957.

– 'The Language of Poetry.' Excerpt from *Anatomy of Criticism* (1957). Cited in *Explorations in Communication,* edited by Edmund Carpenter and Marshall McLuhan, 43–53. Boston: Beacon Press, 1960.

– *The Modern Century*. Toronto: Oxford University Press, 1967.

Galbraith, John Kenneth. *The New Industrial State.* Boston: Houghton Mifflin, 1967.

Gardner, Gary. 'The Challenge for Johannesburg: Creating a More Secure World.' In *State of the World 2002: Special World Summit Edition,* by The Worldwatch Institute, 3–23. New York: Norton, 2002.

Georgescu-Roegen, Nicholas. *Analytical Economics: Issues and Problems.* Cambridge, MA: Harvard University Press, 1966.

– *The Entropy Law and the Economic Process.* Cambridge, MA: Harvard University Press, 1971.

Golley, Frank Benjamin. *A History of the Ecosystem Concept in Ecology: More Than the Sum of the Parts.* New Haven, CT: Yale University Press, 1993.

Goodland, Robert. 'The Case the World Has Reached Limits.' In *Population, Technology, and Lifestyle,* edited by Robert Goodland, Herman E. Daly, and Dalah El Serafy, 3–22. Washington, DC: Island Press, 1992.

Gordon, Scott. *The History and Philosophy of Social Sciences.* London: Routledge, 1994.

Gore, Al. Introduction to *Silent Spring,* by Rachel Carson, xv–xxvi. New York: Houghton Mifflin, 1994.

Gottlieb, Roger S., ed. *This Sacred Earth: Religion, Nature, Environment.* New York: Routledge, 1996.

Goudie, Andrew. *The Human Impact on the Natural Environment,* 5th ed. Cambridge, MA: MIT Press, 2000.

Gowdy, John, and Susan Mesner. 'The Evolution of Georgescu-Roegen's Bioeconomics.' *Review of Social Economy* 56 (1998): 136–56.

Grove-White, Robin. 'The Environmental "Valuation" Controversy: Observations on Its Recent History and Significance.' In *Valuing Nature?: Economics, Ethics and Environment,* edited by John Foster, 21–31. London: Routledge, 1997.

Hardin, Garrett. 'Second Thoughts on "The Tragedy of the Commons."' In *Valuing the Earth: Economics, Ecology, Ethics,* edited by Herman Daly and Kenneth Townsend, 145–51. Cambridge, MA: MIT Press, 1993.

– 'The Tragedy of the Commons.' In *Valuing the Earth: Economics, Ecology, Ethics,* edited by Herman E. Daly and Kenneth N. Townsend, 127–43. Cambridge, MA: MIT Press, 1993. First published in *Science* 162, 13 December 1968, 1243–8.

Hargrove, Eugene C. *The Foundations of Environmental Ethics.* Englewood Cliffs, NJ: Prentice Hall, 1989.

Hayek, F.A. *The Road to Serfdom.* 1944. Chicago: University of Chicago Press, 1994.

– Hayek, F.A. 'The Use of Knowledge in Society.' *American Economic Review* 35, no. 4 (1945): 519–30.

Hayles, N. Katherine. *How We Became Posthuman: Virtual Bodies in Cybernetics, Literature, and Informatics.* Chicago: University of Chicago Press, 1999.

Heaton, Herbert. *Economic History of Europe,* rev. ed. New York: Harper and Row, 1948.

Hines, Colin. *Localization: A Global Manifesto.* London: Earthscan, 2000.

Hobbes, Thomas. *Leviathan*. 1651. Edited by Richard Tuck. Cambridge: Cambridge University Press, 1991.

Hodgson, Geoffrey. 'Economics, Environmental Policy and the Transcendence of Utilitarianism.' In *Valuing Nature?: Economics, Ethics and Environment*, edited by John Foster, 48–63. London: Routledge, 1997.

Hubbert, M. King. 'Exponential Growth as a Transient Phenomenon in Human History.' In *Societal Issues, Scientific Viewpoints*, edited by Margaret A. Strom, 75–84. New York: American Institute of Physics, 1987. Reprinted in *Valuing the Earth*, edited by Daly and Townsend, 112–26.

Innis, Harold A. *The Bias of Communication*. Toronto: University of Toronto Press, 1951.

Jacobs, Jane. *The Nature of Economies*. Toronto: Random House Canada, 2000.

– *Systems of Survival: A Dialogue on the Moral Foundations of Commerce and Business*. New York: Vintage, 1992.

Jevons, William Stanley. *The Theory of Political Economy*. 3rd ed. London: Macmillan, 1888.

Johnson, Paul. *A History of Christianity*. New York: Atheneum, 1976.

Jonscher, Charles. 'Notes on Communication and Economic Theory.' In *Communication and Economic Development*, edited by D.M. Lamberton and M. Jussawalla, 60–9. Elmsford, NY: Pergamon Press, 1982.

Knudstson, Peter, and David Suzuki. *Wisdom of the Elders*, Toronto: Stoddart, 1992.

Koerner, Lisbet. *Linnaeus: Nature and Nation*. Cambridge, MA: Harvard University Press, 1999.

Kuwako, Toshio. 'The Possibility of Environmental Discourse in Aristotle.' In *Philosophy and Ecology*, edited by Boudouris and Kalimtzis, 112–20.

Lee, Keekok. 'Aristotle: Towards an Environmental Philosophy.' In *Philosophy and Ecology*, edited by Boudouris and Kalimtzis, 121–8.

Leiss, William. *The Domination of Nature*. 1972. Montreal & Kingston: McGill-Queen's University Press, 1994.

Leopold, Aldo. *A Sand County Almanac, and Sketches Here and There*. New York: Oxford University Press, 1948.

Lerner, Max. Introduction to *The Wealth of Nations*, by Adam Smith, edited by Edwin Cannan, v–x. New York: Random House, 1937.

Lippmann, Walter. *Public Opinion*. New York: Free Press, 1922.

Lomborg, Bjorn. *The Skeptical Environmentalist*. Cambridge: Cambridge University Press, 2001.

Lyons, Oren. 'An Iroquois Perspective.' In *Environmental Discourse and Practice: A Reader*, edited by Lisa M. Benton and John Rennie Short, 15. London: Blackwell, 2000.

MacGillivray, Alex. *Rachel Carson's* Silent Spring. Hauppauge, NY: Barron's, 2004.

Machlup, Fritz. *Knowledge: Its Creation, Distribution, and Economic Significance.* Vol. 1, *Knowledge and Knowledge Production.* Princeton, NJ: Princeton University Press, 1980.

– *The Production and Distribution of Knowledge in the United States.* Princeton, NJ: Princeton University Press, 1961.

MacNeill, Jim. 'Strategies for Sustainable Development.' *Scientific American* 261, no. 3 (1989): 154–65.

Macpherson, C.B. Introduction to *Leviathan,* by Thomas Hobbes, 9–70. London: Penguin Books, 1968.

– *The Political Theory of Possessive Individualism: Hobbes to Locke.* London: Oxford, 1962.

– *Democratic Theory: Essays in Retrieval.* Oxford: Clarendon Press, 1973.

Malthus, Thomas Robert. *An Essay on the Principle of Population as it Affects the Future Improvement of Society, With Remarks on the Speculations of Mr. Godwin, M. Condorcet, and Other Writers.* London: J. Johnson, 1798. Reprinted in *The Works of Thomas Robert Malthus,* vol. 1, *An Essay on the Principle of Population,* edited by E.A. Wrigley and David Souden. London: William Pickering, 1986.

– *An Essay on the Principle of Population; Or, A View of its Past and Present Effects on Human Happiness; With an Inquiry Into Our Prospects Respecting the Future Removal or Mitigation of the Evils Which It Occasions.* 1803. Edited by Donald Winch. Cambridge: Cambridge University Press, 1992.

Marshall, Alfred. *Principles of Economics: An Introductory Volume.* 8th ed. London: Macmillan, 1947. First edition published in 1890.

Mattelart, Armand, and Michele Mattelart. *Theories of Communication: A Short Introduction.* London: Sage, 1998.

McDermott, Timothy. Introduction to *Thomas Aquinas, Selected Philosophical Writings.* Selected and translated by Timothy McDermott. Oxford: Oxford University Press, 1993.

McGinn, Anne Platt. 'Reducing Our Toxic Burden.' In *State of the World 2002,* by The Worldwatch Institute, 75–100. New York: Norton, 2002.

Meadows, Donella H. 'Changing the World through the Informationsphere.' In *Media and the Environment,* edited by Craig L. LaMay and Everette E. Dennis, 67–80. Washington, DC: Island Press, 1991.

Milani, Brian. *Designing the Green Economy: The Postindustrial Alternative to Corporate Globalization.* Lanham, MD: Rowman & Littlefield, Inc. 2000.

Mirowski, Philip. *More Heat Than Light: Economics as Social Physics, Physics as Nature's Economics.* Cambridge: Cambridge University Press, 1989.

Mitchell, Wesley C. *Types of Economic Theory: From Mercantilism to Institutionalism,* vols. 1 and 2, edited by Joseph Dorfman. New York: Augustus M. Kelley Publishers, 1967, 1970.

Morley, David, and Kevin Robins. *Spaces of Identity: Global Media, Electronic Landscapes and Cultural Boundaries.* London: Routledge, 1995.

Myerson, George, and Yvonne Rydin. *The Language of Environment.* London: UCL Press, 1996.

Mumford, Lewis. *The Pentagon of Power: The Myth of the Machine.* vol. 2. New York: Harcourt, Brace, Jovanovich, 1970.

Murchie, Guy. *The Seven Mysteries of Life: An Exploration in Science & Philosophy.* Boston: Houghton Mifflin, 1978.

Nadeau, Robert L. *The Wealth of Nature: How Mainstream Economics Has Failed the Environment.* New York: Columbia University Press, 2003.

Naess, Arne. 'The Shallow and the Deep, Long Range Ecology Movements: A Summary.' *Inquiry* 16 (1973): 95–100.

Neuzil, Mark, and William Kovarik. *Mass Media & Environmental Conflict: America's Green Crusades.* London: Sage, 1996.

Nisbet, Robert. *History of the Idea of Progress.* New York: Basic Books, 1980.

Nora, Simon, and Alain Minc. *The Computerization of Society, A Report to the President of France.* Cambridge, MA: MIT Press, 1980.

Norgaard, Richard B. 'Passion and Ecological Economics: Towards a Richer Coevolution of Value Systems and Environmental Systems.' In *New Dimensions in Ecological Economics: Integrated Approaches to People and Nature,* edited by Stephen Dovers, David I. Stern, and Michael D. Young, 23–34. Cheltenham, UK: Edward Elgar, 2003.

Odum, Eugene. *Fundamentals of Ecology.* 3rd ed. Philadelphia: W.B. Saunders, 1971.

O'Neill, John. 'Value Pluralism: Incommensurability and Institutions.' In *Valuing Nature?: Economics, Ethics and Environment,* 75–88. Edited by John Foster, London: Routledge, 1997.

Passmore, John. *Man's Responsibility for Nature: Ecological Problems and Western Traditions.* New York: Scribner's, 1974.

Pearce, D., A. Markandya, and E. Barbier. *Blueprint for a Green Economy.* London: Earthscan Books, 1989.

Perring, Charles. *Economy and Environment: A Theoretical Essay on the Interdependence of Economic and Environmental Systems.* Cambridge: Cambridge University Press, 1987.

Pigou, A.C. *The Economics of Welfare,* 4th edition. London: Macmillan, 1932.

Polanyi, Karl. *The Great Transformation: The Political and Economic Origins of Our Time.* 1944. Boston: Beacon Press, 1957.

Ponting, Clive. *A Green History of the World: The Environment and the Collapse of Great Civilizations*. New York: Penguin Books, 1991.

Pool, Ithiel de Sola. *Technologies without Boundaries: On Telecommunications in a Global Age*. Cambridge, MA: Harvard University Press, 1990.

Porat, Marc. *The Information Economy: Definition and Measurement*. Special Publication 77–12(1). Washington, DC: Office of Telecommunication, U.S. Department of Commerce, 1977.

Porat, Marc. *The Information Economy: Definition and Measurement*, Special Publication 77–12(1). Washington, DC: Office of Telecommunication, U.S. Department of Commerce, 1977. In *Information Economics and Policy in the United States*, edited by Michael Rogers Rubin, 16–25. Littleton, CO: Libraries Unlimited, 1983.

Raphael, D.D., and A.L. Macfie. Introduction to *The Theory of Moral Sentiments*, by Adam Smith, 1–52. Indianapolis: Liberty Press, 1982.

Rist, Gilbert. *The History of Development: From Western Origins to Global Faith*. London: Zed Books, 1997.

Robbins, Lionel. *An Essay on the Nature and Significance of Economic Science*. 2nd ed. London: Macmillan, 1935.

– *The Theory of Economic Policy in English Classical Political Economy*. Macmillan: London, 1952.

Roosevelt, Theodore. 'Conservation, Protection, Reclamation, and Irrigation.' Excerpt from State Papers as Governor and President 1899–1909. Reprinted in *Environmental Discourse and Practice: A Reader*, edited by Lisa M. Benton and John Rennie Short, 110–13. Oxford: Blackwell, 2000.

Royal Society of Canada. *Elements of Precaution: Recommendations for the Regulation of Food Biotechnology in Canada: An Expert Report on the Future of Food Biotechnology*. Ottawa: Royal Society of Canada, 2001.

Ruben, Brent. 'General Systems Theory.' In *Approaches to Human Communication*, edited by Richard Budd and Brent Ruben, 120–144. Rochelle Park, NJ: Hayden, 1972.

Ruth, Matthias. *Integrating Economics, Ecology and Thermodynamics*. Dordrecht: Kluwer, 1993.

Saul, John Ralston. *The Unconscious Civilization*. Toronto: Anansi, 1995.

Saussure, Ferdinand de. *Course in General Linguistics*. 1916. Edited by Charles Bally and Albert Sechehaye. Translated by Wade Baskin. New York: McGraw-Hill, 1966.

Schumacher, E.F. *Small Is Beautiful*. London: Abacus, 1974.

Scitovsky, Tibor. *Welfare and Competition*. Revised edition. Homewood, IL: Richard D. Irwin, 1971.

Seligman, Ben B. *Main Currents in Modern Economics: Economic Thought since 1870.* New York: Free Press of Glencoe, 1962.

Shannon, Claude E., and Warren Weaver. *The Mathematical Theory of Communication.* Urbana: University of Illinois Press, 1949.

Simon, Julian. *The Ultimate Resource II.* Princeton, NJ: Princeton University Press, 1998; also available at http://www.africa2000.com/RNDX/chapter003.html.

Smith, Adam. *An Inquiry into the Nature and Causes of the Wealth of Nations.* 1766. Edited by Edwin Cannan. New York: Modern Library, 1937.

– *The Theory of Moral Sentiments.* 1759. Edited by D.D. Raphael and A.L. Macfie. Oxford: Clarendon Press, 1976.

Söderbaum, Peter. *Ecological Economics,* London: Earthscan, 2000.

Spencer, Herbert. *A System of Synthetic Philosophy.* Vol. 1 – *First Principles,* 6th ed. 1904. Reprinted in *The Works of Herbert Spencer.* Osnabruck: Otto Zeller, 1966.

Stigler, George. 'The Economics of Information.' *Journal of Political Economy* 69, no. 30. Reprinted in George Stigler, *The Organization of Industry.* 171–90. Homewood, IL: Richard D. Irwin, 1968.

– 'Information in the Labor Market.' *Journal of Political Economy* 70 (1962). Reprinted in George J. Stigler, *The Organization of Industry*. Homewood, IL: Irwin, 1968. 191–207.

– *Memoirs of an Unregulated Economist.* New York: Basic Books, 1988.

Stigler, George, and Gary Becker. 'De Gustibus Non Est Disputandum.' *American Economic Review* 67, no. 2 (1977): 75–90.

Sumner, William Graham. *Social Darwinism: Selected Essays of William Graham Sumner.* Edited by Stow Persons. Englewood Cliffs, NJ: Prentice-Hall, 1963.

Suzuki, David, with Amanda McConnell. *The Sacred Balance: Rediscovering Our Place in Nature.* Vancouver: Greystone Books, 1997.

Tamari, Meir. 'Judaism and the Market Mechanism.' In *Religion, Economics and Social Thought,* edited by Walter Block and Irving Hexham, 393–421. Vancouver: Fraser Institute, 1986.

Tansley, Alfred George. 'The Use and Abuse of Vegetational Concepts and Terms.' *Ecology* 16, no. 3 (1935): 284–307.

Tawney, R.H. *Religion and the Rise of Capitalism: A Historical Study*. New York: Mentor, 1954.

Thompson, E.P. *The Making of the English Working Class.* Harmondsworth, UK: Pelican Books, 1968.

Thoreau, Henry David. *Walden and Other Writings by Henry David Thoreau.* Edited by Joseph Wood Krutch. New York: Bantam Books, 1962. *Walden* first published in 1854.

Toffler, Alvin. *The Third Wave.* New York: William Morrow, 1980.

Tuck, Richard. 'Introduction' to *Leviathan*, by Thomas Hobbes, edited by Richard Tuck, Cambridge: Cambridge University Press, 1991.

United Nations Environment Programme. *Global Environment Outlook 3: Past, Present and Future Perspectives.* London: Earthscan, 2002.

United Nations. World Commission on Environment and Development (Brundtland Commission). *Our Common Future.* Oxford: Oxford University Press, 1987.

Vatn, Arild, and Daniel W. Bromley, 'Choices without Prices without Apologies.' In *The Handbook of Environmental Economics*, edited by Daniel W. Bromley, chapter 1. Oxford: Blackwell, 1995.

Wallace, Alfred Russel. *Contributions to the Theory of Natural Selection: A Series of Essays.* 1870. New York: AMS Press, 1973.

Weber, Max. *The Protestant Ethic and the Spirit of Capitalism.* 1904–5. Translated by Talcott Parsons. New York: Scribner's, 1976.

Webster, Frank. *The New Photography.* London: J. Calder, 1980.

– Webster, Frank. *Theories of the Information Society*. New York: Routledge, 1995.

Wiener, Norbert. *The Human Use of Human Beings: Cybernetics and Society*. 1950. Republished by Avon Books: New York, 1967.

Weizsäcker, Carl Friedrich von. *The Unity of Nature.* New York: Farrar, Straus and Giroux, 1980.

White, Lynn, Jr. 'The Historical Roots of Our Ecological Crisis,' *Science*, vol. 155, 10 March 1967, 1203–7. Reprinted in *This Sacred Earth: Religion, Nature, Environment*, edited by Roger S. Gottlieb, 184–93. New York: Routledge, 1996.

Willis, Ian. *Economics and the Environment: A Signalling and Incentive Approach.* St Leonards, Australia: Allen and Unwin, 1997.

Wogaman, J. Philip. 'Theological Perspective on Economics.' In *Morality of the Market*, edited by Walter Block, Geoffrey Brennan, and Kenneth Elzinga, 35–59. Vancouver: Fraser Institute, 1985.

Worster, Donald. *Nature's Economy: A History of Ecological Ideas.* 2nd edition, Cambridge: Cambridge University Press, 1994.

Young, R.M. 'Malthus and the Evolutionists: The Common Context of Biological and Social Theory.' *Past and Present* 43 (1969): 109–45.

Internet Sources

Alcouffe, Alain, Sylvie Ferrari, and Horst Hanusch. 'Marx, Schumpeter and Georgescu-Roegen: Three Conceptions of the Evolution of Economic Systems' Toulouse, France: Université des Sciences Sociales, 2004. http://www.univ-tlse1.fr/LIRHE/.

Barlow, John Percy. 'A Declaration of the Independence of Cyberspace.' 1996. http://www.eff.org/~barlow/Declaration-Final.html.

BBC. 'Big Boost for US Military Spending. 24 January 2002. http://news.bbc.co.uk/1/hi/world/americas/1778681.stm.

Bell, Michelle L., Aidan McDermott, Scott L. Zeger, Jonathan M. Samet, and Francesca Dominici. 'Ozone and Short-term Mortality in 95 US Urban Communities, 1987–2000.' *Journal of the American Medical Association* 292 (17 Nov. 2004): 2372–9. http://jama.ama-assn.org/cgi/reprint/292/19/2372.

Bentham, Jeremy. *An Introduction to the Principles of Morals and Legislation.* 1789. Extracts available at http://college.hmco.com/history/west/mosaic/chapter13/source412.h tml.

CDC. Media Relations. 'CDC Telebriefing Transcript.' 31 January 2003. http://www.cdc.gov/od/oc/media/transcripts/t030131.htm.

Canada. 'Sustainable Development Information Systems.' 2004. http://www.sdinfo.gc.ca/main_e.cfm.

Canada. 'Departmental/Agency Strategies: Industry Canada.' 2002; http://www.sdinfo.gc.ca/federal_sd_resources/strategies_display_e .cfm?id=18.

Canada. 'Departmental/Agency Strategies: Environment Canada.' 2002. http://www.sdinfo.gc.ca/federal_sd_resources/strategies_display_e.cfm?id=13.

Canada. National Round Table on the Environment and the Economy. 'What We Do.' n.d. http://www.nrtee-trnee.ca/eng/overview/Who-we-are_e.htm.

Case University, Online Ethics Center for Engineering and Science at Case Western Reserve University. 'Rachel Carson's Story./' n.d. http://onlineethics.org/moral/carson/1-bgrnd.html.

Centre for Atmospheric Science. 'The Ozone Hole Tour: Part 1, The History Behind the Ozone Hole.' n.d. http://www.atm.ch.cam.ac.uk/tour/part1.html.

Coblentz, Bruce. 'Vulnerability to Extinction.' n.d. http://www.orst.edu/instruct/fw251/notebook/extinction.html.

Costanza, Robert, et al. 'The Value of the World's Ecosystem Services and Natural Capital.' *Nature,* 387 (15 May 1997): 253–60. http://www.uvm.edu/giee/publications/Nature_Paper.pdf.

Darwin, Charles. *The Origin of the Species.* 1859. http://www.literature.org/authors/darwin-charles/the-origin-of-species/chapter-03.html.

Environmental Defence and the Canadian Environmental Law Association (Pollution Watch). *Shattering the Myth of Pollution Progress in Canada: A National Report.* December 2004. http://www.pollutionwatch.org/pub/natreport2004.jsp.

Friends of the Earth. 'Shell Record Profits at Expense of People and Planet.' May 2003. http://www.foe.co.uk/resource/press_releases/shell_record_profits _at_ex.html.

– 'Tomorrow's World.' 1997. http://www.foe.co.uk/campaigns/sustainable_development/publicatio ns/tworld/tw-in-10.html.

Friends of the Earth, Public Citizen. *NAFTA Chapter 11 Investor-to-State Cases: Bankrupting Democracy: Lessons for Fast Track and the Free Trade Area of the Americas.* Washington, DC: Public Citizen's Global Trade Watch, 2001. http://www.citizen.org/publications/release.cfm?ID=7076.

Greenpeace. 'We Must Stop the War on the Planet.' Earth Summit 2002. http://archive.greenpeace.org/earthsummit/background.html.

Hubbert, M. King. 'M. King Hubbert on Growth.' Testimony before the Subcommittee on the Environment of the Committee on Interior and Insular Affairs House of Representatives. 6 June 1974 http://www.technocracy.org/articles/hub-gro.html.

International Petroleum Industry Environmental Conservation Association (IPIECA), International Association of Oil and Gas Producers (OGP). *Industry as a Partner for Sustainable Development.* 2002. http://www.uneptie.org/outreach/wssd/contributions/sector_reports/sectors/oil-gas/oil-gas.htm.

Lahanas, Michael. 'Theophrastus of Eresos: Father of Botany and Ecology.' October 2004. http://www.mlahanas.de/Greeks/Theophrast.htm.

Leopold, Aldo. 'The Land Ethic.' 1948. http://www.tipiglen.dircon.co.uk/landethic.html.

Marx, Karl. 'Part 1: The Commodity.' *A Contribution to the Critique of Political Economy.* 1859. http://www.marxists.org/archive/marx/works/1859/critique-pol-economy/ch01.htm.

Multinational Monitor Online. *From Stewards to Shareholders.* 1993. http://multinsationalmonitor.org/hyper/issues/1993/03/mm0393-09.html.

Naess, Arne. 'The Shallow and the Deep, Long Range Ecology Movements: A Summary.' Originally published in *Inquiry* 16, Oslo, 1973. http://www.alamut.com/subj/ideologies/pessimism/Naess_deepEcology .html.

Natural Resources Defense Council. 'The Bush Administration's Slash & Burn Environmental Budget.' 2001. http://www.nrdc.org/legislation/abudget03.asp.

Nisbet, Matthew. 'The Skeptical Environmentalist: A Case Study in the Manufacture of News.' 2003. http://www.csicop.org/scienceandmedia/environmentalist/.

Online Ethics Center for Engineering and Science at Case Western Reserve University. 'Rachel Carson's Story.' http://onlineethics.org/moral/carson/main.html.

Oosthoek, Jan. 'Environmental History: Between Science and Philosophy.' 2001. http://forth.stir.ac.uk/~kjw01/philosophy.html.

Organization for Economic Co-operation and Development (OECD), Nuclear Energy Agency. 'Chernobyl: Assessment of Radiological and Health Impacts,' *2002 Update of Chernobyl: Ten Years On,* http://www.nea.fr/html/rp/chernobyl/chernobyl.html.

Pesticide Action Network North America. 'Chemical Trespass: Pesticides in Our Bodies and Corporate Accountability.' May 2004. http://www.panna.org/campaigns/docsTrespass/chemical/Trespass2004 .dv.html.

Public Citizen. 'The Ten Year Track Record of the North American Free Trade Agreement Undermining Sovereignty and Democracy.' 2004. http://www.citizen.org/documents/NAFTA_10_democracy.pdf.

Rippel, Barbara. 'Tradable CO_2 Emissions Permits: Problems with the "Perfect" Solution?' A study prepared for the National Consumer Coalition under the auspices of Consumer Alert. 25 November 1997. http://www.consumeralert.org/pubs/Study/ets.htm.

Royal Dutch Shell. *People, Planet, Profits: The Shell Report 2001.* www.shell.com/static/royal-en/ downloads/shell_report_2001.pdf.

Sagoff, Mark. 'Do We Consume Too Much?' *Atlantic Monthly,* June 1997, 80–96. http:// www.puaf.umd.edu/faculty/papers/sagoff/consume.pdf.

Schafer, Kristin S., Margaret Reeves, Skip Spitzer, Susan E. Kegley, Pesticide Action Network North America. *Chemical Trespass: Pesticides in Our Bodies and Corporate Accountability.* May 2004. 8, 9. http://www.panna.org/resources/resources.html.

Sengbusch, Peter. 'What Is an Ecosystem?' University of Hamburg, Ecology Online, 2003. http://www.biologie.uni-hamburg.de/b-online/e54/54a.htm.

Simon, Julian. *The Ultimate Resource II.* Princeton, NJ: Princeton University Press, 1998. http://www.africa2000.com/RNDX/chapter003.html.

Steffen, Melinda. 'Protectionism or Legitimate Regulation? A Hope for Clarity in the Murky Waters of Chapter Eleven's Expropriation Provisions.' n.d. http://www.kentlaw.edu/perritt/honorsscholars/steffen.html

Thinkquest. The Environment: A Global Challenge. 'Biotic Communities.' http://library.thinkquest.org/26026/Science/biotic_communities.ht ml?tqskip1=1.

United Nations, Convention on Biological Diversity. 'Sustaining Life on Earth: How the Convention on Biological Diversity Promotes Nature and Human Well-Being.' n.d. http://www.biodiv.org/doc/publications/guide.asp.

United Nations. *Johannesburg Summit 2002. Global Challenge, Global Opportunity, Trends in Sustainable Development.* 2002. www.earthscape.org/pi/nid01

United Nations, Johannesburg Summit 2002. 'With a Sense of Urgency,

Johannesburg Summit Sets an Action Agenda.' 3 September 2002. http://www.johannesburgsummit.org/html/whats_new/feature_story38. htm.

United Nations. 'Stockholm Declaration on the Human Environment.' Adopted 16 June 1972. http://www.unesco.org/iau/sd/stockholm.html.

United States, Department of Health and Human Services, Centers for Disease Control and Prevention. *Second National Report on Human Exposure to Environmental Chemicals*, January 2003. http://www.cdc.gov/exposurereport/.

Van den Bergh, Jeroen C.J.M. 'Ecological Economics: Themes, Approaches, and Differences with Environmental Economics.' Discussion Paper #00-080/3. Amsterdam: Tinbergen Institute, University of Amsterdam, 2000, note 1. http://www.tinbergen.nl/scripts/papers.pl?paper=00080.rdf.

Wesley, John. 'Causes of the Inefficacy of Christianity.' Sermon 16, Dublin. 1789. http://gbgm-umc.org/umhistory/wesley/sermons/serm-116.stm.

White, Lynn, Jr. 'The Historical Roots of Our Ecological Crisis.' *Science*, 10 March 1967, 1203–7. Reprinted in Roger S. Gottlieb, ed., *This Sacred Earth: Religion, Nature, Environment.* New York: Routledge, 1996, 184–93. http://www.geocities.com/Yosemite/Falls/6185/lynwqhite.htm.

Wiegleb, G. 'Lecture Notes on the History of Ecology and Nature Conservation.' 2000. http://www.tu-cottbus.de/BTU/Fak4/AllgOeko/erm/erm1.htm.

World Bank. *Sustainable Development in a Dynamic World.* World Development Report 2003. http://econ.worldbank.org/wdr/wdr2003/.

World Business Council for Sustainable Development. 'About the WBCSD.' n.d. http://www.wbcsd.org/templates/TemplateWBCSD1/layout.asp?type=p&M enuId=NjA&doOpen=1&ClickMenu=Lef.

World Business Council for Sustainable Development and Greenpeace International. 'Climate Change and the Kyoto Protocol.' 2002. http://www.environment.gov.za/sustdev/jowsco/paraEvents/ClimateCh ange.html.

World Conservation Union. 'Species Extinction.' n.d. http://www.google.ca/search?q=cache:blLpxtqATZUJ:www.iucn.org/wss d/files/media%2520brief/mb_species.pdf+IUCN+Extinction+media+Brie f&hl=en.

'Word IQ.' n.d., http://www.wordiq.com/definition/Efficiency_%28 economics%29.

Yale Law School. 'Bretton Woods Agreements.' http://www.yale.edu/lawweb/avalon/decade/decad047.htm.

Index